''Sam Weller introduces to Mr. Pickwick
the leading characters in Mr. Dickens' novels.''

DICKENS 1970

Dickens sketched in February 1870 by 'Spy' (Leslie Ward)

DICKENS
1970

CENTENARY ESSAYS BY

WALTER ALLEN · MARGARET LANE

PAMELA HANSFORD JOHNSON · C. P. SNOW

BARBARA HARDY · RAYMOND WILLIAMS

JOHN HOLLOWAY · ANGUS WILSON

Edited by Michael Slater
(Hon. Editor, *The Dickensian*)

STEIN AND DAY/*Publishers*/New York

First published in 1970
Copyright © 1970 Chapman & Hall
Library of Congress Catalog Card No. 74-126972
All rights reserved
Printed in the United States of America
Stein and Day/Publishers/7 East 48 Street, New York, N.Y. 10017
SBN 8128-1325-1

CONTENTS

ILLUSTRATIONS

INTRODUCTION

'Chapman and Hall,' wrote Dickens in a copy of the first edition of *Pickwick Papers* presented by him to Edward Chapman in 1839, 'are the best of booksellers past, present or to come; and my trusty friends.' Five years later, it is true, outraged by a tactless remark of William Hall's and grievously disappointed by the profits realized on the *Christmas Carol*, he abruptly broke with the firm and made his printers, Bradbury and Evans, his publishers. But when they, too, in due course offended him, he returned to Chapman and Hall who then remained his sole publishers for the last twelve years of his life. And ever since their names have been as firmly linked with Dickens's in the public mind as those of Cruikshank or of Phiz.

It is fitting, therefore, that among all the books called forth by the commemoration of Dickens's death a hundred years ago this month one should appear bearing the same imprint as that famous fourth number of *Pickwick* which introduced Sam Weller to the reading public and began his creator's career as the most astonishing best-seller in all our literature.

Like the volume produced by Chapman and Hall to honour the Pickwick Centenary in 1936, which was co-edited by my predecessor, that great Dickensian, Walter Dexter, this book takes a composite form. It gathers together a number of distinguished writers and critics, united by their common admiration for Dickens's genius, to take a fresh and personal look at some major themes and aspects that have long been central to any serious discussion of his work. Each essay is published here for the first time. Each contributor writes about an aspect of Dickens that particularly interests him but the essays seemed to group themselves naturally into the three sections presented here.

The first three deal primarily with what we might call the critic's Dickens, the towering literary artist. It is appropriate that the first essay in this section, as in the whole book, should be Professor Allen's richly evocative analysis of Dickens's comedy, for a recognition of his extraordinary comic genius (here Chaucer and Shakespeare alone are his peers) is surely basic to all appreciation of his work; as his biographer (and one of his earliest and best critics), John Forster, wrote, 'His leading quality was humour'. But, while this has always been acknowledged by any Dickens critic worth his salt, Dickens's admission to the House of Fiction is a much more recent event; by this I mean that an adequate appreciation of his formal and structural powers has had to wait for the great efflorescence of sensitive and intelligent Dickens criticism witnessed by the last two decades. Professor Hardy concerns herself with this aspect of the novels and, in the course of her essay, has incisive and illuminating things to say about Dickens's artistic development, and about the charge of caricature so often levelled at his mode of characterization. Along with the discovery that his novels cannot be dismissed as a herd of Jamesian 'loose baggy monsters' has gone the discovery of Dickens the Symbolist. This has led to the word 'symbol' being a good deal overworked in some recent Dickens criticism and the time is ripe for some stimulating first-principles investigation of it, of the kind provided here by Dr Holloway.

The second group of essays focusses on the liberal's Dickens, the powerful satirist of Victorian society, the champion of the pathetic victims of the Industrial Revolution and other nineteenth-century phenomena. Here again, some first-principles investigation is in order and Dr Williams in his essay outlines a frame of reference within which discussion of this aspect of Dickens's work might usefully be carried on. My own essay looks at Dickens's treatment of the contemporary sources for the most concentrated piece of socially committed fiction that he ever wrote, published in the midst of the Hungry 'Forties. Finally, C. P. Snow submits a celebrated instance of Dickens's social satire, the Circumlocution Office, to a searching examination and suggests why such intensely topical work still has power over us today.

But Dickens was not concerned exclusively with man as a social animal. He is perhaps above all the novelist of the family, deeply concerned with the ordinary everyday relationships of men, women and children, 'the story of our lives from year to year'. The essays in the last section of this book discuss the treatment in his novels of the domestic affections, of the relations between the sexes, and of children and childhood. Here we approach the very heart of Dickens, the enjoying and suffering human creature, and biography comes to the aid of literary criticism. The subjects studied by Miss Margaret Lane and Professor Wilson have, of course, always been recognized as central preoccupations in all Dickens's work (though they have not often, perhaps, been as fully explored as they are here) but it is still widely believed that Dickens left the sexual life quite out of account in his depiction of the human condition; Miss Pamela Hansford Johnson's essay indicates how misleading a view this is.

It is perhaps no accident that all the essays in this last section are contributed by writers who are themselves distinguished novelists. But there is a further significance in the presence in this book of so many notable fellow-practicioners of Dickens's art. The roll-call of major novelists who have testified to their reverence for Dickens and, often, shown his influence in their work is a long and impressive one, including writers as diverse as Tolstoy and Kafka, Wells and Dostoievsky, Proust and Priestly. It might almost tempt us to dub Dickens 'the novelist's novelist' if this did not make him sound too rarefied. For he is, overwhelmingly and demonstrably, the reader's novelist too. His popularity with patrons of lending libraries and buyers of paperback editions shows no more signs of waning than does his popularity with the literary profession.

Although, with the passing of 1970, we may expect some abatement of the flood of publications relating to Dickens, new and worthwhile studies of the man and his work will undoubtedly continue to appear. The interest he has for us as artist, as social critic, and as fellow-man, can never be exhausted. The praise spoken of him by one of his aides on his spectacular reading tours has stood the test of time triumphantly; 'The more you want of the Master, the more you will find in him'.

June 1970   MICHAEL SLATER
                                                      Birkbeck College, London

Note : The text used for all quotations from Dickens's novels made in the course of these essays is that of the New Oxford Illustrated Edition of his works.

PART
ONE

THE
ARTIST

WALTER ALLEN

THE

COMEDY

OF

DICKENS

'Endless fertility in laughter-causing detail is Mr Dickens's most astonishing peculiarity.' That is Bagehot, not the novelist's most wholehearted admirer, in 1858,[1] before two of the greatest novels had been written; and throughout the shifting critical opinions and changes of critical emphasis Dickens has been subjected to for more than a century, it remains the central, the inescapable fact about him, the one thing that is fundamental to everything else. Admittedly, notions of what constitutes laughter-causing detail have varied from critic to critic. Bagehot, anticipating the view that dominated Dickens criticism until rather less than thirty years ago, scarcely found it at all in the later works, 'of which,' he said, 'we should not like to have to speak in detail.' But Dickens's work, from first to last, from *Pickwick Papers* to *Our Mutual Friend* and *Edwin*

---

[1] 'Charles Dickens', *National Review*, vol. vii, pp. 548-86. Reprinted in Bagehot's *Literary Studies*, vol. ii, 1879.

Drood, is much more of a piece than one would suppose either from Bagehot or from much more recent writers for whom the great Dickens is the late Dickens. The laughter-causing detail may have changed its form and purpose in the later novels, though this is by no means invariably so, but it is always there, except perhaps in *A Tale of Two Cities*, and Shaw is much nearer the mark than Bagehot when, writing an introduction to *Hard Times* in 1912, he says:

> At the same time, you need not fear to find Dickens losing his good humour and sense of fun and becoming serious in Mr. Gradgrind's way. On the contrary, Dickens in this book casts off, and casts off for ever, all restraint on his wild sense of humour. He had always been inclined to break loose: there are passages in the speeches of Mrs. Nickleby and Pecksniff which are impossible as well as funny. But now it is no longer a question of passages: here he begins at last to exercise quite recklessly his power of presenting a character to you in the most fantastic and outrageous terms, putting into its mouth from one end of the book to the other hardly one word which could conceivably be uttered by any sane human being, and yet leaving you with an unmistakable and exactly truthful portrait of a character that you recognize at once as not only real but typical.

We know from documentary evidence how the British reading public of all classes was mowed down by laughter as soon as the Wellers came into the *Pickwick Papers*, and there is a sense in which everything in Dickens, the obsessions and the symbols, are implicit in the *Pickwick Papers*. But even though Dickens's vision may have darkened with the passing years, the comedy does not diminish either in quality or in quantity. If Bagehot and most critics up to and including Hesketh Pearson, in his 1949 biography, found the later novels less funny, it must have been either because they misconstrued the nature of the comedy or for reasons Shaw suggests in his essay on *Hard Times*:

> . . . England is full of Bounderbys and Podsnaps and Gradgrinds; and we are all to a quite appalling extent in their power. We either hate and fear them or else we are them, and resent being held up to odium by a novelist. We have only to turn to the article on Dickens in the current edition of the *Encyclopaedia Britannica* to find how desper-

ately our able critics still exalt all Dickens's early stories about individuals while ignoring or belittling such masterpieces as *Hard Times, Little Dorrit, Our Mutual Friend,* and even *Bleak House* (because of Sir Leicester Dedlock), for their mercilessly faithful and penetrating exposures of English social, industrial, and political life; to see how hard Dickens hit the conscience of the governing class; and how loth we still are to confess, not that we are so wicked (for of that we are rather proud), but so ridiculous, so futile, so incapable of making our country really prosperous. *The Old Curiosity Shop* was written to amuse you, entertain you, touch you; and it succeeded. *Hard Times* was written to make you uncomfortable; and it will make you uncomfortable (and serve you right) though it will perhaps interest you more, and certainly leave a deeper scar on you, than any two of its forerunners.

Comedy is the main instrument by which Dickens inflicts the 'deeper scar', but it is irrelevant that Podsnap is a less comfortable, a less delightful creation than Pickwick. Both are superb comic characters, even though the latter has one foot in fairyland, while the other is an expression of what Lauriat Lane, Jr., calls, in his introductory essay to *The Dickens Critics* (1961), Dickens's dark vision of social reality. An age that has coined the phrase 'black comedy' ought to be able to accept the greatness of the comedy of the later Dickens; but I suspect that even for comparatively sophisticated readers the first association comedy has is with the opposite of blackness. I know from experience how difficult it is to bring home to undergraduates the fact that *Crime and Punishment*, for instance, is among other things a comic novel, that Dostoievsky intended this, and that the comedy is an integral part of the book, an indispensible factor in its total impact and total meaning. But where Dickens is concerned, a *caveat* is necessary. In the earlier novels, from *Oliver Twist* onwards, there was always an element of black comedy, but in the later the black comedy never takes over entirely. The Dickens who delights in the seemingly spontaneous flights of his characters into language at once poetic and absurd is always there. Dickens is always Dickens; and though to account for Dickens's comedy is certainly not the whole of Dickens criticism, Lane says nothing less than the truth when he remarks 'To grasp Dickens' meaning wholly, critics must grasp the meaning of his humour.'

[2]

A rough literary genealogy for Dickens is not difficult to devise, and though it will not by any means cover the whole of his talent it may illuminate some aspects of it. One of his ancestors was Ben Jonson and another, Smollett; and Earle Davis, in *The Flint and the Flame* (1963), has convincingly added to them an artist much smaller and much more obscure, the early nineteenth-century actor and mimic Charles Mathews. Writers in the line of descent from Dickens include Shaw, who was steeped in him, and novelists as diverse as H. G. Wells and Wyndham Lewis. One says 'line of descent', but whether one has in mind Dickens in relation to his forbears or later writers in relation to Dickens, it is necessary to remember that temperamental affinity is more important than influence in the simple sense. Certainly Dickens knew and admired Jonson's plays, some of which he produced and acted in in his amateur theatricals; and he had revelled in Smollett from early boyhood. But what he had in common with both was what he had in common with the Wells of *Tono-Bungay* and *Mr Polly* and with Wyndham Lewis. It may be summed up in Lewis's famous statement:

> The *external* approach to things (relying on evidence of the *eye* rather than of the more emotional organs of sense) can make of 'the grotesque' a healthy and attractive companion... Dogmatically, then, I am for the Great Without, for the method of *external* approach.[1]

The word 'grotesque' is to the point here, for the comic and the grotesque lie very close together and are often indeed, as in much caricature, the same thing. It may be useful to set side by side three instances of the external approach to character, all of which may be called grotesque. Here is Lismahago, from Smollett's *Humphrey Clinker*:

> He would have measured about six feet in height, had he stood up-right; but he stooped very much; was very narrow in the shoulders, and very thick in the calves of his legs, which were cased in black spatterdashes. As for his thighs, they were long and slender, like

[1] *Men Without Art*, 1934, pp. 127-8.

those of a grasshopper; his face was, at least, half a yard in length, brown, and shrivelled, with projecting cheekbones, little grey eyes of the greenish hue, a large hook nose, a pointed chin, a mouth from ear to ear, very ill furnished with teeth, and a high narrow forehead, well furnished with wrinkles.

Here, from *The Revenge for Love*, is Lewis's rendering of a Spanish peasant girl:

She was walking very slowly: she was walking with the orthodox majesty of the women of those unspoilt districts – their skulls flattened with heavy pitchers – with a hieratic hip-roll that bore her away no quicker than a tortoise showing off its speed at the mating season ... She and Don Alvaro were the only people in sight. Don Alvaro spat and waited for a few more revolutions of the hips to bring this slowly-ploughing traditional vessel of Old Spain (built to accommodate, in capacious quarters, the fiery man-child below, and at the same time, several pints of water upon top – incubator and caryatid at once) to the tramlined thoroughfare for which it was headed. At the corner this slowly trampling contraption turned, on its own centre, with a sultry swirl of the skirt, and started to walk back.

And here is Dickens, in *Martin Chuzzlewit*:

... The office-door was wide open, and in the doorway was the agent: no doubt a tremendous fellow to get through his work, for he seemed to have no arrears, but was swinging backwards and forwards in a rocking-chair, with one of his legs planted high up against the door-post, and the other doubled up under him, as if he were hatching his foot.

He was a gaunt man in a huge straw hat, and a coat of green stuff. The weather being hot, he had no cravat, and wore his shirt collar wide open; so that every time he spoke something was seen to twitch and jerk up in his throat, like the little hammers in a harpsichord when the notes are struck. Perhaps it was the Truth feebly endeavouring to leap to his lips. If so, it never reached them.

Two grey eyes lurked deep within this agent's head, but one of them had no sight in it, and stood stock still. With that side of his face he seemed to listen to what the other side was doing. Thus each profile had a distinct expression; and when the movable side was most in action, the rigid one was in its coldest state of watchfulness.

7

It was like turning the man inside out, to pass to that view of his features in his liveliest mood, and see how calculating and intent they were.

Each long black hair upon his head hung down as straight as any plummet line; but rumpled tufts were on the arches of his eyes, as if the crow whose foot was deeply printed in the corners had pecked and torn them in a savage recognition of his kindred nature as a bird of prey.

In each of these passages the effect is to dehumanise. Lewis reduces his Spanish woman to a mechanism, a 'contraption', to use his own word: Smollett and Dickens create grotesques in the strict, original sense of the word, for the grotesque denotes the interweaving of human and animal forms. Lismahago is made into a creature something like a grasshopper; Mr Scadder becomes a bird of prey.

It may be objected that, inasmuch as Mr Scadder's is a satirical portrait executed in concentrated contempt, it is the less typical of Dickens's method of presenting character. And of course the contempt does control the choice of images through which Scadder is embodied for us. Nevertheless, it seems to me that Dickens's method here is wholly parallel with those he uses in the depiction of characters for whom he has no contempt at all. Always the emphasis is on physical or sartorial oddity and idiosyncracy, and it is almost as though for Dickens these are themselves guarantees of the real. Take, for instance, his representation of a character he much admires, one suspects rather more than most of his modern readers do, Tom Pinch, one of Dickens's 'good' men:

An ungainly, awkward-looking man, extremely short-sighted, and prematurely bald, availed himself of this permission; and seeing that Mr Pecksniff sat with his back towards him, gazing at the fire, stood hesitating, with the door in his hand. He was far from handsome certainly; and was drest in a snuff-coloured suit, of an uncouth make at the best, which, being shrunk with long wear, was twisted and tortured into all kinds of odd shapes; but notwithstanding his attire, and his clumsy figure, which a great stoop in his shoulders, and a ludicrous habit he had of thrusting his head forward, by no means redeemed, one would not have been disposed (unless Mr Pecksniff said so) to consider him a bad fellow by any means. He was perhaps about thirty, but he might have been almost any age between sixteen and sixty: being one of those strange creatures who never decline into an ancient appearance, but look their oldest when they are very young, and get it over at once.

Throughout his work, Dickens's main approach to character, what one feels is normal to him, is the external approach. It is not the only one, of course. It does not account for, among others, Steerforth or Arthur Clennam or Eugene Wrayburn, all successful characterizations in a relatively naturalistic mode. But, merely because of this, they strike one as exceptions to the general rule, which is that the external approach, the emphasis on oddity and idiosyncracy, operates whenever his creative sympathies are engaged. It is, indeed, a sign that his creative sympathies *are* engaged; so that it is manifest not only in his comic characters, whether purely humorous like Pickwick, the Wellars, Micawber and the rest, or satirical, as with Pecksniff and Podsnap, but also through a wide spectrum of characters from the purely humorous to the monstrous and melodramatically wicked. To all these the external approach is fundamental; to the comic, by which I mean, in the simplest terms of definition, those characters to whom the immediate response is laughter, whether they are characters we or Dickens 'approve of' or not; to the multitude of figures that exist on the periphery of the comic, such as Newman Noggs or even Jaggers, the most enigmatic of his inventions; and the figures often called melodramatic, such as Quilp, Jonas Chuzzlewit and Carker. And it is surely significant that the characters with which Dickens most signally fails, young women such as Rose Maylie, Kate Nickleby and Ruth Pinch, are precisely those that are not approached externally. It is as though they are sacrosanct by virtue of their youth, sex, innocence and class, qualities that appear to inhibit criticism and the external approach that is the expression of his criticism. Conspicuously they lack idiosyncracy; it seems that if they were in any way odd they would be less than perfect.

Which means that the difference between the characters we think of as primarily comic and those we think of as sinister or melodramatic is often no more than a hair's breadth. Obvious instances are Fagin, Quilp and Jonas Chuzzlewit again, and Uriah Heep.

They are seen in all their minute peculiarities of physiognomy, stance and gesture, with a quite abnormal clarity and intensity of vision, so much so that it seems to me impossible not to agree with Santayana:

> When people say Dickens exaggerates, it seems to me they can have no eyes and no ears. They probably have only *notions* of what things and people are; they accept them conventionally at their diplomatic value. Their minds run on in the region of discourse, where there are masks only, and no faces, ideas and no facts; they have little sense for those living grimaces that play from moment upon the countenance of the world.[1]

It has become a commonplace to say that Dickens retained all his life the child's-eye view of human beings, but the idea is still worth pursuing for the light it throws on the nature of his comedy. The child's eye is innocent because what it sees is not blurred by associations; it sees with the shock of pristine freshness; and for the child the unfamiliar is always odd and perhaps even frightening. Grown-ups, on the other hand, take other people for granted; familiarity blunts the sense of novelty. The child says: 'Mummy, look at that funny man!' and he is right to see the man as funny. It is unlikely he will seem so to the child's mother. The child sees swaying on the man's shoulders a highly polished pink egg with a great red beak sticking out of the middle of it and underneath the beak a tangle of hair like a frayed scrubbing brush. The mother does not so much see the features themselves as remember the words that name them; for her, the man is merely bald, with a large reddish nose and a walrus moustache, and he merges into memories of all the other bald men with red noses and walrus moustaches she has seen in her life. Besides, it is rude to pass personal remarks, which means in this instance to comment on the physical peculiarities that distinguish one man from another. The child is shushed and told not to be rude. The process of depriving him of his innocent eye is already in being.

Inevitably, children live in a world inhabited by persons who seem, in retrospect, born to take their place in the novels of Dickens.

---

[1] Santayana, *Soliloquies in England*, 1922, pp. 65-6.

An instance of this is the way we all, I suspect, saw our school-masters. For children, grown-ups are incomprehensible, incalculable, arbitrary in their exercise of authority, creatures governed by whim, eccentric in the literal sense of the word since they move in orbits different from theirs and largely unknown to them. So, if he has any personality at all, the schoolmaster is likely to appear to his pupils as a comic oddity, as a freak or even a monster – and schoolmasters are aware that a carefully cultivated eccentricity can be a powerful teaching aid. In any case, the pupils will be aware, as the master himself is not, of the small idiosyncrasies that pass next to unnoticed by adults, and will relish them, the purely personal ways of standing or walking, the habitual tricks of speech and gesture, the way, perhaps, that he tugs at the lobe of his ear in moments of abstraction. Boys will magnify these largely unconscious patterns of behaviour until they take on the proportions of the grotesque; and then the boy's vision of the man may become something almost unrecognizable to grown-ups as an image of a human being. The master is made into a comic figure in spite of himself, and often, of course, he is rendered the more comic the more frightened the boys are of him or the more impressive his personality. Humour, the sense of the comic, is a powerful protection against the fearful and awe-inspiring. Humour tames them, puts them in their place, in a curious way makes them acceptable and at times even lovable.

This childish vision is part of Dickens's. Nevertheless, the parallel between Dickens and the child is valid only to a limited degree. The extraordinary intensity of his vision, however much it may seem akin to the child's, has to be explained, if it can be explained at all, in other ways. G. H. Lewes's remarks, in his essay on the novelist written in 1872,[1] which is in part a personal reminiscence, remain suggestive. Lewes writes:

> He was a seer of visions; and his visions were of objects at once familiar and potent. Psychologists will understand both the extent and the limitations of the remark, when I say that in no other perfectly sane mind (Blake, I believe, was not perfectly sane) have I

[1] 'Dickens in Relation to Criticism', *Fortnightly Review*, February 1872, pp. 141-54.

observed vividness of imagination approaching so closely to hallucination. Many who are not psychologists may have had some experience in themselves, or in others, of that abnormal condition in which a man hears voices, and sees objects, with the distinctness of direct perception, although silence and darkness are without him; these *revived* impressions, revived by an internal cause, have precisely the same force and clearness which the impressions originally had when produced by an external cause.

Lewes illustrates his argument by examples from the hallucinations of the insane and then, having emphasised that he has 'never observed any trace of the insane temperament in Dickens's work, or life,' goes on:

> ... nevertheless, with all due limitations, it is true that there is a considerable light shed upon his works by the action of the imagination in hallucination. To him also *revived* images have the vividness of sensations; to him also *created* images have the coercive force of realities, excluding all control, all contradiction. What seems preposterous, impossible to us, seemed to him simple fact of observation. When he imagined a street, a house, a room, a figure, he saw it not in the vague schematic way of ordinary imagination, but in the sharp definition of actual perception, all the salient details obtruding themselves on his attention. He, seeing it thus vividly, made us also see it; and believing in its reality however fantastic, he communicated something of his belief to us. He presented it in such relief that we ceased to think of it as a picture. So definite and insistent was the image, that even while knowing it was false we could not help, for a moment, being affected, as it were, by his hallucination.

Lewes is attempting to explain the nature of the compulsion Dickens lays upon us to accept his world. But what especially interests me now is the sentence in the second passage I have quoted: 'When he imagined a street, a house, a room, a figure, he saw it not in the vague schematic way of ordinary imagination, but in the sharp definition of actual perception, all the salient details obtruding themselves on his attention.' Lewes is here implying, I believe correctly, that Dickens's approach to the fabric of things, the inanimate, was the same as his approach to human beings and that its results were recorded with similar and idiosyncratic intensity. One thinks of the description of the fog with which *Bleak*

House opens or of that of Miss Havisham's bridal chamber at Satis House; but examples are endless. This means that Dickens's characters and the environments in which they have their being are all of a piece. Often, too, it is as though the fabric of things is being rendered almost as if it were itself human. Take the view from the roof of Todgers's, in *Martin Chuzzlewit*:

> ... if the day were bright, you observed upon the housetops, stretching far away, a long dark path: the shadow of the Monument: and turning round, the tall original was close behind you, with every hair erect upon his golden head, as if the doings of the city frightened him. Then there were steeples, towers, belfries, shining vanes, and masts of ships: a very forest. Gables, house-tops, garret-windows, wilderness upon wilderness. Smoke and noise enough for all the world at once.
>
> After the first glance, there were slight features in the midst of this crowd of objects, which sprung out from the mass, without any reason, as it were, and took hold of the attention whether the spectator would or no. Thus, the revolving chimney-pots on one great stack of buildings seemed to be turning gravely to each other every now and then, and whispering the result of their separate observation of what was going on below. Others, of a crook-backed shape, appeared to be maliciously holding themselves askew, that they might shut the prospect out and baffle Todgers's ...

Or again, from the description of the Podsnaps' dinner-party, in *Our Mutual Friend*:

> Everything was made to look as heavy as it could, and to take up as much room as possible. Everything said boastfully, 'Here you have as much of me in my ugliness as if I were only lead; but I am so many ounces of precious metal worth so much an ounce; – wouldn't you like to melt me down?' A corpulent straggling epergne, blotched all over as if it had broken out in an eruption rather than been ornamented, delivered this address from an unsightly silver platform in the centre of the table. Four silver wine-coolers, each furnished with four staring heads, each head obtrusively carrying a big silver ring in each of its ears, conveyed the sentiment up and down the table, and handed it on to the pot-bellied silver salt-cellars. All the big silver spoons and forks widened the mouths of the company expressly for the purpose of thrusting the sentiment down their throats with every morsel they ate.

13

Just as Dickens's method of rendering human beings results in their almost becoming things, so the similar method he uses of rendering things results in their almost becoming human. They are seen, as it were, as comic in their own right, or as sinister, menacing, suggestive of evil, or both.

[3]

Dickens was, as Lewes says, a seer. But he was just as much something else, for which there is no equivalent word. And it is here that any real comparison with Smollett and Wyndham Lewis breaks down. His visual sense, his delight in externals in all their peculiarities, does not exist by itself, in isolation. Rather, it is one element in a double process that functions as one. Here again Lewes is helpful. 'Dickens,' he writes, 'once declared to me that every word said by his characters was distinctly *heard* by him.' Whether this was literally true we cannot know. What is true is that all Dickens's successful characters, major and minor alike, speak in idioms uniquely personal to them as individuals. They are as intensely realized in their speech as their external appearance and mannerisms.

What Dickens is doing may be shown by a contrast with Smollett. In the way of comic creation Smollett did nothing better than Hawser Trunnion in *Peregrine Pickle*. Trunnion is one of the great English comic characters. But he has his genesis in a simple joke executed with infinite ingenuity. Commodore Trunnion is the retired naval officer who, back on dry land, insists on living as far as possible as though he were still on the bridge of one of His Majesty's ships at sea. He is, as it were, a triumph of the inability, indeed of the absolute refusal, to adjust. He continues in his retirement to feel, think, talk, behave entirely in terms of his profession of naval officer. This is the beginning, end and whole of the joke, which is based on the simplest of incongruities. As Smollett exploits it, it is a wonderful joke, and it reaches its peak in the passage in which Trunnion sets out on his wedding morning to navigate his way to church on horseback and is caught up *en voyage* in a fox-hunt. To say that the conception and execution of Trunnion's adventures are entirely mechanical is not to criticize Smollett's achievement. It is the unrelenting exploitation of a single classic comic situation, that of the sailor on dry land. Trunnion says nothing that is not in character, but the character – the sailor on dry land, both nouns existing as it were in the abstract – is the narrowest conceivable. Trunnion is the simplest kind of Jonsonian humour; and what he says – the translation, for instance, of his horse into a frigate – is implicit in the basic situation. To maintain the nautical metaphor, Trunnion is firmly anchored to his creator's intellectual conception of him.

This is not Dickens's way – as, indeed, the case of Captain Cuttle establishes. He is also presented as the sea-animal on land; but there is no such automatic, mechanical relationship between his externals and the way he habitually talks. His speech, which is invariably *sui generis*, is as it were liberating like that of Dickens's comic characters generally: it sets him in a dimension additional to any Smollett achieves with his characters. It has often been pointed out that the speech of Dickens's *dramatis personae* is akin to soliloquy; it is the language of personal obsession, the expression of the characters' permanent fantasy of themselves. And it is on the wings of their speech that Dickens's characters soar and rise above and clear of the intellectual conceptions in which many of them no doubt had their origin. It can make them extraordinarily rich, so rich as creations as to make the old accusations that used to be levelled against them as being caricatures or 'flat' characters obvious nonsense, so far short as adequate descriptions of them or as explanations of the effect they have on us such critical terms fall.

Mr Pecksniff is a case in point. He has, of course, always been recognized as one of Dickens's supreme achievements in the comic. He is a hypocrite – but having said that, one has said merely the first and most obvious thing about him, for in his complexity he is much more. He is not to be equated, for instance, with Tartuffe. Beyond any other character in *Martin Chuzzlewit*, he is at the centre of the novel, at the centre of the whole web of intrigue. *Martin Chuzzlewit* is a novel on the theme of selfishness – and, of course, unselfishness, which appears as much less convincing. And Pecksniff, besides being a hypocrite, is the absolutely selfish man. He is, one is tempted to say, the complete embodiment and dramatization of solipsism. He is a man for whom the external world and other people scarcely exist; he is armoured by, imprisoned in, his immense self-assurance. He is impregnable and invincible, as his last recorded utterances in the novel indicate:

'I know the human mind, although I trust it. That is my weakness. Do I not know, sir;' here he became exceedingly plaintive, and was observed to glance towards Tom Pinch; 'that my misfortunes bring this treatment on me? Do I not know, sir, that but for them I never should have heard what I have heard today? Do I not know that in the silence and the solitude of night, a little voice will whisper in your ear, Mr. Chuzzlewit, "This was not well. This was not well, sir!" Think of this, sir (if you will have the goodness), remote from the impulses of passion, and apart from the specialities, if I may use that strong remark, of prejudice. And if you ever contemplate the silent tomb, sir, which you will excuse me for entertaining some doubt of your doing, after the conduct into which you have allowed yourself to be betrayed this day; if you ever contemplate the silent tomb, sir, think of me. If you find yourself approaching to the silent tomb, sir, think of me. If you should wish to have anything inscribed upon your silent tomb, sir, let it be, that I – ah, my remorseful sir! that I – the humble individual who has now the honour of reproaching you, forgave you. That I forgave you when my injuries were fresh, and when my bosom was newly wrung. It may be bitterness to you to hear it now, sir, but you will live to seek a consolation in it. May you find a consolation in it when you want it, sir! Good morning!'

In its inspired dottiness this is wonderful in its own right. But there is more to it than this. It is dramatically right, and in the most masterly way, for it is the finally clinching manifestation and revelation of the Pecksniff that cannot be pinned down as simply a hypocrite but is nothing less than a moral monster, a monster of self-regard. His self-regard, his unfalteringly bland self-approval and self-complacency, are fundamental to his hypocrisy, and it is the psychological truth of this that makes him so much more complex and interesting a character than the hypocrite of classical comedy. Our joy in what he says and how he says it should not blind us to the fact that the matter and manner alike of what he says are functional. For Pecksniff, language is the means by which everything, however hostile, in the world outside him is turned into food for the gratification of his insatiable appetite for self-praise, of his moral superiority:

16

'It is to be lamented,' said Mr. Pecksniff, with a forgiving recollection of Mr. Spottletoe's fist, 'that our friend should have withdrawn himself so very hastily, though we have cause for mutual congratulation even in that, since we are assured that he is not distrustful of us in regard to anything we may say or do while he is absent. Now that is very soothing, is it not?'

'Pecksniff,' said Anthony, who had been watching the whole party with peculiar keenness from the first: 'don't you be a hypocrite.'

'A what, my good sir?' demanded Mr. Pecksniff.

'A hypocrite.'

'Charity, my dear,' said Mr. Pecksniff, 'when I take my chamber candlestick to-night, remind me to be more than usually particular in praying for Mr. Anthony Chuzzlewit; who has done me an injustice.'

And even when, in moments of crisis, Pecksniff's language soars into lunatic poetry, as when he announces Tom Pinch's defection to old Martin Chuzzlewit:

'Oh! bad, bad, bad!' said Martin, laying down his book. 'Very bad! I hope not. Are you certain?'

'Certain, my good sir! My eyes and ears are witnesses. I wouldn't have believed it otherwise. I wouldn't have believed it, Mr. Chuzzlewit, if a Fiery Serpent had proclaimed it from the top of Salisbury Cathedral. I would have said,' cried Mr. Pecksniff, 'that the Serpent lied. Such was my faith in Thomas Pinch, that I would have cast the falsehood back into the Serpent's teeth, and would have taken Thomas to my heart. But I am not a Serpent, sir, myself, I grieve to say, and no excuse or hope is left me.'

the very extravagence, the lunacy of language and logic, seem purposive. It is as though Pecksniff is deliberately enveloping himself in a fog of nonsense in order to obscure the issue, to destroy the possibility of communication and to protect himself against truth and reality, much as the cuttle-fish in the presence of enemies isolates itself in a cloud of sepia. Pecksniff's launchings out into the linguistically absurd are a form of self-justification. Dickens leaves nothing undone or unsaid that will emphasise Pecksniff's absurdity; but I think we do Dickens an injustice if we take Pecksniff as being merely absurd. He is a moral monster, created with deep psychological penetration, and he is revealed in all his complexity in the words that Dickens puts into his mouth.

[4]

There is a passage in *Great Expectations* in which, it seems to me, Dickens momentarily shows us the secret springs of his creative imagination in its simplest and most primitive form. It is in chapter 9, which begins:

> When I reached home, my sister was very curious to know all about Miss Havisham's, and asked a number of questions. And I soon found myself getting heavily bumped from behind in the nape of the neck and the small of the back, and having my face ignominiously shoved against the kitchen wall, because I did not answer those questions at sufficient length.

Pip goes on, under the inquisition of Mr Pumblechook, to produce his fantasy of life at Satis House:

> 'Now, boy! What was she adoing of, when you went in to-day?' asked Mr. Pumblechook.
> 'She was sitting,' I answered, 'in a black velvet coach.'
> Mr. Pumblechook and Mrs. Joe stared at one another – as they well might – and both repeated, 'In a black velvet coach?'
> 'Yes,' said I. 'And Miss Estella – that's her niece, I think – handed her in cake and wine at the coach-window, on a gold plate. And we all had cake and wine on gold plates. And I got up behind the coach to eat mine, because she told me to.'
> 'Was anybody else there?' asked Mr. Pumblechook.
> 'Four dogs,' said I.
> 'Large or small?'
> 'Immense,' said I. 'And they fought for veal-cutlets out of a silver basket.'
> Mr. Pumblechook and Mrs. Joe stared at one another again, in utter amazement. I was perfectly frantic – a reckless witness under the torture – and would have told them anything.
> 'Where *was* this coach, in the name of gracious?' asked my sister.
> 'In Miss Havisham's room.' They stared again. 'But there weren't any horses to it.' I added this saving clause, in the moment of rejecting four richly caparisoned coursers, which I had had wild thoughts of harnessing.
> 'Can this be possible, uncle?' asked Mrs. Joe. 'What can the boy mean?'
> 'I'll tell you, mum,' said Mr. Pumblechook. 'My opinion is, it's a sedan-chair. She's flighty, you know – very flighty – quite flighty enough to pass her days in a sedan-chair.'

Pip is not the young Dickens. He had already appeared as David Copperfield. But all the circumstances in which *Great Expectations* was written, along with the ambiance of the story itself, make it reasonable to see Pip as very closely related to his creator, as a surrogate figure. Pip's fantasy of Satis House is not, in fact, any more fantastic than what he has already seen and taken part in there; but it is fantasy all the same, and it seems to spell out the primary qualities of Dickens's imagination, which isolated and emphasized the intrinsically odd, the astonishing and the bizarre, and delighted in the juxtaposition of incongruities and in wild departures from the expected. If we take the world as depicted in the fiction of say, Trollope or George Eliot as being representative of ordinary vision, which most of us would assume we possess, since it is on that assumption that we call it ordinary, then Dickens's depiction of the world is obviously very extraordinary indeed. When we recognize in Dickens the world as commonly observed we see that it is as it were only the launching-pad for his flights of fantastic invention. What results is a panorama of the lives of men and women in society not less 'real' than Trollope's or George Eliot's but intensely more dramatic, composed of much greater contrasts of light and dark, a world of extremes, in which everything is heightened and, ordinary vision would say, exaggerated. It is not because of that less true than Trollope's or Eliot's. We are all, by contrast with Dickens, more or less in the position of Sam Weller, with his: 'Yes, I have a pair of eyes, and that's just it. If they wos a pair o' patent double million magnifyin' gas microscopes of Hextra power, p'raps I might be able to see through a flight o' stairs and a deal door; but bein' only eyes, you see, my wision's limited.' Our wision's equally limited. But in the end, the criticism of life and society which proceeds from Dickens's pair of patent double magnifying gas microscopes of Hextra power seems to me more profound and more satisfying than that either of Trollope or George Eliot.

It is common form to say that Dickens's progress as an artist was from the delighted acceptance of the world his imagination revealed to him to an increasingly radical dissatisfaction with it; in other words, that his imagination darkened as he grew older. In general

terms, this is true; but the progress, as I have suggested, was not
an even one; and it is always necessary to remember that even as he
was writing the later parts of *Pickwick Papers* he was also writing
Oliver Twist, which, relatively crude though it is, demonstrates at
the outset of his career his affinities with Dostoievsky. It may be
useful to set the two novels side by side, for together they throw
much light on the diversity of Dickens's modes of comedy and of
comic-character creation.

Pickwick Papers is one of the most remarkable works ever written.
It is probably still most people's first introduction to Dickens, which
means that it is generally read first in childhood; and it remains the
chief source of the Dickens of the popular imagination, the Dickens
whose achievement is summed up in the adjective Dickensian, with
its attributes of high spirits, jolliness and benevolence. My own
belief is that to see it in its true light it needs to be re-read after one
has read the later Dickens, for in significant ways it stands apart
from the rest of his work. As Steven Marcus, to whom all students
of Dickens are indebted, has said:

> *Pickwick Papers* is the novel in which Dickens achieved the very
> thing we tend to think is the exclusive right of only the greatest,
> most mature, most fully consummated artists: he achieved trans-
> cendence. By transcendence I mean a representation of life which
> fulfils that vision, which men have never yet relinquished, of the
> ideal possibilities of human relations in community, and which, in
> the fulfilment, extends our awareness of the limits of our humanity.[1]

Dickens, in other words, began his career with the expression of
his ideal vision of man and society and, over the years, found it more
and more contradicted by the realities of the society in which he
lived. Yet, in a real sense, a good deal of what was to preoccupy the
later Dickens, the social critic and satirist, is present in *Pickwick
Papers*. Mr Pickwick is caught up, in all innocence, in the machinery
of the law; he is the victim of unscrupulous lawyers. A large part of
the action takes place in the Fleet Prison. The innocent are gulled
by dissenting ministers, the professional representatives of the principles of plain living and high thinking. And so on. The main

---

[1] Steven Marcus, *Dickens: from Pickwick to Dombey*, 1965, p. 17.

difference between it and the works that followed is again stated by Steven Marcus: '*Pickwick Papers* is Dickens' one novel in which wickedness, though it exists, is not a threat.' It makes, of course, all the difference in the world. It means that in *Pickwick Papers* we are in the realm of pure humour as in no other book ever written except perhaps *Alice in Wonderland*. As a comic work, it is almost wholly devoid of satire. It has, admittedly, its rogues and villains – Mr Jingle and Job Trotter, Dodson and Fogg, the Rev. Mr Stiggins. But we do not think of them as rogues and villains. We think of them as purely comic creations; and so they are. Their absurdity exists in its own right, as a good thing in itself. It is as though Dickens is so enchanted by the spectacle of human absurdity that he has created from his observation of the world that his critical impulse, the impulse to satirise, is inhibited. He is disarmed by his own comedy and content to laugh; for his characters justify themselves, even redeem themselves, by their very power to provoke laughter.

The treatment of Mr Stiggins is interesting here. Mr Stiggins, it will be recalled, is strong for providing the infant Negroes of the West Indies with flannel waistcoats and preaches at the United Grand Junction Ebenezer Temperance Association: deploring with Mrs Weller Mr Tony Weller's iniquities, he drinks his pineapple rum and fills up his pint-and-a-half bottle with it before he departs. Dickens does not satirise Stiggins; the simple fun that arises from the simple contrast between principle and exploitation of principle, which leads to practices clean contrary to principle, is enough for him. But fifteen years later, in *Bleak House*, he drew the character of another religious humbug, Chadband; and Chadband he does satirise. Chadband is the target for Dickens's contempt:

> 'Peace, my friends,' says Chadband, rising and wiping the oily exudations from his reverend visage. 'Peace be with us! My friends, why with us? Because,' with his fat smile, 'it cannot be against us, because it must be for us; because it is not hardening, because it is softening; because it does not make war like the hawk, but comes home unto us like the dove. Therefore, my friends, peace be with us! My human boy, come forward!'

It is Jo, the crossing-sweeper, he is beckoning, and Jo, the lonely exiled child, exists for him only as an object which triggers off his ludicrous eloquence. But in *Pickwick Papers* there is no Jo, or any character like him. By comparison with the novels that follow, *Pickwick Papers* displays a world 'as innocent as Beatrix Potter's'.[1] Its comedy has no designs on us and no ulterior motive. Its true intent, quite simply, is all for our delight. Which is why, for the first and the last time in Dickens we are in the realm of pure humour, which comes out at its plainest in the characters of Pickwick himself and of the Wellers, Dickens's first great astonishers in the comic use of language. Both are great poets in their own right, as their mastery of imagery shows.

There are no such figures in *Oliver Twist*, and the nature of the novel makes it impossible that there should be. *Oliver Twist* does have designs on us, palpable designs. It is an 'exposure' novel, and what Dickens himself seems to have been principally interested in exposing was what he called 'the miserable reality' of crime. He saw the novel as a work of realism, a debunking of the romanticising of crime current in the popular fiction of the day. But Fagin and Bill Sikes are not figures that we should expect to find in the realistic novel as we normally understand it. They have the intensity, the superreality, of figures in nightmare. They are poetic conceptions; and in their great last scenes, Sikes at bay before the mob on Jacob's Island, Fagin in the dock and in the death cell, they become heroic, almost tragic figures. Sikes is never comic, and I suspect that the modern reader does not see Fagin as comic, either; but he sees himself as comic and succeeds in making even Oliver laugh. He is not called 'the merry old gentleman' for nothing, but his vein of merriment is part of his sinisterness.

But there is the other side of the novel, which is linked to the miserable reality of the criminal underworld by the workhouse, the breeding-place of crime. The workhouse, or rather the consequences of the New Poor Law of 1834, is the second object of Dickens's exposure. Whether he was fair to the New Poor Law scarcely matters now. What he was protesting against, as he was to go on doing for the rest of his life, was the conception of life that he believed was held by those responsible for the Poor Law, the statisti-

[1] W. H. Auden's phrase. See 'Easily, my dear, you move, easily your head', *Look Stranger!*, 1936, p. 50.

cal view of man, which sees him as comparable with a machine that can be kept in working order, i.e., alive, by the injection into it of a carefully calculated minimum of energy-producing fuel – calories we might say today. Mr Bumble expresses it in his own terms when he is summoned by the Sowerberries to deal with Oliver after his attack on Noah Claypole:

> 'It's not Madness, ma'am,' replied Mr. Bumble, after a few moments of deep meditation. 'It's Meat.'
>
> 'What?' exclaimed Mrs. Sowerberry.
>
> 'Meat, ma'am, meat,' replied Bumble, with stern emphasis. 'You've over-fed him, ma'am. You've raised a artificial soul and spirit in him, ma'am, unbecoming a person of his condition: as the board, Mrs. Sowerberry, who are practical philosophers, will tell you. What have paupers to do with soul or spirit? It's quite enough that we let 'em have live bodies. If you had kept the boy on gruel, ma'am, this would never have happened.'
>
> 'Dear, dear!' ejaculated Mrs. Sowerberry, piously raising her eyes to the kitchen ceiling: 'this comes of being liberal!'

We know what Mrs Sowerberry's liberality has consisted of – 'all the dirty odds and ends which nobody else would eat.'

That *Oliver Twist* is an exposure of a conception of man and its consequences that Dickens detested governs the nature of the comedy. It is angry, even savage, and Bumble, who is at its centre, is rendered ridiculous, one feels, because it is only by being able to see him as ridiculous that Dickens can bear to contemplate him at all. He is the first instance in Dickens of savage caricature, and it is worth stressing that he is caricatured not simply because he is a beadle. He is any unimaginative and corrupt underling to whom bureaucracy has given power, seen from the point of view of one of his victims. He is a representative figure, as Dickens's savage caricatures tend to be, Uriah Heep, for instance, in whom Dickens concentrates one of his most damaging criticisms of Victorian society. 'I'm not fond,' David Copperfield tells him, 'of professions of humility.'

> 'There now!' said Uriah, looking flabby and lead-coloured in the moonlight. 'Didn't I know it! But how little you think of the rightful umbleness of a person in my station, Master Copperfield! Father and

me was both brought up at a foundation school for boys; and mother, she was likewise brought up at a public, sort of charitable, establishment. They taught us all a deal of umbleness – not much else that I know of, from morning to night. We was to be umble to this person, and umble to that; and to pull off our caps here, and to make bows there; and always to know our place, and abase ourselves before our betters. And we had such a lot of betters! Father got the monitor-medal by being umble. So did I. Father got made a sexton by being umble ... "Be umble, Uriah," says father to me, "and you'll get on. It was what was always being dinned into you and me at school; it's what goes down best. Be umble," says father, "and you'll do!" And really it ain't done bad!' ...

'... I am very umble to the present moment, Master Copperfield, but I've got a little power!'

Heep, the representative victim of early nineteenth-century good works having his own back on the nineteenth century, is sinister as well as comic. And it seems to me that much light is thrown on Dickens's conception not only of Heep but also of his figures of savage caricature generally, by Heep's 'I am very umble to the present moment, Master Copperfield, but I've got a little power!' It is power, little or otherwise, that is the especial target of Dickens's most ferocious contempt. One thinks of Squeers, of Gradgrind and Bitzer and Bounderby, the 'Bully of humility' with his 'infection of moral claptrap,' his 'I can see as far into a grindstone as another man; farther than a good many, perhaps, because I had my nose well kept to it when I was young. I see traces of the turtle soup, and venison, and gold spoon in this. ... By the Lord Harry, I do!' One thinks of Podsnap, in whom all the self-complacency and self-righteousness of Victorian middle-class respectability are compounded.

It seems to me that the savagery of these characterizations can scarcely be over-estimated. It is as though, for Dickens, the possession of power, or, rather, the arbitrary exploitation of power, is the absolutely unforgivable thing; and on those who possess it he pours all his resources of ridicule and contempt. But they remain monstrous and terrifying, and are meant to be.

Lack of power, effective power, on the other hand, is disarming. Dickens's comic characters, at any rate after *Pickwick Papers*, are rarely morally admirable. Silas Wegg, for instance – and the instance is a useful one since he appears in Dickens's last completed work – is a rogue, but the satirical intention that one assumes was originally in Dickens's mind when he conceived the character is all but forgotten as the novel proceeds. Wegg is softened by humour; his viciousness becomes very much a secondary consideration, almost lost in Dickens's sheer exuberant joy in the character he is creating. And joy in turn begets a kind of sympathy, even love, so that in the end characters like Wegg exist for their own sake, without reference to moral considerations. The sign that this has happened is the comic poetry these characters utter. Such a remark as that Silas Wegg makes to Mr Venus, 'Since I called upon you that evening when you were, as I may say, floating your powerful mind in tea,' is surely as ultimately unanalysable and mysterious as a line of great lyric poetry; and when we come across it, and comparable felicities in Dickens, we know that the current of satire, of moral indignation, has been inhibited. The character has been translated in a realm in which moral considerations are irrelevant. The comic becomes an aspect of Dickens's charity, indeed in these instances it is the expression of his charity. The supreme example of this, of course, is Mrs Gamp, with whom, dirty gin-sodden old midwife and layer-out of corpses as she is, Dickens soars into great poetry, for if her characteristic flights of fantasy are not great poetry one doesn't know what else to call them:

'Now, ain't we rich in beauty this here joyful arternoon, I'm sure. I knows a lady, which her name, I'll not deceive you, Mrs Chuzzlewit, is Harris, her husband's brother bein' six foot three, and marked with a mad bull in Wellington boots upon his left arm, on account of his precious mother havin' been worrited by one into a shoemaker's shop, when in a sitiwation which blessed is the man as has his quiver full of sech, as many times I've said to Gamp when words has roge betwixt us on account of the expense – and often have I said to Mrs Harris, "Oh, Mrs Harris, ma'am! your countenance is quite a angel's!" Which, but for Pimples, it would be. "No, Sairey Gamp," says she, "you best of hard-working and industrious creeturs as ever was underpaid at any price, which underpaid you are, quite diff'rent. Harris had it done afore marriage at ten and six," she says, "and wore it faithful next his heart 'till the colour run, when the money was declined to be give back, and no arrangement could be come to. But he never said it was a angel's, Sairey, wotever he might have thought." If Mrs Harris's husband was here now,' said Mrs Gamp, looking round and chuckling as she dropped a general curtsy, 'he'd speak out plain, he would, and his dear wife would be the last to blame him! For if ever a woman lived as know'd not wot it was to form a wish to pizon them as had good looks, and had no reagion give her by the best of husbands, Mrs Harris is that ev'nly dispogician!'

[5]

Nevertheless, even when one has produced samples, in terms of characterization, of Dickens's comic genius, the difficulty of presenting the totality of his comic genius remains, and is probably insoluble. To quote speeches from the Wellers, Pecksniff, Mrs Gamp, Podsnap and the rest is inevitably to abstract them from the novels in which they appear. It takes no account of the ceaseless invention that informs their being, the delighted surprise that for the reader attends them continually in their progress. It takes no account, in other words, of their cumulative effect. It ignores, also, the contexts in which they appear, for, however much we may abstract them in memory, they exist in nothing like a void in the novels. On the contrary, they exist in contexts characterized by quite extraordinary density of specification, to use James's phrase. They are at the centre of crowded scenes, of great set pieces of wonderfully sustained comic drama, the trial of Mr Pickwick, the goings-on at Todgers's, the dinner-party at the Podsnaps, to quote three instances only from a list that could be virtually endless.

And there is something else, of which all this is an aspect: the sheer prodigality, the inexhaustible fecundity of Dickens's comic invention. I have concentrated on a mere half dozen comic figures; but again the list is virtually endless. Some of them appear only once or twice in the course of a novel; they are marginal or peripheral, thrown in, one might say, for good measure, though, more truly, because Dickens, caught in the throes of creation, simply could not stop creating. But they immortalize themselves with a phrase, Mr Turveydrop's 'Wooman, lovely wooman, what a sex you are!' or Trabb's boy's 'Don't know yah, don't know yah, 'pon my soul don't know yah!' or the anonymous butcher in *Martin Chuzzlewit* telling

Tom Pinch, 'with some emotion', that meat 'must be humoured and not drove'.

The nature, indeed, the crowdedness of the fantastically crowded canvases that are Dickens's novels may be illustrated, I think, by a comparison, however unfair it may seem, with novels by later writers who have seen themselves as being in a very real sense in the Dickens tradition. *The History of Mr Polly* is Wells at his closest to Dickens, and it contains two memorable comic characters, Uncle Pentstemon and Mr Polly himself, whose 'Second Dear Departed I've seen. Not including mummies,' surely has the genuine ring. The eponymous hero of V. S. Pritchett's *Mr Beluncle* is also a character in the Dickens mould. Both works are considerable achievements, highly serious, highly entertaining. They exist firmly in their own right. Yet, when one puts them side by side with Dickens's novels one realizes their comparative poverty – comparative, of course, only to Dickens. One feels that in any Dickens novel, Uncle Pentstemon, Mr Polly or Mr Beluncle, admirable though they are and would remain, would have been merely one comic figure among many, a dominant figure, perhaps, in a corner of the total canvas.

In the presence of this fantastic prodigality, this superabundance of invention, all that can be said, though I think even more justly, is what Dryden said of Chaucer: 'Here is God's plenty.' The world that Dickens creates is his own, absolutely his own, and is vast both in range and variety. It is almost as difficult to see steadily and to see whole as life itself. This makes all critical approaches to Dickens partial. Yet the different truths they discover are not mutually exclusive. Recent interpretations of Dickens that stress his affinities with Dostoievsky and Kafka, interpretations that, once made, seem self-evident, do not negate the truths contained in Chesterton's interpretation. Both are right, and they are not incompatible. But always, as a check on the findings of Dickens criticism, we have to come back to what is fundamental to him, the element without which Dickens would not be Dickens, the comic genius, Bagehot's 'endless fertility in laughter-causing detail.'

BARBARA HARDY

THE
COMPLEXITY
OF DICKENS

Dickens possesses such variety and richness that at times he may seem to run into the danger of being all things to all people. He has appealed to the illiterate, the child, the common reader, and the literary critic. He has been described as theatrical, poetic, analytic, journalistic, symbolist, explicit, realist, surrealist, Marxist, Christian and existentialist. Critics of all schools and philosophers of many, have found the right material or the right image in his fiction. And if at times his very openness, breadth, and informality of thought have made him easily assimilated by all the schools, there is perhaps something to be said for seizing the significance of this, rather than carping, as we count up the numerous visions and revisions of his genius.

In order to account for any one of his great novels, we do have to see many aspects of the man and the artist. He is one of our greatest comic writers, and his actual range of comedy, which includes all kinds and colour of jokes, farce, humour, wit, and satire, is probably only overreached by Shakespeare. He is a great caricaturist and we may want at times to use of him the phrase T. S. Eliot used of Ben Jonson, when he called him an artist 'of the surface'. But only at times. For if he can represent the social surfaces of men, places, objects, and institutions, brilliantly, harshly, and powerfully, Dickens can also plumb the depths, both of sensation and feeling. We need to put his black passions beside the comedy, and see the psychological insight that may be implied even in his surfaces and theatrical set-pieces. He is one of the most shrewd and sharp reporters in English literature, and adds to the reporter's observation the journalist's deliberate manipulation and entertainment of his readers. He is a social critic, of individual institutions and of a whole society, and his art of characterization can only be truly understood if we see that he is creating and re-creating the distortions he saw around him, and against an ideal which can perhaps best be seen as an image of his belief in original virtue.

He was also capable of extremely bad writing, banal plots, wooden characters, and pretty meaningless stories, situations and conclusions. We really need to include his extremes of goodness and badness in an account of the complexity of his art. To some extent, this may be accounted for by the pressures of time and space, but it seems to me most likely that it is explained by the unusually large quantity of his vitality that got into his fiction. If we compare literary output with the larger life, it is usually striking how small a slice of the human experiences and interests – of the whole man – gets into the writing. With Dickens, the external evidence of his life and his other interests reveals how little he left out.

His art is a heterogeneous one, but not in the way that Sterne's *Tristram Shandy* or Joyce's *Ulysses* are heterogeneous. Sterne and Joyce are both artists whose literary artifice is conspicuous, very highly controlled, and constantly, self-consciously, discussed and analyzed. Their eclecticism exists in the interests of a discussion of art. For all Dickens's foresight and serial planning, for all his extreme awareness of the reader and of himself, he seems to belong to that great and admirable class of writers who share a tremendous literary innocence, who are not carefully shaping their art for their fellow-artists, the critics, or the artist in themselves, and who are indeed not writing about art – writers like the Brontës, Hardy, Lawrence. They are not by any means lacking in a concern for art, but, paradoxically perhaps, it is a concern overridden by their larger humanity. It seems significant that they do not attempt large-scale literary satire, often show rough edges and undigested discursive elements, and at times write appalling English prose.

Dickens's art and his humanity sometimes complexly serve each other, are sometimes complexly at odds with each other. His art is complex in its profound and superficial attempts to order a social and personal narrative, and in its attempt to come at life – or to create life – seriously and comically. I want to look at three aspects of this complexity, all of which show the surface and depth, the comedy and the seriousness. Like all the great Victorians (except perhaps Charlotte Brontë) he usually tells a complex story, made out of many strands, many characters, many places, many stories, and many themes. In the ordering of such multiple actions, he is serious and comic, writing caricature and character, telling a social and a personal story.

[2]

It is well known that *Pickwick Papers* (1836–7) is organized so as to present a split between the comic and the serious. In the inset tales that are read, discovered, and presented, Pickwick and his friends are given a literary supplement to their tour of England, and it is a dark, grim, tragic supplement, telling of madness, crime, death, poverty, despair. In the main action and adventures, there is also some poverty, crime, and wretchedness but it is either resolved or comically distanced. There is another minor but conspicuous source of the underworld, in the black humour of Jingle's telegraphese and Sam Weller's anecdotes, which present a world of deaths, murders, marital disaster, servants' wretchedness, fear, pain, drugs, horror. 'There's nothin so refreshin as sleep, sir, as the servant-girl said afore she drank the egg-cupful of laudanum': can stand as the type. The blandness with which Sam's comparisons are received makes plain one of the chief formal characteristics of

Dickens's first work of fiction, its rich discreteness. Its comedy lies apart from its pathos, and indeed the various kinds of comedy – jokes, farce, comedy of humours, visual anecdote, social satire – often lie apart from each other. The episodic structure of the action, with its many narrative interruptions, shows Dickens's form at its most informal. But the novel – it had better be called a novel, after all – also shows the breadth of his interests and the variety of his skills.

If we jump to the other end of Dickens's career, to *Our Mutual Friend*, the last complete novel (1864–5), we find a dramatic expansion and synthesis of comedy and serious action. Here is the scene from Book IV, Chapter xv where Rogue Riderhood has at last hunted down Bradley Headstone to his schoolroom. Bradley first sees Riderhood's approach in the boys' eyes, 'reading in the countenances . . . that there was something wrong' and there follows a strong scene where the comic surface is sinister in its brittle play and irony. He asks if he can question the children, and Bradley has to agree:

> 'Oh! It's in the way of school!' cried Riderhood. 'I'll pound it, Master, to be in the way of school. Wot's the diwisions of water, my lambs? Wot sorts of water is there on the land?'
> Shrill chorus: 'Seas, rivers, lakes, and ponds.'
> 'Seas, rivers, lakes, and ponds,' said Riderhood. 'They've got all the lot, Master! Blowed if I shouldn't have left out lakes, never having clapped eyes upon one, to my knowledge. Seas, rivers, lakes, and ponds. Wot is it, lambs, as they ketches in seas, rivers, lakes, and ponds?'
> Shrill chorus (with some contempt for the ease of the question): 'Fish!'

Riderhood then reaches the climax, and flourishes the telltale bundle of clothes he has fished out of the river. This mingling of the comic and the melodramatically serious has a nervous *bravura* which virtually absorbs comedy in the grim irony of Riderhood's trap. But there is more to it than that: Riderhood is putting on an ironic performance, which terribly teases and flouts the schoolmaster, but the performance also acts as a kind of dreadful parody of pedagogy, and of the whole futile discipline, rules and drilling that have narrowed Bradley, the passionate man, to what he is. It is an institutional satire that reveals the man, but it is also a marvellous exhibition of the triumphant confidence of the comic villain, enjoying his moment, and having that kind of comic flourish and enjoyment of vitality that we find in the denouements of Ben Jonson. So, although the comedy seems to be absorbed in a grotesque melodrama and revealing satire, it is still something recognizably comic. Riderhood has had a comic dimension all along, but the sheer contrast here between his free-playing energy and the man incapable of humour, wit, or freedom, makes its incisive psychological definition. This is the kind of complex mingling of the comic, the horrible, and the pathetic that is typical of late Dickens.

However, it can make impressive appearances in a quieter, more reticent way too. Here is an example from *Bleak House* (1852-3). It is a description of the sickbed of Sir Leicester Dedlock; we begin with Sir Leicester speaking about Lady Dedlock:

> 'My Lady is too high in position, too handsome, too accomplished, too superior in most respects to the best of those by whom she is surrounded, not to have her enemies and traducers, I dare say. Let it be known to them, as I make it known to you, that being of sound mind, memory, and understanding, I revoke no disposition I have made in her favour. I abridge nothing I have ever bestowed upon her. I am on unaltered terms with her, and I recall – having the full power to do it if I were so disposed, as you see – no act I have done for her advantage and happiness.'
>
> His formal array of words might have at any other time, as it has often had, something ludicrous in it; but at this time it is serious and affecting. His noble earnestness, his fidelity, his gallant shielding of her, his general conquest of his own wrong and his own pride for her sake, are simply honourable, manly, and true. Nothing less worthy can be seen through the lustre of such qualities in the commonest mechanic, nothing less worthy can be seen in the best-born gentleman. In such a light both aspire alike, both rise alike, both children of the dust shine equally.
>
> Overpowered by his exertions, he lays his head back on his pillows, and closes his eyes; for not more than a minute; when he again resumes his watching of the weather, and his attention to the muffled sounds. In the rendering of those little services, and in the manner of their acceptance, the trooper has become installed as necessary to him. Nothing has been said, but it is quite understood. He falls a step or

two backward to be out of sight, and mounts guard a little behind his mother's chair.

The day is now beginning to decline. The mist, and the sleet into which the snow has all resolved itself, are darker, and the blaze begins to tell more vividly upon the room walls and furniture. The gloom augments; the bright gas springs up in the streets; and the pertinacious oil lamps which yet hold their ground there, with their source of life half frozen and half thawed, twinkle gaspingly, like fiery fish out of water – as they are. The world, which has been rumbling over the straw and pulling at the bell, 'to inquire', begins to go home, begins to dress, to dine, to discuss its dear friend, with all the last new modes, as already mentioned.

Now, does Sir Leicester become worse; restless, uneasy, and in great pain. Volumnia lighting a candle (with a predestined aptitude for doing something objectionable) is bidden to put it out again, for it is not yet dark enough. Yet it is very dark too; as dark as it will be all night. By-and-by she tries again. No! Put it out. It is not dark enough yet.

I have chosen this passage, in its way very unremarkable, bland, and quiet compared with many, as a typical extract from the mature Dickens, showing his restraint, his relaxation, and his complexity. In an early novel, particularly in *Pickwick Papers*, *Nicholas Nickleby*, *The Old Curiosity Shop* and *Barnaby Rudge*, we could not find such restrained complexity. Here the Dickensian powers of wit and caricature are present, but are subdued to the occasion. Sir Leicester's gentlemanliness and his formality, together with that legalistic formality which colours so much of the language of the novel, are all expressed in his controlled crescendo, elaborate parenthesis, inversions and legal phrases. But it is not a dead or a deadlocked language any more because Dickens is now employing it to express the manliness that is larger than gentlemanliness, a nobility that has nothing to do with pedigree. The sheer quality of its loyal and loving feelings and its precision of statement, does exactly what Dickens tells us it does, shines through the 'formal array' of his words that might have seemed 'ludicrous'. The caricature of style is subdued. And with it, the caricature of formality in the man. Subdued also is the wit that is so obtrusive and exuberant elsewhere (at the beginning of the novel, for instance) darting out only in the description of the oil lamps with a typical Dickensian precision, as he explains the literal source of his conceit, 'fiery fish out of water – as they are', referring to the whale-oil. It is subdued also in satire in the last quiet collocation 'to discuss its dear friend, with all the last new modes'. After all, the world has been to inquire, and does put its friend before the last new modes.

Subdued also is pathos and moral exaltation, both given a long leash in early Dickens and by no means quite absent from *Bleak House*. Sir Leicester's formal style is used for the words of loyalty, forgiveness, generosity and love. It controls and realistically individualizes the moral climax. Sir Leicester's pathetic struggles with his illness are realized and sharpened by the use of silly old Volumnia and by the flash of his still-surviving commanding peremptoriness, the more abrupt for sliding in without quotation marks in 'No! Put it out.'

As my qualifications have had to make clear, this fusion and mixed colouring of comedy, moral earnestness, and pathos is by no means the rule in *Bleak House*, where we could also find passages of unrelieved sentiment and moral exclamation, mostly in passages dealing with Esther and Jarndyce. Even there we might think Dickens is trying to individualize nobility, both in the archness of Esther and the grotesque eccentricity of Jarndyce, though as it happens, the archness of Dame Trot and the Growlery and the East Wind plays in with the excessive moral display of love and sacrifice, sweetens rather than gives an edge. But in the quoted passage, there is a new co-operation of humour, pathos and solemnity. Its very quietness and relaxation is part of the complexity; this is no flourishing performance, but the performer's brilliance is dimmed, like the lights, his loudness quietened, like the street noises. Dickens is learning what his great model Jonson might have taught him earlier – decorum.

My subject is form, not language, or I would say much more about this quietening and relaxation of Dickens's verbal brilliance towards the end of his writing. (It is very marked, for instance, in *Edwin Drood*.) I must, however, make it absolutely clear that the quietness is not invariable: perhaps the most celebrated instance of Dickensian brilliant comic language comes from the opening of this novel. Gissing talks about the spirited wit of the first paragraph of *Bleak*

House as an inappropriate display of cheerfulness. The Gissing comment is quoted by Robert Garis, in one of the best books written about Dickens, and Garis goes on to propose that though the inappropriateness here is not typical, and must be inadvertent, the passage itself is 'thoroughly representative. Whenever Dickens is at his best this odd thing happens; all the landscapes, all the dramatic scenes come to us in a voice in which we hear an infectious delight in what it, itself, is doing – infectious because the pleasure often spills on to the material itself' (*The Dickens Theatre*, p. 16). Though I admire Garis's book, and much as I agree with much of his analysis, my view of Dickens's comic complexity is in conflict with Garis's thesis. As I hope I have illustrated, certain grave crises in the later novels can evoke a subduing of both the comic effect and, with it, the self-exhilarated performance. It is at times as though the Irrepressible were recognizing and trying out the possibilities of repression. Such repression and restraint passes unrecognized by Garis. Moreover, I would not accept Gissing's comment, or Garis's use of it, without some demur. Dickens seems to me to be piling up his vigorous conceits, like the Megalosaurus, the deposits of mud 'accumulating at compound interest', the snow-flakes 'gone into mourning for the death of the sun' and so forth with a strong contemptuous flippant humour which, far from being inappropriate, leads up to the moment when it must cease, with the words, 'Jarndyce and Jarndyce has passed into a joke. That is the only good that has ever come of it. It has been death to many, but it is a joke in the profession.'

It seems to me no accident that Dickens attacks the well-known legal habit of misplaced humour. He instances the 'good things' said in 'select port-wine committee after dinner in hall', the articled clerks who have been in the habit of 'fleshing their legal wit upon it' and winds up with the joke made by the last Lord Chancellor who corrected and capped Mr Blowers's joke about something happening when 'the sky rained potatoes' by substituting 'or when we get through Jarndyce and Jarndyce'. Garis and Gissing seem to me to be wrong about Dickens's cheerfulness at the beginning. Each joke is a grim one, and what cheerfulness may be native to joking seems to me to have a decided edge to it. Moreover, the jokes are

36

used to punctuate very serious unjoking remarks. The whole has a verve and vigour which adds up to anger and contempt, and to which the jokes seem to contribute. Some of the wit is a form of spitting contempt, very like that used of the Circumlocution Office in *Little Dorrit*, a form of admission of silliness, as when Tite Barnacle's eyeglass and his language flop about, or, here, when the barristers are deflated satirically by the conceits about 'tripping one another up on slippery precedents' or bobbing up 'like eighteen hammers in a piano forte'. The humour strikes me, to sum up, as wry, bitter, and contemptuous. If there is enjoyment here it may be that of effectively knocking your opponents, but there seems to be nothing inadvertent about that. Dickens makes grim jokes, and in a section where he is discussing the whole question of indecorous joking. The one 'cheerful' joke, about the Megalosaurus, is the exception to the rule, the only free fanciful spurt of fun in the whole grim chapter.

I am arguing, in fact, that what we often feel as the disappearance of the old free, wild humour from middle and late Dickens is a sign of his control of humour. It is there, but it is combined with seriousness in a way, after all, which we are quite used to – as was Dickens – in Ben Jonson and Swift. However, to speak of 'his control of humour' is to look only superficially at one symptom of a larger and more fundamental control. Dickens also comes to control other aspects of his art that showed themselves in separate assertiveness in the early novels.

[3]

Closely allied to his humour, and at times inseparable from it, is Dickens's grotesque caricature. It is one of his chief means of depicting 'evil,' which we can perhaps roughly but not too inaccurately describe as nature corrupted and deformed. In his British Council Pamphlet, *Charles Dickens* (*Writers and Their Work*: No. 37) K. J. Fielding dismisses T. A. Jackson's comment[1] on Dickens's flat characters in the following terms: 'Jackson came to the conclusion, in all seriousness, that Dickens drew his characters "in the flat" because that is how they actually were, crushed out of shape by the pressure of capitalist society.' I suggest that it is worth

[1] *Charles Dickens: The Progress of a Radical*, 1937, p. 253.

37

taking Jackson's conclusion a little more respectfully than this. From *Sketches by Boz* onwards, Dickens seems to be presenting caricature in terms of a social distortion of 'natural' values. He shows officials shaped and simplified – 'flattened' as Jackson said – by their roles, by their greeds, by their professions, all of which he saw as a simplification, distortion or narrowing of the unconditional 'natural' man. Dickens believed in original virtue. One of his favourite observations, starting very early in *Oliver Twist*, is to compare the natural man, the hopelessly corrupt social distortion, and – somewhere in between – a caricature with some implied natural inner life. As a model for this, we can look at one of his eloquently compressed vignettes from *Sketches by Boz*, called 'The Pawnbroker's Shop'. At the end of this sketch Dickens uses the scenic division (a device he continues to exploit) of the shop. In a split-scene sketch he presents two girls, one still virtuous and the other 'whose attire, miserably poor but extremely gaudy' 'bespeaks her station'. The virtuous girl, with her mother, is pawning a gold chain and a 'Forget-me-not' ring and the prostitute catches sight of the trinkets and bursts into tears. Another variation, in fact, of the theme of Holman Hunt's 'The Awakening Conscience'. But Dickens is very careful to use his sentimental genre-piece to make a point about social corruption. He infers that the first girl is no novice, because of the way she and her mother answers questions and bargain with the pawnbroker. They have some delicacy, standing back to 'avoid the observation even of the shopman' but are not too humiliated, 'for want has hardened the mother, and her example has hardened the girl, and the prospect of receiving money coupled with a recollection of the misery they have both endured from a want of it' has made them what they are. The prostitute represents a further stage in what Dickens calls degradation, but there are still 'chords in the human heart' which vibrate to past associations. In case we have still not got the point, or may mistake this for a contrast between virtue and vice, Dickens dissolves the antithesis and presents a series:

> There has been another spectator, in the person of a woman in the
> common shop; the lowest of the low; dirty, unbonneted, flaunting,

and slovenly. Her curiosity was at first attracted by the little she could see of the group; then her attention. The half-intoxicated leer changed to an expression of something like interest, and a feeling similar to that we have described, appeared for a moment, and only a moment, to extend itself even to her bosom.

Being Dickens, he ends by explicit comment, asking 'how soon these women may change places' and seeing all three as representing different stages of deterioration.

In the novels, where this kind of brief expressive image gives place to extensive dramatization of character and action, the process of social determination is made plainer. But the vibrating 'chords in the human heart' continue to vibrate significantly. Bumble's heartless pompous greed is created by the work he does for a heartless institution, unjustly ordered and inhumanly formalised, and, within the uniforms, clearly on the make. But Oliver's 'So very lonely!' can make even Bumble clear his throat. Dickens's favourite reflection of the socially 'flattened' character is a subtle one, as indeed Jackson realized, being no naive Marxist, but as critical of E. M. Forster's definition of 'flat' characters as Fielding is of his. So Uriah Heep reveals the social pressure by his awareness of society's demand for the effective humour of 'umbleness'. Wemmick acts out, in a split *persona* and a split scene, that inner awareness of role determination which is just glimpsed in Vholes's constant reference to daughters and fathers. Jaggers reveals his inner 'natural' man in glimpses and then, at the end, in plain collaboration with the good. Dickens is from beginning to end interested in the assumption of a social clothing, mask, habit, role, which may stifle the inner life entirely, or still allow it a little inner breathing space. Many of his caricatures are nothing but surfaces; no one glimpses the inner life of a Gamp, a Pecksniff, a Quilp, though, as in Jonson's humours, the ferocity of their animation suggests a large energy and life compelled into tight bonds. Pecksniff and Quilp are, like Volpone, allowed libido as well as mercenary humour, and this expands caricature in the direction of life.

I want to stress here that Dickens's complexity of characterization tends to show itself in the same form that we saw in the scene from the 'Pawnbroker's Shop'. He creates a series where at one extreme may be a full or fairly full nature, at the other a totally corrupt one, and in the centre a significant mixture. We see this series, which resembles but is not identical with the static model of the Pawn-broking scene, in terms both of psychological and social realism. If we feel, with E. M. Forster, that the realistic art of fiction is dependent on psychological realism, that is, on the creation of complex, dynamic, and mobile characters, we shall see this psychological series or scale as a form which allows Dickens to be satiric and comic, using the necessary and effective simplifications of satire and comedy, together with the complex creations that imitate the characters and the actions of men. This way of looking at Dickens is understandable, and perhaps indeed inevitable, for people who come to him with the slightly patronising air of readers of George Eliot and Henry James, prepared for the worst but also eager to seize on the best – by which they will mean those things that most resemble the great psychological creations of their ideal. But it is not the best way to understand Dickens. Jackson seems to me to be much nearer the truth, seeing, as he does, that the complexity of Dickens is the complexity of an artist committed most seriously and profoundly to a critical rendering of society, and of men formed in and by that society.

This is not the same thing as saying that Dickens is a Marxist novelist. On the contrary – and this was something Jackson could not see – Dickens put into his novels, though not into the Pawn-broking scene – the unconditioned virtue, a saintlike and intact ideal that resisted any idea of environmental pressure. All the novels depended on such ideals, though the social reporting of *Sketches by Boz* did not. Dickens, like most of us, told himself a fiction about the actual workings of society, and out of it created that scale where human nature slid inevitably into greed, brutality, degradation. He also created another fiction about the powerful human nature that could resist the environment. Hence Oliver Twist, Little Nell, Florence and Paul, Agnes, Little Dorrit, Esther, and Lizzie Hexam. I will simply observe in passing that children and women were easier models for the unconditioned virtue, could be seen in a more insulated environment, but that though this may explain the age and sex of Dickens's typical saints, he surrounds them with threats and attacks from the corrupting world. Kate Nickleby and Madeline, two saintly girls, are held up for sale by evil to evil, Quilp pursues Nell, Monks tries to engineer Oliver's corruption, Uriah Heep aspires to Agnes. It is as if Dickens is recognizing the need to face the corruption that these characters resist and puts it strongly into the action. It is also as if he realizes the attraction that the good holds for the evil, sexually and morally. Underlying his moral action are the more resonant myths, of the snake in Eden, Mephistopheles and Faust. For some reason, he drops this vicious pursuit of the incorruptible in the later novels; Esther Summerson, Little Dorrit, and Lizzie have their trials, but are not so terrifyingly up against the aggressive evil world. Even Bradley Headstone, a marvellous study in complex role-determination, cannot stand in such contrast to Lizzie as Quilp to Nell. Slowly the 'evil' itself becomes humanized.

But even in the early novels it is the sense of social determination that creates the whole range of Dickens characters, from the saints to the monsters. Those characters who inhabit the central part of his sliding scale are the most interesting instances of his complexity. This middle range seems to give him most trouble, for his imagination shows itself most readily and easily in the extremes of impersonation. It is tempting to see a development in the novels, and I would say that such characters as Arthur Clennam in *Little Dorrit* and Wrayburn in *Our Mutual Friend* show an emotional complexity and restraint very different from anything that has gone before. But as usual with Dickens, generalizations about development are difficult to maintain: how easy it would be to dismiss the badness of early Dickens, his maudlin presentation of goodness, his sheer bad writing, the highly-strung but banal pastoral landscape, the tedious story, the stereotyped juvenile lovers, the contrived obstacles that make up what passes for narrative action – how easy, were it not for *Oliver Twist* and the action of comedy and criminal psychology in *Pickwick Papers* and *Nicholas Nickleby* – far less evident, alas, in *The Old Curiosity Shop* or *Barnaby Rudge*. How easy it would be to talk about the complex psychology of late Dickens heroes and heroines, did not Edith Dombey show the same self-division as Louisa Gradgrind, did Lizzie Hexam not show an ideality very like Nell's, did Pip's complexity not prove, on close inspection, to rely very largely on narration rather than drama. Still, Pip is an excellent instance of the movement away from nature, beginning as he does with 'natural' love and giving, corrupted as he swiftly is, by Estella's nurtured and self-conscious corruptibility.

Even in an early novel like *Nicholas Nickleby* (1838-9) we find the character of Ralph Nickleby, whose complexity can stand as another instance of Dickens's complexity, or his complex awareness of nature and social shaping. We may at first sight take Ralph's detestation of Nicholas for an instinctive loathing of goodness by evil, but the novel eventually lets us know that there is a much more plausible and simple human cause in Ralph's re-awakened sexual jealousy. Part of the complexity of this characterization – standing out, as it does, in an action with few complex characters – lies in the way in which Dickens slowly unfolds causality and, with it, nature. He begins with a brief and unrevealing summary of the Nickleby family history, disclosing little about the elder brother. But Ralph is slowly disclosed as a monster who has been made monstrous by a social structure built on the values of mercenariness and greed. Throughout the novel Dickens lets us see slivers of light in and into Ralph, who is, we are told at first, a man whose heart has rusted, and is 'only a piece of cunning mechanism, and yielding not one throb of hope, or fear, or love, or care, for any living thing' but which turns out to be capable, after all, of one or two throbs.

This renewal of the natural heart provides an instance of another kind of contrast in Dickens, between his success and failure in expression and symbol. Chapter XIX ends with a small incident, rather reminiscent of the pawned forget-me-not brooch and 'The Awakening Conscience': Kate has just got into the coach after the dinner-party at Ralph Nickleby's, and as the door closes, a comb falls out of her hair. Ralph picks it up, and sees her face picked out in the lamplight, especially a 'lock of hair that had escaped and curled loosely over her brow'. Ralph is moved by 'some dormant train of recollection', reminded of his dead brother's face 'with the very look it bore on some occasion of boyish grief'. Dickens then rises into the crescendo and climax:

Ralph Nickleby, who was proof against all appeals of blood and kindred – who was steeled against every tale of sorrow and distress – staggered while he looked, and went back into his house, as a man who had seen a spirit from some world beyond the grave.

But, as it happens, Dickens has already shown Ralph as a little moved, and the earlier instance is one of those tiny realistic touches which are worth ten of the more melodramatic scenes from the inner life. Slightly earlier, at the end of Ralph's dinner-party, Kate is weeping, and Dickens makes the point that Ralph is vulnerable – not very, but slightly – because his ruling passion is for the moment not involved:

> Ralph would have walked into any poverty-stricken debtor's house, and pointed him out to a bailiff, though in attendance upon a young child's death-bed, without the smallest concern, because it would have been a matter quite in the ordinary course of business, and the man would have been an offender against his only code of morality. But, here was a young girl, who had done no wrong save that of coming into the world alive; who had patiently yielded to all his wishes; who had tried hard to please him – above all, who didn't owe him money – and he felt awkward and nervous.

It is moments like these, even in this not very good novel, which create a sense of emotional wholeness and sequence in the flat characters. They also show the human surplus, the vital remnants of nature not wholly perverted. Notice how completely unsentimental this last observation is; it even allows us a flash of contempt for Ralph, the denatured man being invoked in order to explain the surplus touch of nature. It contrasts strongly with the incident of the lock of hair in the lamplight which belongs less to the truthful observations of psychology than to the crude melodrama of the inner life.

The knowledge of the inner life, I am arguing, is a source of Dickens's complexity, or, to say it another way, has its roots in his complex awareness of social nature as against what he sees as untarnished and unfallen nature. A similar contrast might be found in Dombey, between his final, ideal, stereotyped, pathetic and redeemed old age (made more shadowy by those shadow-figures of angel-children so shamelessly evoked by Dickens on the last page of *Dombey and Son, Martin Chuzzlewit*, and *Nicholas Nickleby*) and the many marvellous earlier touches, his moments of resentment of Florence, his silences, and his distaste and embarrassment when he visits Edith in her boudoir, where her jewels and clothes are cast about in socially and sexually contemptuous disarray. Or there is the stage in Richard Carstone's downward progress when he is still able to distinguish what he was from what he is becoming. He speaks of his 'litigious, contentious, doubting character' as if it were still separate from him. He expresses his willingness to listen to Esther on any subject other than Chancery, and she comments 'As if there were any other in his life! As if his whole career and character were not being dyed one colour!'

Richard's moment of hesitation, when he feels himself still larger than his ruling passion, while Esther sees it absorb him, is placed in a scene of considerable structural control, where comedy, moral seriousness, and natural description are all made to respond to each other. One of the difficulties in speaking of Dickens's pastoral reinforcement of character, which begins with *Pickwick Papers*, and is very prominent in *Oliver Twist* and *The Old Curiosity Shop*, is connected with his extremely flat and banal handling of description. The pastoral point is made repeatedly, and makes very plain what Empson, in *Some Versions of Pastoral*, calls the role of the child as Swain. It joins to emphasise the unconditioned and unconditional nobility of the child, but does so in a stereotyping of sweetness, simplicity, and rural innocence. The effect should be a symbolic reinforcement but tends instead to be a prettifying, a reduction, a heart-shaped frame with flowers and ivy round the dear child-face. A real move ahead typical of the mature Dickens comes, I suggest, in the pastoral of *Bleak House*, though the pretty rural reduction is by no means entirely successful, and is at the end, I believe, a diminution of the complexity of the novel. The little Yorkshire cottage cannot truly answer the bleakness of the House of England.

There are moments in this novel when Dickens seems to realize separately and bring together responsively the different aspects of his symbolism, where the pastoral achieves a complex stature and so truly strengthens the moral discourse and the psychology. In Chapters XXXVI and XXXVII Esther is staying in the country, near

Chesney Wold, to recuperate after her smallpox. The simple physical contrast between foul and sweet air introduces the pastoral. Esther's pleasure in nature (to which she is always symbolically related by name) is made through the recognition of the fresh sensations after an illness. It is made fairly simply, without too much excited accompaniment: 'I found every breath of air, and every scent, and every flower and leaf and blade of grass, and every passing cloud, and everything in nature, more beautiful and wonderful to me than I had ever found it yet.' If we feel the presence of Romantic stereotyping here, we must admit that Dickens is trying hard to use the sensuousness of this nature to say something about human nature. Next, Esther feels the pitying touch of a child after the clumsy question about why she is no longer a pretty lady, and comments: 'There were many little occurrences which suggested to me, with great consolation, how natural it is to gentle hearts to be considerate and delicate towards any inferiority'. The comment is followed by the successfully individualized Wordsworthian anecdote – and for once I think Wordsworth can be evoked without summoning a blush to the cheek of the reader – about the bride who is a good scholar but makes a mark instead of signing her name in the marriage register because her husband cannot write. The emphasis placed on what is morally *natural*, partly because Dickens is looking at social distortion, and partly because he is concerned with hierarchy and class. When Sir Leicester eventually sticks by Lady Dedlock, it is because of natural 'nobility' like this.

In this pastoral section all aspects cohere: the sensations of rural life, the natural landscape, and the recuperation after health form the preliminaries to Esther's natural discovery of her natural mother, a discovery marked by the only natural unbending on the part of Lady Dedlock. Their recognition scene is not a mere stereotype but emphasizes Lady Dedlock's social de-naturing and Esther's natural loving response. Dickens points out that this response is natural; involving no revival of early associations. Even the supernatural is given a natural status, though a dreadful one, in the moment when Esther realizes that hers is the ghost's footstep in the Walk.

Comedy plays its role too. Just as Richard's revelation is made most appropriately in a country air, to which his remaining natural self responds, while it makes its doom clear, so Skimpole, called by Richard 'Fresh and greenhearted' comes along to add his significant and stereotyped gush to the pattern:

> 'In old times, the woods and solitudes were made joyous to the shepherd by the imaginary piping and dancing of Pan and the Nymphs. This present shepherd, our pastoral Richard, brightens the dull Inns of Court. . . . '

Richard's divided self is made very clear as Skimpole's superficial and mistaken chatter about 'the shepherd-youth, a friend of mine' (who transmutes the legal abuses into 'something highly fascinating') is contrasted with Richard's recognition, 'This is a lovely place. . . . None of the jar and discord of law-suits here!' The total responsiveness of all the parts in this episode is continued when Esther asks Mr Vholes if he would like to live in the country, and he says he would – 'You touch me on a tender string'. The imagery in this section is coloured by pastoral, from its absence in Lady Dedlock's metaphor of her 'desert' to Esther's final view of Ada at the end of Chapter XXXVII, which attaches this local contrast of nature and aridity to the larger bleakness and waste:

> I look along the road before me, where the distance already shortens and the journey's end is growing visible; and, true and good above the dead sea of the Chancery suit, and all the ashy fruit it cast ashore, I think I see my darling.

The pastoral in *Bleak House* gives a complex enlargement to the caricature and the character.

[4]

Up to now, I have been looking at Dickens's structural powers, or lack of power, in aesthetic terms, though always in terms of the aesthetic of fiction. But there is one major source of disunity which has been haunting this essay, and which is not simply a failure in creating an artistic order. In Dickens's novels, as I have been saying or implying, there is a frequent gap between the story of an individual's history and moral *Bildung*, on the one hand and the portrait of a society, on the other. In *Pickwick*, despite what Pickwick says about learning from experience, we do not see him changed or changing. To sum it up crudely, the Pickwickians have seen more that they expected but neither Eatanswill nor the Fleet has undermined their celebratory optimism. In the early novels, this lack of representativeness in the individual drama was perhaps made possible by Dickens's tendency to discuss individual institutions. Even in *Pickwick* where he moves from one institution to another, and takes in law, education, medicine, politics, the prison, there is no coherent sense of a corrupt system. When we say this, we are not judging Dickens by the standards of political thinkers, but by his own. In the last novels, perhaps beginning with *Dombey and Son*, we feel that his terrible bird's-eye-view of history (past in present) is, like Carlyle's, an indictment not of institutions but of a whole society. We may well come to feel a growing, rather than a diminishing, failure of social illustrativeness on the part of his human histories. We have seen so much of bleakness and desolation in *Bleak House*, seen so much diagnostic passion exposing government, religion, law, the aristocracy, the establishment as a whole, that a happy ending, even for Esther and Allan, even faintly muted by Richard's deterioration and death, seems too complacent. We have been through a novel that has insisted on teaching us that parts cannot be separated from whole, that Mrs Jellyby should not separate her social vision from what is close to her, that the smallpox is a leveller, that we cannot live in isolation. The novel has made us feel the interpenetrations of social morality and makes it extremely difficult for us to endorse its conclusion. We can only do so by cutting off and isolating the part from the whole, which is what we have been learning not to do. Even Sir Leicester Dedlock has glimpsed this meaning. The one part of the novel that does not respond to the complexity of the whole is its end.

By the test of final responsiveness, however, Dickens does succeed in *Hard Times*, *Little Dorrit* and *Great Expectations*.

The end of each of these three novels – including the revised happier ending of *Great Expectations* – is a refusal to pitch the celebration of the individual indecorously high. Let me take as my chief example, the end of *Hard Times* (1854). It is the only conclusion in all Dickens that allows only the reserved 'happy ending'

of peace, of passion spent, of the end of disaster. It has no damaging
bright glow of a future happiness for Louisa. Sissy's happy ending
is not damaging, both because she has never been an actively, only
a symbolically, prominent character; also because her happy
marriage is brought in to emphasize Louisa's lack of glow. For once,
even the children on the last page are tolerable:

> Herself again a wife – a mother – lovingly watchful of her children,
> ever careful that they should have a childhood of the mind no less
> than a childhood of the body, as knowing it to be even a more beauti-
> ful thing, and a possession, any hoarded scrap of which, is a blessing
> and happiness to the wisest? Did Louisa see this? Such a thing was
> never to be.
>
> But, happy Sissy's happy children loving her; all children loving
> her; she, grown learned in childish lore; thinking no innocent and
> pretty fancy ever to be despised; trying hard to know her humbler
> fellow-creatures, and to beautify their lives of machinery and reality
> with those imaginative graces and delights, without which the heart
> of infancy will wither up, the sturdiest physical manhood will be
> morally stark death, and the plainest national prosperity figures can
> show, will be the Writing on the Wall, – she holding this course as
> part of no fantastic vow, or bond, or brotherhood, or sisterhood, or
> pledge, or covenant, or fancy dress, or fancy fair; but simply as a duty
> to be done, – did Louisa see these things of herself? These things
> were to be.
>
> Dear reader! It rests with you and me, whether, in our two fields of
> action, similar things shall be or not. Let them be! We shall sit with
> lighter bosoms on the hearth, to see the ashes of our fires turn grey
> and cold.

There is a formality and solemnity in the language, and its quiet
and reserve, like that of Sir Leicester's loving if legalistic statement,
which is one of those triumphs of the late Dickens style, a *vox humana*
with a difference, not too deep, shrill or ecstatic, and a turning away
from grand climax. The moral suggestiveness is optimistic, but not
only does the quieter language underline the mere spectator's solace
that remains for Louisa, but also points two ways for the Dear reader.
Though the last sentence speaks for the better way, it does so in the
unradiant imagery of death, with no heavenly sunset glow but gray
ashes, just right for Coketown. Coketown can be remembered in
the last lines of *Hard Times* as the slums are not at the end of *Oliver*

Twist or *Bleak House*, and this is right, since the human discovery has not cancelled out the world of Coketown.

Such balance and complexity are not found only on the last page. *Hard Times* is a novel where there is a fine responsiveness between the central human case and the social indictment. This does not mean that it is an unflawed novel, for its sub-plot, which is a very interesting attempt at industrial analysis and action of a kind Dickens never tries elsewhere, is weak both in its social grasp and its presentation of passions. But the main line of action conducts and combines the particular and the social generalization in a sensitive unity. Mr Gradgrind and Louisa are so plainly cut out of the same complexly patterned material that one hesitates to ascribe fictional roles, like 'heroine' or 'villain' to them. They show finely and subtly Dickens's belief in unfallen nature and his concern for social distortion. That inner spark in Ralph Nickleby is bigger and brighter in father and daughter. From the first, Gradgrind is distinguished, like the hesitant pastoral Richard, from his ideology, even though his story shows a conversion after deterioration. Like Mrs Jellyby and Turveydrop, he is one of Dickens's warped but very pleasant people, and though Mrs Jellyby and Turveydrop are socially 'flattened' characters, they are an advance on the earlier stereotyping where to be wicked was either to be markedly horrid, like Quilp or Ralph or the Murdstones, or to be a hypocrite. Dickens shows that corrupted people can be quite genuinely nice.

The niceness of Gradgrind is rather different, implying a complex inner life. Dickens tells us in Book I Chapter v, where Gradgrind uses 'what he meant for a reassuring tone' that 'his character was not unkind, all things considered; it might have been a very kind one indeed, if he had only made some round mistake in the arithmetic that balanced it'. Gradgrind is a case of well-meaning error, and though he acts in conformity with his mistaken beliefs, the distinction between the natural vitality and the theory-determined man is made very clear. It is particularly clear in the scene in Book I Chapter xv when he persuades Louisa to marry Bounderby – or, rather, does not dissuade her from marrying him:

> Silence between them. The deadly statistical clock very hollow. The distant smoke very black and heavy.

49

'Father,' said Louisa, 'do you think I love Mr. Bounderby?'

Mr. Gradgrind was extremely discomfited by this unexpected question. 'Well, my child,' he returned, 'I – really – cannot take upon myself to say.'

'Father,' pursued Louisa in exactly the same voice as before, 'do you ask me to love Mr. Bounderby?'

'My dear Louisa, no. No. I ask nothing.'

'Father,' she still pursued, 'does Mr. Bounderby ask me to love him?'

'Really, my dear,' said Mr. Gradgrind, 'it is difficult to answer your question – '

The scene is beautifully managed, beginning with Louisa's formal pressing of the question. The re-formulations and repetitions turn Louisa's life-and-death questioning into a parody of a pedagogic interrogation. This time Gradgrind the pedagogue is on the wrong side of the examination, though he evades it by an eloquent dismissal of its terms as he rejects the meaningfulness of the 'fanciful', 'fantastic', and 'sentimental' word 'love'. Both his first brief faltering answers and his growing confidence when he moves on to his own ground show the gap between the distortion and the whole man. Dickens shows the division again when he says that Louisa might have wavered and confided, if Gradgrind had not built artificial barriers 'between himself and all those subtle essences of humanity which will elude the utmost cunning of algebra until the last trumpet ever to be sounded shall blow even algebra to wreck'. He shows it again, perhaps most sadly, when Louisa clutches at metaphor, direct communication having failed:

'Are you consulting the chimneys of the Coketown works, Louisa?'

'There seems to be nothing there but languid and monotonous smoke. Yet when the night comes, Fire bursts out, father!' she answered, turning quickly.

'Of course I know that, Louisa. I do not see the application of the remark.' To do him justice, he did not, at all.

The caricature in *Hard Times* is seen most precisely as a man's self-inflicted distortion, though they are also clearly related in their mechanism to the forces and need of the industrial society. In Gradgrind, and Bounderby, the caricature is what the character, in the fullest sense, has made itself. In Louisa's case it is seen largely as the product of education. Both Gradgrind and Louisa are like the picture illustrating Oscar Wilde's theory of masks, where the characters move and converse hidden behind the social guise and cover. Dickens's point, of course, is that character becomes diminished and distorted in a commitment to the mask. The balance between the inner life and the mask, character and caricature, is a complex statement about education and ideology, and not a comic simplification, and it leads into a conclusion which the same complexity is found. There is no sense of simplification, of the part flourishing at the expense of the whole, but the recognition that moral triumphs are rare, expensive, and subject to mortality.

The complexity of Dickens is not like the complexity of George Eliot, or Henry James, but because it makes some recognition and dramatisation of the largeness, wholeness, innerness, and fluidity of human beings, it proffers itself dangerously for a comparison with the psychological novel proper, a form of fiction much less concerned with social criticism. On the other hand, Dickens is much too serious in psychology and social thinking – I am not confusing seriousness with depth – to be dismissed or described as a great performer. His complex insights are not always satisfactorily resolved and unified. When T. A. Jackson said that Dickens suffered from an excess of form, he had a point. Dickens drew limits round his actions and analyses, and the limits – often of story or moral pattern – are often arbitrary. In some of the later novels, where language becomes much more fully and individually sensitive, and is able to reveal the individuality of caricature and the connections between parts, the comedy is joined with the seriousness, the type with the individual, and – rare and hard achievement – the portrait of society with the portraiture of people. Dickens's complexity begins by being a complex series of separately assertive intents, passions, statements; it moves towards some measure of integration. I would not say that he presents us with E. M. Forster's ideal of a more ordered and manageable world, but his disintegrations and integrations alike convince one of his sensitive awareness and rendering of the difficulties of being a sensuously, morally and historically conscious man.

JOHN HOLLOWAY

DICKENS
AND THE
SYMBOL

By now there is general recognition that Dickens was a novelist of a radically different kind from, say, Jane Austen or George Eliot or Trollope. He must be read in a different spirit from them – one more open, tolerant and exploratory and less tied to sobriety, exactitude or mere calm sense. The remark is no sooner made than it calls for qualification, but something like it is not really in question; and if, leaving the qualifications aside since they are not obscure or difficult, one considers how this more open and poetic dimension in Dickens's work has been given an account of, clearly the main way in which this has been done has been by reference to his 'use' of symbolism.

I put the word 'use' in quotation marks, because there seem to be two main directions in which the symbolism has been explored, and two critics who suggest themselves as examples of these both rely much upon it. Of these two directions, Lionel Trilling's essay on

Little Dorrit well illustrates the first.[1] Reduced to its baldest essential, the distinctive interest here becomes almost a quantitative one. The critic offers to assist the common reader, in that he shows him a certain symbolic significance coming *more often* in the book than that common reader may have seen for himself:

> The subject of *Little Dorrit* is borne in upon us by the informing symbol, or emblem, of the book, which is the prison. The story opens in a prison in Marseilles. It goes on to the Marshalsea, which in effect it never leaves. The second of the two parts of the novel begins in what we are urged to think of as a sort of prison, the monastery of the Great St. Bernard. The Circumlocution Office is the prison of the creative mind in England . . . in a score of ways the theme of incarceration is carried out . . . Symbolic or emblematic devices are *used* by Dickens to one degree or another in several of the novels of his late period, but nowhere to such good effect as in *Little Dorrit* . . .

It is true that Professor Trilling goes on to attribute the 'good effect' to something other than the frequent repetition of the 'informing symbol': but the sense of connection between frequency, between density of 'use', and effectiveness is clear enough in the passage as a whole. All in all it is not unfair to say that this essay is a very superior example of a kind of criticism which, though it is by no means without its merits, exposes itself to the limiting observation that after a time, each fresh point it makes is likely to be *less important than the last*. Professor Trilling was far too astute to have taken his reader right through that 'score of ways', because after the first three or four items, triviality would have supervened.

The other direction in which symbolic criticism of Dickens has gone is well represented by J. C. Reid's *The Hidden World of Charles Dickens* (1962). In this kind of analysis the primary stress is not on how often the symbols come: though that they come frequently is indeed part of what is stressed. The primary stress has regard to their place of origin. Professor Reid, in a most interesting essay which marshals for us a great many useful points of detail (and which it is no part of my purpose to denigrate), argues that Dickens's

[1] *Sewanee Review*, 1950. Reprinted as Introduction to *Little Dorrit* in the *New Oxford Illustrated Dickens* edition.

symbols are drawn from two distinguishable though maybe not distinct areas of human culture or consciousness: partly they are from folk-lore and popular culture, partly they are true archetypes of the subconscious.

> Dickens's novels supply us with countless examples of familiar fairy-tale figures ... Dickens sometimes uses two characters as complementary in a way recalling similar patterns in folk-lore ... In other cases, Dickens uses the 'Double' archetype in a single person. (*op. cit.*, pp. 23, 28, 29).

And so on: the word 'use' is once again conspicuous, and the limiting factor in this kind of criticism must be equally so. It is, that while one senses at once how Professor Reid's material must somehow have much relevance to the merit and value of Dickens's work, the question of exactly how retains its interest: the mere presence of 'fairy-tale stereotypes', as no less of archetypes, is no guarantee of any merit whatsoever. Archetypes and 'stereotypes' will turn up in worthless fiction as readily as in good. Anyone who is in doubt over this need only consider whether he himself could not, at short notice, write a story himself, and introduce into it *one more* such entity than he can count in any given novel by Dickens, if he were offered a sufficient fee. But would this give his piece a marginal advantage over Dickens's? It would not. Professor Reid perceives that archetypes and stereotypes do not of themselves ensure quality, but he cannot save himself from entanglement at this point in his discussion:

> At the same time, Dickens was writing novels, not fairy-stories, and everywhere his moral and social ideas are presented not as abstractions but in terms of character and action ... his archetypal figures and folk-lore figures are filled out with the rich details of his fancy ... These are not the anonymous, monotonously stereotyped and featureless traditional figures; they are real people ... Yet ... He can, while writing a social commentary and a novel, also write a parable that calls up deep-rooted traditional responses ... (p. 22).

This approach creates problems as great as any it solves. That Dickens's novels fall within the area of what might loosely be termed 'the literature of the common people' is now admitted as a major fact about them. But it is a fact which can diagnose merit once merit is established. It cannot prove in the first place, and by itself, that merit is there.

Earlier in this essay the fact that these two critics both spoke of how Dickens 'used' symbols was noted, because when a critic begins to think of his author like that he is beginning to think about him mechanically. C. S. Lewis, in one of his infrequent lapses, spoke of Milton's 'manipulation' of his reader; and we have the same kind of lapse here. This may be the right language for a best-seller; but if so, it is not the right language for a great work of the imagination. There is a dimension in major literary art which one might point to by saying that the 'method' uses the author almost as much as he uses it; a fact which I should like to illustrate through examination of merely one brilliant, disruptive, disturbing image in *Dombey and Son*.

In Chapter xlv of that novel, the second Mrs Dombey is in angry, anguished conversation with her husband's 'trusty agent' Carker. The trusty agent, long smarting under the humiliating subservience imposed on him by Dombey, and infatuated by the beautiful and imperious Edith, stands before her now, gloating inwardly over her admission that he has succeeded in exposing her to humiliation. She asks him why he has humiliated her, and Dickens, with the sexual insight and discreet frankness which the attentive reader finds so often in his work, tells us that the answer was, so that he could listen to her rehearse what he had done to her:

> Had she not been blinded . . . she would have seen the answer in his face. . . .
>   She saw it not . . . She saw only the indignities and struggles she had undergone . . . As she sat looking fixedly at them, rather than at him, she *plucked the feathers from a pinion of some rare and beautiful bird, which hung from her wrist by a golden thread, to serve her as a fan, and rained them on the ground.*

No doubt Dickens might be said to be 'using' the conventional or even archetypal symbol of captured bird for captive soul or trapped woman: and 'using' the image of the golden thread, in much the same way, for the money which had led Edith to commit herself to Dombey. Yet the power of the image, which seems to me entirely beyond dispute, lies in what is mysterious, enigmatic and contradictory about it, not in these trite significances that were 'used' also in the Victorian drawing-room ballad. What has Edith to do with a beautiful bright-coloured 'rain' upon the ground? Or with currents of fresh air that the bird's wing makes as a fan? Who is 'pinioned' to what? What is one to make of the sudden vividness with which one thinks of a *caged* bird, 'looking fixedly' in imagination (as we easily bring ourselves to speak) at a reality away from where it is? What has this moment to do with the moment, later in the book, when Edith strips herself of all her own fine feathers – before she flies? How should one take the sudden sense of barbaric opulence, exotic yet macabre, with which the passage invests Dombey's whole society? The overwhelming power of this passage is not explained away by such answers as one might cudgel up to these problems: it can be related only to the sudden half-awareness of them as enigmatic, unanswered questions, as possibilities of meaning which are in themselves less than meanings. In part they are less than meanings because even as they dawn in the mind, what dawns as well is a sense that they can be in dynamic inter-action, but cannot simply and statically co-exist.

In making this distinction, one cannot but recognize that there stands behind it a distinction between two long traditions of thought: an analytical tradition going back to Bentham and beyond, and a synthetic and more dynamic one for which the truly seminal figure is, I fear, Hegel. To the extent that our criticism owes something to Richards and through him to Bentham, it tends rather towards the former model than the latter; and this has relevance to much study of symbolic significances in literature, as undoubtedly it has also had, in respect of moral significances. But one need not have recourse to Hegel, in order to show that the other kind of thinking about symbols was readily available to Dickens himself. Carlyle, writing at almost exactly the same time as Dickens's earliest novels, makes his Professor Teufelsdröckh speak like this:

> ... the benignant efficacies of *Concealment* ... who shall speak or

sing? Silence and Secrecy!... Of kin to the so incalculable influences of Concealment, and connected with still greater things, is the wondrous agency of Symbols. In a Symbol there is concealment and yet revelation: here therefore, by Silence and by Speech acting together, comes a double significance... In the Symbol proper, that we can call a Symbol, there is ever, more or less distinctly and directly, some embodiment and revelation of the Infinite...[1]

These words appeared in *Fraser's Magazine* only three years before *Pickwick* was published. To have them in mind for Dickens' symbolism is eminently reasonable. A few years earlier again, Coleridge in a note appended to one of the Aphorisms in *Aids to Reflection* (1825 edition, p. 254, n.) had written:

> ... in the fullest force of the word, Symbol, rightly defined, viz, A Symbol is a sign included in the Idea which it represents ... an actual *part* chosen to represent the *whole* ... the Symbolical is hereby distinguished *toto genere* from the Allegoric and Metaphorical.

Those accustomed to think along Benthamite lines rather than Hegelian ones may not at once see how far-reaching are these claims. But a passage which Coleridge wrote only a few years earlier brings this out:

> ... by a Symbol I mean, not a metaphor or allegory or any other figure of speech or form of fancy, but an actual and essential part of that, the whole of which it represents. Thus our Lord speaks symbolically when he says that the eye is the light of the body.[2]

One finds it a little too easy, perhaps, blithely to take these words as having only a kind of attractive suggestiveness; as vaguely indicating something psychically more capacious and accommodating than metaphor or allegory, and as enabling the literary consciousness to assert its difference from the scientific or rational in broad and blanket terms. The situation is other, and intellectually more strenuous, than that. An essential part of what Coleridge or anyone else must mean by the relation of symbolizing is that it is

---

[1] *Sartor Resartus*, Book III, Chapter iii.
[2] *The Statesman's Manual*, Appendix B.

different from the relation of identity, of being-identical-with. Therefore, if the true symbol is necessarily a part of what it symbolizes, it necessarily stands in two relations to itself: being identical with itself, and symbolizing itself (for this is necessarily part of what it does, in symbolizing the whole). But, *prima facie*, these are mutually incompatible; the symbolizing relation *entails otherness*. The identical begins to look as if it is not-identical; yet as soon as it does so, we remember that it is also itself after all. The way Coleridge invites us to think does not have merely a cloudy abundance, but a paradoxical structure: the logic of which invites us to become aware of fuller significance in something like an ordered drama of (to revert to Carlyle's terms) revelation and concealment. Nor can one overlook the close similarity between what Coleridge says about the structure he creates, and what Hegel himself creates when he distinguishes mechanical thinking from another kind:

> ... Conceptual thinking goes on in quite a different way. Since the concept ... is the very self of the object ... it is a self-determining active concept ... [the] inert passive subject really disappears ... Thus the solid basis which ratiocination found in an inert subject, is shaken to its foundations ... Ideational thinking [briefly, this is a form of mechanical thinking] ... is checked in its course, since that which has in the proposition the form of a predicate is itself the substance of the statement. Starting from the subject, as if this were a permanent base on which to proceed, it discovers, by the predicate being in reality the substance, that the subject has passed into the predicate, and has thereby ceased to be subject.[1]

Subject passes into predicate, and thereby ceases simply to be subject, within a structure like what Coleridge sets up when he sees symbol as passing into symbolized, and thereby ceasing to be symbol in abstraction from symbolized. 'Why not at once Symbol and History?' Coleridge asks immediately before the passage in *Aids to Reflection* quoted above; '– or rather, how should it be otherwise?' The facts of social life are symbols not in contradistinction to being social facts, but *in* being social facts.

I have already expressed doubt about one aspect of Trilling's remark that symbolic devices are 'used' by Dickens 'in several of

[1] *Phenomenology of Mind*, transl. J. B. Baillie, 1966. Preface: pp. 118-9.

the novels of his late period'; but it seems also that something for which the most reasonable word is 'symbolism', is if anything most prominent not in those late novels, but in some of the earlier ones. Here, Dickens's 'History', his detailed delineation of the integrated spectrum of life, is less developed than it is, say, in *Bleak House*, or *Little Dorrit*: and the importance of something of another kind is all the clearer.

Oliver Twist and *The Old Curiosity Shop* stand in a curious relation one to the other. Each leaves one with a sense that the fiction Dickens was narrating in the book is one with which he has a strong personal involvement: he must have *needed* to enact the drama of a child threatened and hurt by an old man; or at least, one who seems old to him. It may be that this reflects Dickens's own childhood sense of his relation to the father whose improvidence brought such keenly-felt degradation (on the blacking factory) on the son. The crucial fictional line in *The Old Curiosity Shop* recalls Chaucer's *Prioress's Tale*: for just as Freud argues that in the dream-work, contiguity takes the place of causality and therefore means causality, so the two decisive events of the novel, the death of the child and the death, if not directly at the hands of justice, at least as the direct consequence of being caught up with by justice, of the Jew (Dickens never says outright that Quilp is a Jew, but his portrait of an unctuous and devious middleman–financier, and perhaps something of his stature, are reminiscent of the conventionalized myth; and the original illustrations to the novel unquestionably give him a Jewish physiognomy) must be related by the reader until he sees the one as in essence punishment for the other. There is a curiously perennial, mythic structure, below whatever personal involvement dictated.

In *Oliver Twist* the central nerve of the fiction is strikingly the same. It is impossible to link the hanging of Sikes, or the sentence on Fagin, as related simply to murdering Nancy, or to being an accessory and a fence. Rather, these are the means whereby Dickens weaves a mythic story into a fabric of social portraiture. The vital facts about Sikes and about Fagin is that each is Enemy of the Child; and each thus has a part to play in polarizing, as it were, the drama of the book.

This structure, in each book, might (as I said) seem to have a more than literal significance, and exist on a mythic or symbolic plane. *Symbol* would then be Child and Old Man, and *Symbolized* would be . . . it would be easy to complete the sentence: but I do not do so, precisely because it is what it is not easy to add that I wish to make my especial concern. The point is, that precisely by as much as one supposes that the account of the Symbolized which might complete such a sentence is a completion in the full sense, precisely by that much does one imply that the symbolic dimension of the novel in question is something which could be expressed merely by *an other and simpler version of the tale.* The social portraiture might go, but the symbolism would survive if the novel in its fullness were replaced by a fable version of the novel. This implication is contrary to Coleridge's assertion that Symbol and History (which means, in this context, veridical social portraiture) *are one:* and that the Symbol is an actual and essential part of what is symbolized. By the same token, it is contrary to Carlyle's assertion that a symbol is a symbol by virtue of the very fact that it is at once both revelation *and concealment.*

This line of thought gains strength from the fact that it would do the greatest violence to either of these novels to treat them as if they consisted of a core of mythical narrative, which wove a meaning at the level of symbol through a discrete and distinct background, the sustained fabric of the book, which had meaning of another kind. This would be grotesque: for the more static parts of both novels, the parts where one might try to express what is going on by saying that the author was creating the setting within which and through which the fable was to transact itself, can no more be seen simply in terms of the concept of realistic literality, than can the fable itself.

The fugue – for that, I suppose, is the psychologist's word for it – upon which Nell and her grandfather embark, is a fugue through a world which cannot possibly be seen as typical and literal representation of nineteenth-century social experience. It comprises the Punch-and-Judy men, 'Grinder's lot' the stilt-walkers, Jerry the Dog-Master, Vuffin and his giant, the sharpers and the bargees, the idyll of the village schoolmaster, Mrs Jarley and her wax-works. 'I won't go so far as to say, that . . . I've seen wax-work quite like life, but I've certainly seen some life that was exactly like wax-work', says Mrs Jarley: seeming thereby exactly to translate Coleridge's definition into the epigrammatic language of the novelist, for the gist of what she says is that wax-work is not like life, but makes up – '*some* life' – a part of it.

These vivid, colourful and rootless people, all movement, activity and oddity, are only part of what is in a sense the *local* of the action; and to some extent one is conscious of them as having a symbolic dimension, rather than being simply picturesqueness and romance, because of the sense of a wider *local*, which is present to the reader from the start, and to which, from first to last, they dialectically belong. This wider *local* begins with the 'long, deserted streets', the 'one dead uniform repose' of the city at dawn as Nell and her grandfather leave it; a repose which transmutes, even as one registers it, into 'noise and bustle', 'the haunts of commerce and great traffic, where many people were resorting, and business was already rife'. Over against the colour and openness of the fair people and travellers stands Miss Brass's kitchen, 'a very dark miserable place, very low and very damp . . . everything was *locked up*; the coal-cellar, the candle-box, the salt-box, the meat-safe, were all padlocked'. This is the home of the 'small servant'. With it one must count the 'dirty little box' of a counting-house where Quilp 'shuts himself in' because he has locked himself in; the locked shop with which the whole story opens; the room in the Brass's house which is taken by the 'single gentleman', and into which he locks himself for long enough to throw the whole household into uproar. With these again, the cell where the turnkey takes Kit and 'locks him up again'; and the 'dimly-lighted sick chamber' up the 'dark and narrow stairs', in which Dick Swiveller and the small servant are incarcerated for so long. Should one count, along with these, ambivalent places, the very temple of virtue itself, the 'chamber, vaulted and old', with 'only one other little room attached', in which Nell and her grandfather find refuge and rebirth after they have 'tried the rusty keys as before; at length found the right one'?

In seeing that the answer to this question is unquestionably Yes because of the ambivalence of this as well as all the other locked places in the novel, one recalls the earlier use of words like 'dynamic' and 'dialectical', and comes (I hope) to a sense of something very important about the contribution of symbolism in Dickens: that symbolism may well contribute primarily to a work not by *augmenting the meaning*, but by *transmuting the nature*, of the book's picture of life. The Brass's kitchen is not only the small servant's virtual prison, but also the base from which she obtains the Brass's secret and brings about the denouement. Quilp's 'Bachelor's Hall' is not only the box where he shuts himself in and then shrouds himself totally up in the blankets of his hammock, but the place from which the water of the life-crammed river washes away the stain that is Quilp, leaving him in the end 'to bleach'. In Chapter v of the novel Dickens had already been at pains to set Quilp's filthy counting-house amid the sails 'glistening in the sun', the water dancing and buoyant', the forest of masts, the fleet of barges, the flood tide, the whole panoply of unfettered motion and travel. The Single Gentleman's locked room turns out to have been the base for all his benevolent activities; the shut-in sick-chamber, scene of Dick Swiveller's regeneration. On the other hand, the fantastic church-house is the place both of Nell's death and her grandfather's regeneration; and I think one must associate it, in spite of its peace and beauty, with the macabre incident when the sexton shows Nell the pit under the trap-door in the church crypt. Yet even that scene closes with thoughts of the next spring, when the pit is to be sealed up and made away with.

It is surely clear that one who attempts, systematically, to elicit augmentations of meaning from all these complex matters will not get far. Dickens seems almost at pains to invest whatever could look like a symbol with a dialectical, self-contradictory potentiality; and this is to say that what we find in the book is what Carlyle told us to look for: 'In a Symbol there is concealment and yet revelation . . . by Silence and Speech acting together.' Coleridge's 'actual and essential part' affords another clue: for while one could as it were detach how Quilp 'drank boiling tea without winking' from what might be termed the whole presentation of that character in literal terms, and say that it was a symbol of his hellish nature, there can be no question of detaching all the matters that have been touched on so far, from the novel as literal presentation: and that for a simple reason. This is, that there would be no literal presentation left. The symbolism is no detachable part of the whole; but an 'actual and essential' part. This is why I spoke of 'transmuting the nature' rather than 'augmenting the meaning'. The symbolism is rather a dimension than an ingredient. What it does is modify literality until the work as a whole stands in a new perspective. What kind of perspective? I used the word 'polarization' some time ago, but the need is perhaps to coin an ugly word and speak of multi-polarization: a mode of presentation by which the world is shown as peopled not with minimal persons (with individuals in the social scientist's sense, if you like, in which an individual is more an *item* than an individual) but with personalities: intensely focussed versions of Innocent Child, Dotard, Devil, Lively Old Man, Honest Boy, Rake and the rest. By the same token, every *local* in which such a personality finds himself (or herself) seems to be transmuted along similar lines, until it is no mere topographical item, no mere nondescript place which one is in once or over a period – but either a Place-of-Adventure on the one hand, or a Prison-House on the other. And in the final analysis, what this kind of transmutation means is not very obscure. To polarize life, to depict it as not individuals inter-related in causality, but person-alities breaking out continually into drama, is simply to take one's stand, in one distinctive way (for of course there are others) against the whole social calculus, the mechanical-science conception of society and life which Dickens always felt as an affront. It is no accident that Carlyle, immediately after his account of symbolism, should go straight on to attack the 'Motive-Millwrights' and how they leave 'only a kind of Digestive, Mechanic life': although in refutation of this, he adds, it is enough for a man simply to 'open his eyes and look'. The symbolic message (if message it can be called) is one only to behold, not to de-code.

In fact, it is no exaggeration to suggest that the picaresque form in which *The Old Curiosity Shop* is to so great an extent constructed is itself a standing challenge to the notion of society as mere nexus and causality. Yet here again one cannot see the form as standing symbolically for a non-systematic something which lies over against it. The form *is* what it speaks of. At the same time, it is essential to realize, as one turns from one work to another, that there is a reason for giving up the symbol-symbolized dichotomy as an adequate critical concept, quite other than any reason which has transpired so far. This is, that one work may seem to point in a certain direction by means of a certain distinctive something in it, and another point in much the same direction but by means of what is almost the opposite of that: almost as if red could stand for danger, and green too.

This invites elucidation. In *The Old Curiosity Shop*, the 'Motive-Millwright' conception of experience is implicitly rejected through a largely picaresque form and through a polarization of setting into Adventure-Scene on the one hand, and Prison-House on the other. The claim that these matters must be seen as concerned with genuine symbolism, and not mere picturesque colour, rests on the unchallengable facts that, taken particular by particular, they must be admitted to have a structure amongst themselves: and taken together, to have something which must certainly be understood in terms of meaning, but which cannot be understood in terms of literal meaning. If one now turns to *Oliver Twist*, the particulars stand in a greatly different light. For just three pages of its length (the opening of Chapter viii) that novel seems to tell the reader that its form is to be the picaresque: and then, abruptly, the notion is emphatically discarded, both straightforwardly and by satire:

> . . . a boy, who had *passed him carelessly* some minutes before, had returned, and was now *surveying him most earnestly* . . .

The careless passing-by of the picaresque is ousted by the earnest surveying of those drawn together into permanent social nexus. Rejection by satire comes on the next page:

> 'I am very hungry and tired,' replied Oliver . . . 'I have been walking these seven days'.
> 'Walking for sivin days!' said the young gentleman. 'Oh, I see. Beak's order . . .'

The life of the destitute 'rover' (this used to mean one who, because he had been displaced from static society, became a wanderer through society in somewhat the picaresque-hero style) is outside the Artful Dodger's Cosmos: all he can do by way of making Oliver's remarks intelligible, is to relate them to the unchanging *local* of the prison-house treadmill. In one phrase, he renders the picaresque form static, and locks it up within the institutions of nineteenth-century society.

But while picaresque adventure is absent in *Oliver Twist*, what made its counterpart (though one dialectically integrated with it) in *The Old Curiosity Shop* is present once again, and to a remarkable degree. Here too, the connecting idea, all the way through, is *prison-house*: Fagin's den ('the walls and ceiling of the room were perfectly black with dirt'); Magistrate Fang's cramped little office; the house in Chertsey that Sikes tries to burgle ('the crib's barred up at night like a jail'); the 'scullery, or small brewing-place, at the end of the passage' into which the criminals push Oliver through the tiny window; the 'bare garret-room, with a dim light burning at the farther end' which lies 'along the passages, and up the stairs' in the workhouse, and in which 'old Sally' dies; even the 'little room ("quite a cottage room")' through the window of which Oliver is seen by Fagin and Monks; the loft in the ruined 'manufactory' by the river, where Monks meets Mr and Mrs Bumble; the tiny garret ('lighted by only one small window in the shelving roof') where Sikes lies ill; and all the other haunts of the thieves, including the last one, the 'upper room' of the house 'strongly defended at door and window' on Jacob's Island, the door 'double locked and chained' and the panels and windows lined with sheet-iron. The last little dark room in the book is Fagin's condemned cell.

It is in these places that the action lies. After the meeting between Oliver and the Artful Dodger, only one important incident is set out of doors. This is the meeting between Nancy, Rose Maylie and Mr Brownlow. It occurs in the dark, at the foot of a flight of stone stairs which lead off London Bridge straight down into the water of the Thames. Cruikshank's illustration well conveys the cell-like incarceration of the place.

But what lies between these dark and claustophobic scenes is also *anti*-Picaresque (no less emphatic term will serve), though in another way. The book is indeed full of outdoor events; yet they insistently take the form of anxious, urgent, foreboding journeys hurriedly taken from one 'prison-house' to another. Oliver's flight; the thieves' secret journey to the house; the Bumbles' trip in storm and dark ('both wrapped in old and shabby outer garments . . . sheltering them from observation') to the rendezvous with Monks; Nancy's distraught hurry from Spitalfields to the West End ('She tore along the narrow pavement . . . "The woman is mad!" said the people'); Sikes's return to kill Nancy ('the robber held on his headlong course, nor muttered a word nor relaxed a muscle'); and his flight after the murder. The polarization is as marked as in *The Old Curiosity Shop*, but instead of being between prison-scenes and adventure-scenes, it is between scenes of incarceration, and transfers from one incarceration to another. Yet the departure from literalism is just as clear, and the emergence of a symbolic dimension much the same.

In writing of *The Old Curiosity Shop* I treated the minor characters as if they belonged rather to the setting than to the persons of the book. More of the characters in *Oliver Twist* must be seen as having a real and substantial part in the action; but for the most part they too must be taken, like the major characters of the other book, not as literal and realistic *members* of society but as *poles* of it. Child, Evil Old Man, Ruffian, Jack-in-Office, Cruel Nurse, Madman, Woman Criminal with a Heart, Spy – these characters in the novel are of course more than *commedia del l'arte* types in society. They are more than that, through the intensity of their realization, which presumably does not warrant labouring; but the crucial point is that veritably they are the opposite of *members* of society. Once again, membership of society and social causality are mesmerized into uniqueness and drama. The characters are *roles* in society, not members of it simply. How much this is distinctive of the book, or rather is constitutive of its whole substance, can perhaps be seen from another standpoint if one constructs what might be called a 'role-catalogue' of the persons between whom the major conversation-pieces one by one occur. That catalogue will tun: Inmate and Master (Chapter II); Orphan, Ruffian and Magistrate (III); Victim and Bully (VI); Good Child and Bad Child

(VIII); Evil Old Man and Victims (IX); Prisoner, Witness and Judge (XI); Castaway and Rescuer (XII); and so on. If the force of the catalogue is not clear, it soon becomes so if one does the same thing for the conversation-pieces in, say, *Pride and Prejudice*. There, after the celebrated opening scene, which (though I think misleadingly) could be called 'Man and Wife' and so treated like those in Dickens, one would have to describe the conversation-scenes in terms like 'some members of a family'; 'some friends and neighbours'; 'some people who meet at a dance'. The difference in the status of the characters is self-evident; but this difference is not there because the Dickensian characters, in that they are more, somehow, than literalism and realism, are symbols 'of' something. If one had to choose a preposition, the least inappropriate thing would perhaps be to say that they were symbols 'amid' – everything: everything, that is, in the book. One is back, once again, with Coleridge's 'actual and essential part'.

The first quarter of *Martin Chuzzlewit* is for Dickens a curiously literal and realistic-seeming novel. His characteristic abundance of detail may be recognized easily enough, and so may the splendid loquacity of some of his characters; but the sense of a firmly-established provincial middle-class *milieu* is strong, and the book is clearly preoccupied with such matters as are more usual with, say George Eliot or Trollope: family affairs and inheritances, the major characters' involvement with their careers. In these earlier pages, the sense that Pecksniff is an architect as much as, though of course not in the style that, Lydgate in *Middlemarch* is a doctor, is quite clear. In all his work, Dickens has no other character of quite this kind. Only the description of Todgers's Commercial Boarding-House, at the beginning of Chapter IX, seems to have a clear potentiality for transposing the novel into a more poetic key.

But it is not until the American part of the book, that a decisive shift of perspective proves inescapable; and even here, that it has indeed become inescapable is sufficiently inconspicuous to have escaped some. Among them is the author of the Introduction in the *New Oxford Illustrated Dickens* edition of this novel: who writes 'It will be found that it is very worth while reading the two parts (that is, the American scenes, and the main body of the work) separately'.

There is never any knowing what folk may find worth while, but it certainly seems worth while to make a point of not doing that, because then, and only then, does the structure of the novel begin to emerge. The America that Dickens depicts is a richly detailed analogue of one part of the world he depicts at home in England: the world of Pecksniffery and Chuzzlewittery. For what, after all, are the values by which Architect Pecksniff and Business-man Chuzzlewit maintain themselves? They are four, and the three most conspicuous ones are Hypocrisy, Cant and Greed. But turn to the American chapters:

> 'Is smartness American for forgery?' asked Martin. (Chap. XVI.)
> 'Lord love you, sir'', [Mark Tapley] added, 'they're so fond of Liberty in this part of the globe, that they buy her and sell her and carry her to market with 'em'. (Chap. XVII.)
> 'Come, come,' said Mr. Norris ... as Martin closed the door, 'the young man has this night beheld a refinement of social manner, and an easy magnificence of social decoration, to which he is a stranger in his own country. Let us hope it may awake a moral sense in him'. (*ibid.*)

– this is essentially Pecksniff: Dickens is at great pains to bring out the parallel. There is the slave-servant who joins up with Mark Tapley, and makes him 'jolly' by recounting his appalling trials; the *whitewashed* rooms everywhere through the National Hotel; the remarkable physical resemblance between hanger-on in the Old World, Mr Montague Tigg, and hanger-on in the New, Mr Scadder the land-agent (it was the illustrations by 'Phiz' that first brought this to my notice, but the text bears it firmly out). Mark Tapley, looking out at the stars and stripes 'hoisted from the house-top' sums up the situation in the closing words of the whole chapter in which the cupidinous falseness of 'America' is finally exposed:

> ... You're a gay flag in the distance. But let a man be near enough to get the light up on the other side and see through you; and you are but sorry fustian! (Chap. XXI.)

'Happy he who can look through the Clothes of a Man (the woollen, and fleshly, and official Bank-paper and State-paper Clothes) into the Man himself', wrote Carlyle of his 'Clothes-Philosophy'.

I said that there were perhaps four dominant qualities in the world of Pecksniff and the Chuzzlewits, and mentioned three of them only. The fourth is *Sterility*. Pecksniff is an architect who cannot design a building, the Chuzzlewits, less even than Dombeys, have only a mean, shabby, incompetent commercial life ('a dim, dirty, smoky, tumble-down, rotten old house . . . in the miserable bedrooms there were files of moth-eaten letters') with, moreover, a secret background of sordid violence. But is Sterility not of the American essence also? – as Dickens distils that precious article for us? Cant about liberty in a land of slavery; cant about an aristocracy of intelligence and virtue, when only one man practices these qualities, and he has to do so in secret; cant about the rich and fertile continent that culminates in the foetid swamp of Eden.

At this point, however, one is forced to recognize a dynamism, an even dialectical complexity in the novel, not unlike what showed itself in *The Old Curiosity Shop*. Eden is no foetid swamp in the sense simply that it is agriculturally unproductive. It is Eden seriously as well as ironically, because it is a source-place of the psyche from which comes Martin's regeneration, and from which he returns to England to succeed where he had failed. Curiously enough, what Martin finds is much what Hegel describes in his account of the dialectical transformations of Master *vis-à-vis* Servant: 'he really finds that . . . it is not an independent, but rather a dependent consciousness that he has achieved'. (*Phenomenology*, pp. 236-7). Moreover, there is a place surprisingly like the American Eden in the English part of the book: it is none other than the wood where Jonas murders Tigg-Montague, with its 'boggy ground', its 'soft and stealthy moss about the trunks of some old trees', its fallen or partly fallen tree-trunks, and everything 'tangling off into a deep green rustling mystery'. But this wood too is not only a scene of death. It is a scene of the event from which the defeat of Jonas, exposure of Pecksniff, and release of Chuffy and Mercy Chuzzlewit follows. Other major *locals* are rendered with similar complex potentiality, where one 'moment' of the scene has a potential which negates the other. Mr Pecksniff's own house is set, in Chapter 11,

70

in the late autumn in 'the fair old town of Salisbury'. The sun has been in mist all day but comes out bright at evening; birds chirp and twitter on the naked boughs; the fallen leaves 'gave forth a pleasant fragrance'; fruit and 'berries that hung like clusters of coral beads' stand side by side with wintry barrenness. Todgers's boarding house is surrounded by – it is an extraordinary image – streams of porters carrying chests of oranges everywhere through the streets; but, at the same time there is the scent everywhere of oranges decaying in the cellars all round. The churchyards are 'all overgrown', but with '*straggling* vegetation'. The cellars are said to be full of wealth – 'silver, brass, or gold, or butts of wine' – but unconnected with Mrs Todgers's own house. The roof-top is cumbered with 'posts and fragments of rotten lines, once intended to dry clothes upon' – but nearby one sees the Monument 'every hair erect upon his golden head', and a 'very forest' of steeples, towers, belfries, shining vanes, and masts of ships'. Even Mr Pecksniff has a spade and garden hat, and says 'I do a little bit of *Adam* still' (Chapter XXIV). Then, if one asks which character most blatantly embodies the hypocrisy, cant, greed, covert violence, and total absence of productiveness that makes up Pecksniffery-Chuzzlewittery, the answer is Mrs Gamp – in her inexhaustible fertility. No doubt it is entirely by accident that Dickens comes near to a Hegelian image in characterizing Mrs Gamp. Hegel (*Phenomenology*, p. 110) refers to the 'clear as noonday' account of experience as 'a synoptic index, like a Skeleton with tickets stuck all over it, or *like the rows of boxes kept shut and labelled in a grocer's shop*'. Mrs Gamp keeps her belongings in rows of tightly-shut hat-boxes (Chapter XLIX); but the boxes have *no bottoms*. And if one asks who is the most pathetic and helpless victim of that System, clearly it is Chuffey. But she it is, and he, the first by mere excess of action and the second by a Dickensian transformation, who decisively release the positive forces in the book and bring in its denouement. At every point, the impetus of the novel is away from the literal-realistic; but equally, it is away from anything where part may be abstracted from part in a symbol and revealed as a schema of symbol and symbolized. The effect is that the whole texture is loosened out, as it were, into another and further dimension; one that by concealment, as well as revelation, suggests open possibilities of meaning, rather than meanings *tout court*.

If this were not so, *Martin Chuzzlewit* would suffer (and so would others of Dickens's novels) from a most far-reaching defect: a radical disparity between the sterile world it depicts, and the profusion and multifariousness of reality in which Dickens seems to indulge whenever he can. A few examples will suffice where many are to hand:

> ... being market-day, and the thorough-fares about the market-place being filled with carts, horses, donkeys, baskets, waggons, garden-stuff, meat, tripe, pies, poultry, and huckster's wares of every *opposite* description and possible variety of character. (Chap. v.)

The word 'opposite' has a certain special interest here.

> A famous Inn! the hall a very grove of dead game, and dangling joints of mutton, and in one corner an illustrious larder.
> Business! Look at the green ledgers with red backs, like strong cricket-balls beaten flat; the court-guides, directories, day-books, almanacks, letter-boxes . . . (Chap. XXVII.)

This of course is in the sterile, bogus office of the Anglo-Bengalee. Its 'Medical Officer' comes out in the same colours:

> His neckerchief and shirt-frill were ever of the whitest, his clothes of the blackest and sleekest, his gold watch-chain of the heaviest, and his seals of the largest. His boots, which were always of the brightest, creaked as he walked. (*ibid.*)

It is not enough simply to argue that Dickens is making hypocrisy plain. That he makes it plain in terms so like what he does when he is making not hypocrisy but abundance and creativity plain, brings a fuller resonance to the passage as a whole. It must be seen along with the account of the lightning through which Jonas travels in the coach with Tigg-Montague:

> The eye, partaking of the quickness of the flashing light, saw in its every gleam a multitude of objects which it could not see at steady

noon in fifty times that period. Bells in steeples, with the rope and wheel that moved them; ragged nests of birds in cornices and nooks; . . . miles upon miles of hedge-divided country. (Chap. XLII.)

Here Dickens is not indulging himself with a little out-of-place scene-painting. The moment is essentially not one only of hate, estrangement and sterility. Dickens sees experience with a poet's eye, and for him there are no such moments. They are not null, because within themselves they are self-annulling; and they are so because experience is not mere system and causality, but almost sacral: a drama of personalities immersed in destruction and yet also in regeneration.

Coleridge, when he wrote about the Symbol, went straight on to say 'the genuine naturalist is a dramatic poet in his own line'; he must have had in mind exactly this distinction between reality as system and as drama. Perhaps it is an accident that he should go straight on to speak of the *self-transformation* necessary to one who should study human life in a truly dramatic-poetic way. But certainly, it is this mode of presentation which makes it possible for Dickens to preoccupy himself with the transformation and self-transformation of his characters as, broadly speaking, none of his contemporaries could do save perhaps Emily Brontë.

Fully to display the importance of these ideas in Dickens's middle novels would require another discussion. The concept of a total change of the personality turns up everywhere; and the contrast with such transformations as interest, say, Jane Austen is inescapable. Jane Austen's transformations come when the scales fall from a character's eyes. 'How differently did everything now appear!', she writes of Elizabeth Bennett after D'Arcy's momentous letter. As for Emma, subject of an equally spectacular *anagnorisis*, 'to thoroughly *understand* her own heart was her first endeavour', and 'the conclusion of the first *series of reflections*' was progress in that. But Dickens writes otherwise: 'I am not the man I was. I will not be the man I must have been' says Scrooge. 'From that time, there sprung up in the old man's mind, a solicitude about the child which never left him': opening words of Chapter LV of *The Old Curiosity Shop*. The death of the Child transmutes into the rebirth of the grandfather. Young Martin is transformed in Eden, Mercy Pecksniff transformed and regenerated through the trials of marriage with Jonas. But it is precisely the texture of openness, of revelation-concealment, which is created in these novels by their dynamic and dialectically complex symbolism, that creates in them their potentiality for transformation of character. To use the word 'dialectical' is no affectation, for it is Hegel himself who has exactly expressed the distinction between human change in Jane Austen terms, as recognition; and in Dickensian terms, as rebirth:

> the exposition ... may be taken as the pathway of the natural *consciousness* which is pressing forward to true *knowledge*. Or it can be regarded as *the path of the soul, which is traversing the series of its own forms of embodiment, like stages appointed for it by its own nature.* (*Phenomenology*, Introduction, p. 135.)

Dickens's use of the symbol not for its addition of meaning, but for its innermost life-quality, transmuting the work as a whole, seems to me to be, more perhaps than anything else in his work, what enables him so abundantly, so inexhaustibly, to represent the second, larger, freer, deeper of these alternatives.

PART TWO

THE CRITIC
OF SOCIETY

RAYMOND WILLIAMS

DICKENS
AND
SOCIAL
IDEAS

We need to begin by recognizing that Dickens is not, in any normal sense, a novelist of ideas. Yet ideas, and attitudes towards ideas, play an important part in his work. In order to define his use of ideas we need to consider, first, some of the general relations between novels and ideas and then, comparatively, some of the particular relations in Dickens and in two or three of his important contemporaries. When this has been done we may be able to clarify what are now often obscure accounts: of Dickens's relations, for example, to utilitarianism, to environment as an influence on character, to religion and to social and political change.

There is an immense variety of relations between novels and ideas, and this must make any analysis tentative. But we can perhaps distinguish and illustrate seven characteristic relations, as a way of reminding ourselves of this actual complexity. Too many discussions of ideas in fiction, or in art generally, seem to fail to get beyond the two or three simplest cases.

Quite the simplest case is that of the novel which openly propagates ideas, or an idea. This is often fairly called propagandist fiction, though the judgment is subject to the usual vagaries of perception of propaganda: his ideas are propaganda, my beliefs are truths. There is a whole body of fiction, and especially of magazine fiction, in Dickens's period, which is overtly of this kind. Consciously improving stories, often barely distinguishable from tracts, were written to instruct the poor in the dangers of theft or intemperance or sexual immorality, a fiction dedicated, one might say, to the training of domestic servants. Where a more serious conscience was engaged, as in the evangelical and other religious novelists such as Mrs Tonna or Mrs Sherwood, the tales belong, however simply, to an older tradition of moral fable or parable. It is wrong, however, to limit this first type to any particular sect or emphasis, or to suppose that this kind of fiction is always trivial. Robert Tressall's *The Ragged-Trousered Philanthropists* is a vigorous socialist novel of this kind: expounding ideas directly in the narrative and through characters, as well as dramatizing a world which shows the need for these ideas. Many of H. G. Wells's later novels, and some of his earlier science tales, are expositions of ideas in the same sense.

The second type has a shifting boundary with the first. We can define it as that in which ideas are not so much propagated as embodied, yet with something of the same root emphasis, in the desire to persuade. It is some indication of the critical complexity of this issue that some undeniably major works have to be considered under this heading. Tolstoy's *War and Peace* is a great novel by any standard and of course includes virtually every kind of writing that has gone into modern fiction. But its organizing centre is an idea about history, directly expressed in the Appendix, to which all the particular and substantial actions can be seen in the end as relating. The form is more mature than that of propagandist fiction, and more experience is gathered – substantially gathered, and not merely as secondary illustrative evidence – to enact and enforce the governing point of view. But it would be evasion to suggest that the central idea is not radically there, as it is also in *Resurrection.* Some of D. H. Lawrence's novels are similar: *Lady*

78

Chatterley's Lover, fairly clearly, or the less successful *The Plumed Serpent*.

We need to remember these two kinds, where the distinction between propaganda and embodiment of an idea is often a matter of detailed working rather than of radical difference of aim, if we are to keep our bearings when we go on into a kind which most of all perhaps, beyond the evident fictional tracts, is seen as the novel of ideas. This third type is the novel in which ideas are argued, are overtly discussed. Here the simplest case is the early work of Aldous Huxley, *Crome Yellow* or *Point Counterpoint*, which are fictional variants of a modern symposium with most representative points of view set out and in a way lived through by the group of characters who have been assembled, primarily, for just this purpose. The method has precedents in Peacock or in Mallock's *The New Republic*, and at its edges is hardly fiction at all but philosophical or critical dialogue. Yet, again, some important novels suggest themselves as belonging to this type. Thomas Mann's *The Magic Mountain* has a similar purpose and organization, distinguished mainly by its greater weight and sustenance. Instead of illustrating various ideas and points of view, in such a way that the illustration, the representativeness seems the main point, it explores the ideas, not so much mimicking as illuminating them. Parts of George Eliot's mature novels have the same quality, notably the arguments about radicalism in *Felix Holt* and about internationalism, of which Zionism is the instance, in *Daniel Deronda*; and of course, quite overtly but in a historical context, *Romola*. Some of George Eliot's other work, for example *Adam Bede* or *Silas Marner*, belongs in the critical area between the first and second types; it is often overtly propagandist, as in Dinah in *Adam Bede*; as often embodied but still directed, as in *Silas Marner* or parts of *Felix Holt* or *Middlemarch*.

Ideas, it is well known, are most recognizable as ideas when they are unfamiliar or new. Other ideas which have become orthodox in a group or in a society take on more readily the appearance of general truths or even of 'common sense', 'maturity' or 'universal human experience'. The novelist who is writing with the grain of his society characteristically uses ideas of this kind, and is then

often described as a 'non-ideological' novelist when the only substantial difference is in this matter of conformity or challenge. Jane
Austen, for example, is full of ideas, for the most part directly and
plainly expressed, but most of them are so taken for granted, as
common standards or conventions by which individual behaviour
or conduct can be seen and judged, that they operate, as ideas,
more passively than actively, although the final weight of the ideas
in the fiction is often no less. A novel by one of her contemporaries,
Godwin's *Caleb Williams*, is distinguishable as 'a novel with an
idea' mainly because the idea is new, and even then, I think, it
would not stand out so clearly if Godwin had not also written
Political Justice. Defoe's *Robinson Crusoe*, it is now generally
recognized, is radically organized by an idea of the independent
economic individual: historically a contentious and provocative
idea, which over a distance of centuries allows us to challenge but
more crucially to recognize it, yet at the time so much with the grain
of its world that it could appear evident truth or, more decisively,
as in the case of any successful idea, not an idea at all but simply
characteristic and normal behaviour, a sensible and admirable way
to live.

Here again, of course, there is a difficult border area. Some of the
most effective embodiments of an idea in fiction create so immediate
and convincing a reality that it is only by analysis, and then with a
certain artificiality, that the shaping idea can be separated out.
When a novelist is using widely accepted ideas this is especially
likely to be the case. The idea as such may never have entered his
mind, while he was creating the character or situation, and this is
just because the idea was part of his mind from a much earlier
stage, as an habitual way of seeing and valuing. Indeed the most
interesting relations between novels and ideas are often of this kind,
when ideas appear, so to say, only as characters, and when ideas as
such may be hardly visible at all. We have seen the importance of
Tolstoy and Lawrence in an earlier type, in which an idea is
embodied in the whole direction of a novel. Each writer also uses
this later method; Tolstoy's *Anna Karenina* is an excellent example,
and parts of Lawrence's *Sons and Lovers* and *The Rainbow*. Here
the characters as it were embody principles, and the action is the

testing of those principles, but our immediate response, as readers, is to the people as created, who both seem and are autonomous (the autonomy depending in the end, though, on what is fundamentally a realized and embodied idea).

A further and related type is that in which the whole fictional world of the novelist is directed by an idea or a complex of ideas, and yet again these are so deeply embodied that they are in effect dissolved, into what seems and is willingly taken as a free-standing world. The most immediate examples of this type are novels like Kafka's *The Trial* and many of his short stories, and Joyce's *Ulysses* and even more *Finnegans Wake*. It is not difficult to offer a more or less exact equivalent, in terms of ideas, to the worlds and actions there created, and in the case of Joyce we know that some of this construction was conscious. But the working of these ideas into fictional reality is so deep and so sustained that in the first instance our response is unmediated and direct.

One final type should be added, though it is very different from any considered hitherto. It seems to be perfectly possible for a writer to hold ideas, even strong ideas, and to express these directly or through particular characters, while at the same time the actions he creates, the values and consequences he explores, bear in quite other directions: a case, we might say, where the writer's opinions outside his writing are different from the ideas he finally embodies in his work. I am using, in this definition, Coleridge's important distinction between opinions and ideas: the former often strongly held and expressed but belonging as it were to the surface of the mind, a kind of small change of thinking; the latter more deeply, even unconsciously established, in ultimately decisive ways. The classic case of this type is, I suppose, Balzac, whose reactionary opinions are surpassed by actions exposed without the limitations those values would normally imply. There are, no doubt, many other cases, and in reminding us of the problem of the level of ideas, in any particular instance, this type returns us to the complexity of the whole inquiry.

I have distinguished then, tentatively, these seven kinds of relation between fiction and ideas: briefly, works in which ideas are *propagated*; in which ideas are *embodied*; in which ideas are *argued*;

in which ideas are *conventions*; in which ideas emerge *as characters*; in which ideas are *dissolved* into a whole fictional world; and in which, over and above the real action and its values, ideas are present as what can properly be called a *superstructure*.

I want now to try to clarify Dickens's uses of ideas in relation to these varying methods. I may be wrong but I think there is not much evidence, in Dickens, of the seventh kind, though it is true and important that where we can compare ideas expressed outside his writing and in the novels there are some significant differences of tone (the examples collected by Professor Collins, in *Dickens and Education*, on his views of children's upbringing and of schools, are relevant here, and there are some other interesting cases in Humphry House's *The Dickens World*.) In general, however, Dickens's ideas are in no way a superstructure, of a kind which the actions of his novels bear away from or contradict. The overall bearings, indeed, are remarkably close.

Other types which we can exclude, where Dickens is concerned, are the third and fourth. For he never really argues ideas, in either a representative or an exploring way. There is frequent mimicry of well-known ideas and tendencies, but this is set against a warm attachment to certain other ideas and tendencies. Nobody could ever feel, reading Dickens, that he is listening to a debate, though we may very often feel that we are reading an *account* of a debate by a passionately committed and polemical reporter; the sort of thing we still often read in newspapers, reporting discussions from a partisan position; and of course this was part of Dickens's own immediate inheritance and practice. Further, it is hardly ever the case that Dickens uses ideas as conventions, in the sense I defined. That use belongs, really, to basically settled societies, and to writers who find the general ideas of their time adequate. Dickens, for the most part, is as far away from this as any writer we could think of.

But the remaining four types all seem possibly relevant. It isn't difficult to collect cases where Dickens is directly propagating ideas, even in the most direct way by address to the reader.

> Dead, your Majesty. Dead, my lords and gentlemen. Dead, Right Reverends and Wrong Reverends of every order. Dead, men and

women, born with Heavenly compassion in your hearts. And dying thus around us, every day. (*Bleak House*, Chap. XLVII.)

Oh for a good spirit who would take the house-tops off, with a more potent and benignant hand than the lame demon in the tale, and show a Christian people what dark shapes issue from amidst their homes, to swell the retinue of the Destroying Angel as he moves forth among them! For only one night's view of the pale phantoms rising from the scenes of our too-long neglect; and from the thick and sullen air where Vice and Fever propagate together, raining the tremendous social retributions which are ever pouring down, and ever coming thicker! Bright and blest the morning that should rise on such a night; for men, delayed no more by stumbling-blocks, of their own making, which are but specks of dust upon the path between them and eternity, would then apply themselves, like creatures of one common origin, owing one duty to the Father of one family, and tending to one common end, to make the world a better place! (*Dombey and Son*, Chap. XLVII.)

So many hundred Hands in this Mill; so many hundred horse Steam Power. It is known, to the force of a single pound weight, what the engine will do; but, not all the calculators of the National Debt can tell me the capacity for good or evil, for love or hatred, for patriotism or discontent, for the decomposition of virtue into vice, or the reverse, at any single moment in the soul of one of these its quiet servants, with the composed faces and the regulated actions. There is no mystery in it; there is an unfathomable mystery in the meanest of them, for ever. – Supposing we were to reserve our arithmetic for material objects, and to govern these awful unknown quantities by other means! (*Hard Times*, Book I, Chap. XI.)

It is of course characteristic of this first type that it can be illustrated by isolated examples, but there can be little doubt that Dickens used this method of direct address, direct propagation of ideas and attitudes, significantly often, and almost always in line with the major directions of his art, rather than as isolated propaganda.

He would not, all the same, be anything like so important a novelist if this were his only method. Several of his novels seem to me excellent examples of the second type, in which a novel is

83

centred around a directing idea, with the same radical desire to persuade yet with a more complicated and more substantial gathering of experience to support the idea, which may or may not be directly stated. *Hard Times* is only the most obvious example. *Dombey and Son*, *Little Dorrit* and *Great Expectations* seem to me even more substantial cases of this kind.

Indeed the question is, really, whether Dickens's use of ideas is not limited to these first two types, in which he is unusually strong and direct, and whether the fifth and sixth types, in which ideas are dissolved into characters or into whole fictional worlds, are not another and different kind of art. It is a matter of critical opinion, obviously, but I think there are several significant cases of ideas dissolved into characters, in the novels before *Dombey and Son* and in *Bleak House* (Micawber, Pecksniff, Sarah Gamp, Skimpole, Lady Dedlock), and indeed that this kind of characterization, a unique and memorable and individual reality which yet has a lasting force as a general meaning or emphasis in life, a general idea, is one of the most evident marks of Dickens's genius. Other readers would choose other characters, but I am concerned particularly with those cases which have not only impressed me but which are different in operation, I think, from the characters who serve as elements of a more directly organized idea (Gradgrind and Bounderby, Dombey and Captain Cuttle, Miss Tox and Merdle, Jo Gargery and Magwitch).

And then, overlapping in actual novels, both with this kind of creation and with organization around a single directing idea, there seem to me to be major cases, in Dickens, of that sixth type in which ideas are so dissolved into a fictional world that our first apprehension of the whole reality thus created is unmediated and direct. There is no quite simple case, but *Our Mutual Friend*, in its main bearings, seems to me essentially a novel of this kind, and one might add, for illustration, the elements represented by Tulkinghorn and Krook in *Bleak House*, by the Clennams in *Little Dorrit*, and by Miss Havisham in *Great Expectations*. Here again Dickens's genius is remarkable, and it is of an essentially different fictional kind from the methods discussed earlier.

Indeed I would say that to discuss Dickens's use of ideas, with any adequacy, we have to be aware of his use of these four major methods, which can often be separated by analysis but which in most of his important works lie closely together, in a particular organization. The simplest illustrations of his ideas can come from the first type – extractable ideas and opinions – or from the second – as has been effectively done with *Hard Times*. But we shall only respond to his full range when we include the other types, and this is not a case of leaving ideas behind for some more substantial art (a common way of putting it in orthodox analysis) but of seeing more clearly how important ideas were to him and at the same time the very particular ways in which they were important.

Another way of arguing this would be by comparing Dickens with some of his most relevant contemporaries. Disraeli, for example, is full of examples of the first type – the propagation of ideas – and is a very good case to consider in relation to the second type – novels organized by a directing idea, as *Coningsby*, *Sybil* and *Tancred* fairly evidently are. The critical point is that Disraeli succeeds only in a minor way in gathering experience around the directing ideas, though he is highly effective in illustration. *Hard Times*, in many ways, is nearer to the methods of Disraeli than any other Dickens novel, which is not to deny its limited success at that level. But *Dombey and Son* and *Great Expectations*, though essentially organized by ideas, have moved further into the substantial embodiment which the second type is at its most important. And there is hardly anything in Disraeli which could be confidently referred to the fifth and sixth types. That is a measure not only of a difference of achievement as novelists, but also, I would say, of the ultimate importance of the operative ideas. In Disraeli these constitute a very clear outlook and indeed a programme. In Dickens there is something more: an involvement of the ideas with a profound and deepening way of seeing life as a whole: that difference one attempts to indicate by distinguishing between illustration and vision.

Elizabeth Gaskell is much nearer to Dickens in her use of the first and second types. *Mary Barton* and *North and South* contain directly propagated ideas and each novel is organized – the latter more clearly – by a directing idea. It was in fact in *Mary Barton* that she came nearest to pushing beyond illustration to vision, and she was driven back by external opposition, from her publisher and friends. *North and South* is clearer just because she has accepted a certain limitation. No creative energy or disturbance is, as it were, unused and troubling. But in *Mary Barton* it had been, in her response to John Barton, the good man who is a murderer, and her revision does not wholly exclude this. Of course as a fine example of the difficult area between the first and second types Elizabeth Gaskell is a serious novelist, whom I continue to admire. But I think she drew back where Dickens went on, and I think this has a great deal to do with the question of creative openness – really creative openness – to ideas.

George Eliot, of course, is the really telling case for comparison. For she is clearly at ease with ideas, and over a very wide range, in a way that Dickens is not. Reading her lucid embodiments of a complex argument, or her precise and scrupulous applications of an interpreting idea, is an experience we cannot hope for in Dickens, and there are moods in which, with its memory in mind, his characteristic uses seem limited to sentimentality and to jeering. But the comparison, in the end, involves more than that. George Eliot is involved with thinking as a form of direct life, and this is her main stress although she can be aware of fixed thought, fixed ideas, as alienated and grotesque. She has difficulties in the relation between her attachment to educated procedures and her very deep fidelity to certain customary and emotional links and bearings; a tension between these modes often disturbs, even at times dis-locates her fiction. And her characters are ordinarily realized in the detailed processes of formation and development, to which thinking and analysis are at once relevant and contingent.

Dickens, on the other hand, creates his characters, with very telling effect, as essentially formed, as the products of experience rather than its immediate processes. And ideas, then, are not so much active and qualifying as parts of a fixed appearance, a fixed mode, against and through which, on a single bearing, his own ideas – the basic points of view of the narrative – operate in directing ways. What is finally rendered is then radically different but, seen in a wider context, no less valuable. He is concerned so much with a kind of false consciousness – the rationalizations of inhumanity, of pretension and deformity – that the alienated and grotesque mode is often directly relevant. So many of the ideas that bore on life in his time are indeed only records of pretension and deformity, and there is often a creative rightness in treating them as such rather than in the limited credit of analysis. From a position in experience like his, it is the consequence of an idea, and not its formal substance, that really tells. And he works more finely than anyone in his time the tension – often the unbearable tension – between orthodox ideas, the ratifying explanations of the world as it was, and the tearing, dislocating, haunting experience which the ideas, in majority, were meant to control.

I do not say this is the only creative way, but we are fortunate to find, in Dickens and George Eliot, writers of genius who take alternative ways through the intense and complex experiences of that society. All the virtues of a positivist analytic and referential mode – the very strengths of intellectual liberalism – are to be found in George Eliot (though she has creative resources, in forms of emotional transcendence and of customary fidelities, beyond the scope of that tradition). All the virtues of an alternative radicalism, of a central human vision of goodness and kindness and fullness of life which then creatively transcends, is made to transcend and surpass, the expositions and rationalizations of temporary interests – a movement, one might say, of conversion rather than persuasion, and of acts of transcendence rather than of conclusion – are to be found in Dickens. Since these different modes are still active alternatives, the contrasted genius of George Eliot and of Dickens is still directly relevant, to our own living and thinking.

[2]

I have been offering to define the ways in which ideas are brought to bear in Dickens's novels, and to compare these ways with others. This essential grasp is then the main critical ground. I want now to go on, from this basis, to Dickens's relations with some major ideas of his time.

Ideas of an active and consequential kind are always in solution in a society. It needs positive intellectual work to examine them as precipitates. Dickens, it is clear, takes his ideas from the currents rather than the sources of this kind of thinking. We can see his important relation to Carlyle, and his significant relation to Cobbett and to the Romantic essayists – Leigh Hunt and Lamb, perhaps Hazlitt – who both popularized and were further popularized in radical journalism. But it is characteristic of Dickens that even here he only takes what he needs. Medievalism, for example, which is a common element in the sources most like him, is left strictly alone. And I think this is part of a general evolution of radicalism, in which the wrongness of that industrial society could at last be stated directly, without the medieval contrast as cover. Yet when we consider that major writers after him – Ruskin and then Morris – still held to medievalism, we have to acknowledge, I think, other contributory elements. There was a vital radicalism which challenged false gods, the idols of early industrial capitalism. But there was another radicalism which challenged, more directly, actual muddle and neglect, and this, in Dickens, is an obviously powerful current. It is with this in mind, and remembering the main sources of the challenge to neglect and muddle, that we have to look again at his real relations to utilitarianism.

The key case, here, is of course *Hard Times*, which has been widely taken as a direct exposure of utilitarianism. But I have noticed, in some of these accounts, a very confused idea of what utilitarianism was, as a reforming movement, and some of the misunderstandings bear directly on Dickens's theme. The main tenets of utilitarianism included the exposure of all institutions to the tests of rational utility, in the interest of the greatest happiness of the greatest number (it was in this spirit that it conducted its major campaigns for legal, social and political reform which unquestionably made the society as a whole more humane), and the possibility of an objective ethics, in which the judgment of right and wrong actions would be dependent on calculation of the amount of pleasure or pain which those actions produce. In its mood, rather than in all of its detailed tenets and procedures, utilitarianism powerfully influenced all radical thought, and in ways not only not different from Dickens but in some respects very like him; he too would have accepted happiness or pleasure as an absolute

88

criterion, as against the emphases of most other contemporary religious and philosophical systems.

Yet Thomas Gradgrind is quite clearly a utilitarian, and of the political party of the philosophic radicals. The word is used in descriptions of him – 'his unbending, utilitarian, matter-of-fact face' (Book I, Chapter xv) – and the emphasis on statistical inquiry and the reliance on 'the strong dispassionate ground of reason and calculation' (Book I, chapter xv) make the identification certain. The education he imposes on Tom and Louisa is very unlike the famous education of John Stuart Mill, but just as Louisa can say 'I never had a child's heart' (Book I, chapter xv) so Mill could say 'I never was a boy; never played at cricket; it is better to let Nature have her way'.

Yet it is a simplification of *Hard Times*, and indeed of Dickens's use of ideas in his novels, if we isolate the system of thinking as the only object of attack. We have to observe, first, how many feelings Dickens had in common with the utilitarian reformers. He shared with them an angry impatience with any conservative idealization of the past (as in the dummy books at Gad's Hill – *The Wisdom of Our Ancestors*. Vol. I, Ignorance; Vol. II, Superstition; Vol. III, The Block; Vol. IV, The Stake; Vol. V, The Rack; Vol. VI, Dirt).[1] He shared also an insistence on legal reform; not only generally, but precisely in *Hard Times*, where the presentation of the problems of divorce, and of the lack of a law which could help such poor men as Stephen Blackpool, is very much in this spirit. He shared a contempt for the aristocracy and its social pretensions, sufficiently instanced in *Hard Times* by Mrs Sparsit and James Harthouse. He shared an impatience with every kind of inherited muddle and neglect – and 'muddle', as Blackpool's diagnosis of his condition, is characteristic. Outside his writing he was of course a friend of Southwood Smith, who had been Bentham's private secretary and who stands with Edwin Chadwick as a type of the utilitarian reform commissioner, in his work on regulations for housing and public health, which Dickens warmly and centrally supported.

Yet Gradgrind, a version of apparently just this tradition, is the very starting point of *Hard Times*. To understand what happens,

[1] See *The Dickensian*, vol. liv, 1958, p. 47.

not only here but more generally in Dickens's use of ideas, we have to look at a contradiction within utilitarianism itself, not so much as an intellectual system as a whole social and political tendency. This is Dickens's characteristic emphasis on the consequences of an idea, rather than on the idea itself. Two of Gradgrind's children are named in his early notes Adam Smith and Malthus, and the names are reminders of a more complicated intellectual and political history. At a certain point in the real history of England during the industrial revolution, the teachings of utilitarianism and of philosophical radicalism became inextricably entwined with the teachings of classical economics and of restraint of the poor. When Dickens was writing, the utilitarian emphasis was a compound of rationalism and *laissez-faire* economics, in spite of the substantial contradiction between an appeal to general utility and a recommendation of non-interference. What can readily be separated as contradictory ideas were in fact combined, as so often in real history, by the urgent and overriding interests of a class. I think that in *Hard Times* Dickens penetrated this contradiction, not analytically but in an act of emotional and substantial recoil and revulsion. He attacked the ideas, that is to say, as part of a more general attack on that practical combination of rationality and exploitation which dominated life in England and which was directly creating new kinds of distress and abuse even while it was reforming many inherited abuses and muddles.

For it is surely this general movement that we find in the novel. Gradgrind the utilitarian is the close friend and ally of Bounderby the brutal and indifferent employer. It is to Bounderby that he gives his daughter in marriage. It is Harthouse, the drifting aristocrat, whom he introduces for political reasons to both Bounderby and Louisa (and with the unintended effect of destroying that calculated marriage). I do not mean that Dickens saw utilitarianism as betraying itself; he rarely started from considerations like that. I mean that he judged the idea, the system, by its alliances and its consequences; by its fruits, as he would always be likely to be the first to say.

What he is then refuting is not so much an idea as a whole social formation. The reliance on reason had been cleansing and liberating, but as the instrument of a class which was both reforming and aggressive it became, in a real history, an alienation, in which the calculation of interest was separated from all other human impulses and ties. This is where, of course, Dickens learned from Carlyle, but also from what he could see happening. As in Bitzer, not thinking but rationalizing, not applying but using an idea:

> his only reasonable transaction in that commodity would have been to buy it for as little as he could possibly give, and sell it for as much as he could possibly get; it having been clearly ascertained by philosophers that in this is comprised the whole duty of man – not a part of man's duty, but the whole. (Book II, Chap. I.)

But what 'philosophers' had ascertained, or tried to ascertain, was an ethical basis. What was being applied, on the authority of the economists but more directly in the interests of a class, was a characteristic form of capitalist trade. The structure of Dickens's handling of the idea is exact: not the analysable content but the consequence.

The use of statistics is another case in point. Dickens would use them, himself, when they helped. But the use he shows in the novel is already alienated, within the pressure of rationalizing an economic system. As Sissy Jupe says:

> 'Then Mr M'Choakumchild said he would try me again. And he said, This schoolroom is an immense town, and in it there are a million of inhabitants, and only five-and-twenty are starved to death in the streets, in the course of a year. What is your remark on that proportion? And my remark was – for I couldn't think of a better one – that I thought it must be just as hard upon those who were starved, whether the others were a million or a million million. And that was wrong too.' (Book I, Chap. IX.)

It is when a statistical technique is used to rationalize that kind of neglect and suffering that the 'statistical clock' is indeed 'deadly'.

Rationality, again, has been made a function of a mode of production, overriding other values. People have been reduced in Coketown to 'Hands' –

> a race who would have found more favour with some people, if
> Providence had seen fit to make them only hands. (Book I, Chap. x.)

The economic system, as Ruskin put it, 'manufactures everything
but men'. That consequence is the basis of its reasoning, rather than
its result. The ideas are ideology rather than grounds for action.

What is then seen is not an idea but a system which uses ideas.
Everything, from system to ideas, is then systematically attacked.
If the system is as it is, all institutions, Dickens believes, will take
on its colour: the dustheap of parliaments, or the trade union which
reduces brotherliness to a generalized antagonism. The only
positive values are personal, outside the system: where a repressed
humanity asserts itself in personal love and care and responsibility,
or breaks out in the fanciful and eccentric play of the Horseriding.
As so often, Dickens sets himself to make the struggling human
feelings defeat the system: the transformation he always had in
mind. But he is enough of his period to add to this central desire a
politic warning:

> Utilitarian economists, skeletons of schoolmasters, Commissioners of
> Fact, genteel and used-up infidels, gabblers of many little dog's-
> eared creeds . . .

(the range of those addressed and warned is already important,
indicating an attack on a whole system of social thinking and practice rather than on an isolated idea)

> . . . in the day of your triumph, when romance is utterly driven out
> of their souls, and they and a bare existence stand face to face,
> Reality will take a wolfish turn, and make an end of you.

This is a revolutionary perspective, when they (the poor) and 'a
bare existence stand face to face'. But notice the mood of the warning. A revolution of the human spirit is necessary, or a bitter and
destructive revolution in human fact. Dickens both sees the cause
and fears the result, holding anxiously and even desperately to those
who go on under pressure loving and caring, and trying in his

created action to extend their influence. It is in these active and consequential ways that he both perceives ideas and attempts to surpass them.

We may now turn to consider some other examples of his use of ideas. One very perplexing case is that of the influence of environment on character. This is very difficult, now, to estimate, because what was, in the nineteenth century, a comparatively new way of thinking – that environment is the decisive influence on character – is in our own time, at least in certain areas, almost taken for granted. It had been preceded, of course, by the much older idea of good or bad families, good or bad stock, in which the character of any individual was seen as being primarily formed. In some cases, these essentially different ideas overlap, but there is ultimately a world of difference between them. Perception of the influence of environment, of social conditions, is deeply related to a particular consciousness of history, within which men are seen as being made. The best known English advocacy of this view, in the early nineteenth century, is Robert Owen's. His insight was so widely accepted, by succeeding generations, that we now scarcely notice its originality:

> The general diffusion of manufactures throughout a country generates a new character in its inhabitants . . . The manufacturing system has already so far extended its influence over the British empire, as to effect an essential change in the general character of the mass of the people . . .[1]

By the time Dickens was writing, this consciousness of the human effects of the industrial revolution had spread so widely that it is an intrinsic element of ordinary ways of seeing the world, which Dickens certainly shares. His description in *Dombey and Son* of the dislocation and then the reorganization of life around the railway, in what had been Staggs's Gardens, is a fine and deeply worked example of this way of seeing the effects of a system.

But we must then distinguish Owen's more particular viewpoint, as expressed in his earliest writings, from this consciousness of

---

[1] *Observations on the Effect of the Manufacturing System*, 1815, p. 5.

environment and influence as it passed into the general mind. In *A New View of Society* and *Observations on the Effect of the Manufacturing System* Owen believed that

> any general character, from the best to the worst, from the most ignorant to the most enlightened, may be given to any community, even to the world at large, by the application of proper means; which means are to a great extent at the command and under the control of those who have influence in the affairs of men.[1]

It was in this mood that as a young man he called on the Prime Minister with a plan to change the moral character of Britain in the next few years.

I recall this emphasis because two later developments now obscure it. Owen himself, finding that the ruling class did not at once adopt his plans, turned to creating alternative institutions which would have the same effect: model schools, factories and industrial villages; trade unions and cooperative societies; experimental communities. That emphasis on an alternative culture fed in, very powerfully, to a growing working-class movement. But, also, from many political positions, the stress of Owen's view of transformation was dismissed as utopian. We may think of this rejection now as mainly marxist: an emphasis on the realities of class relations which rule out any such inspirational shortcut. But of course it was also rejected by many kinds of practical men, who felt that the real world was never to be changed in these ways.

Dickens did not put much faith in alternative institutions. His attitude to the later Owen emphasis is indeed quite regularly hostile. But equally he had very little room for the objections of the practical men of any kind. Because of the development of Owen's thought, and the fact that the later phase is much the best known, I think we have missed Dickens's relation to the mood of the earliest phase. I do not mean that he was directly influenced by early Owen, but that their ideas have an important common content which belongs to the general history of English popular radicalism.

[1] *A New View of Society and Other Writings*, ed. Cole, Everyman's Library, 1927, p. 16.

In the matter of the evil influence of a bad environment, the relation is undoubtedly close. Consider this important passage from *Nicholas Nickleby*:

> But now, when he thought how regularly things went on, from day to day, in the same unvarying round . . . how, in seeking, not a luxurious and splendid life, but the bare means of a most wretched and inadequate subsistence, there were women and children in that one town, divided into classes, numbered and estimated as regularly as the noble families and folks of great degree, and reared from infancy to drive most criminal and dreadful trades; how ignorance was punished and never taught; how jail-doors gaped and gallows loomed, for thousands urged towards them by circumstances darkly curtaining their very cradles' heads, and but for which they might have earned their honest bread and lived in peace; how many died in soul, and had no chance of life; how many who could scarcely go astray, be they vicious as they would, turned haughtily from the crushed and stricken wretch who could scarce do otherwise, and who would have been a greater wonder had he or she done well, than even they had they done ill . . . and yet how the world rolled on, from year to year, alike careless and indifferent, and no man seeking to remedy or redress it . . . (Chap. LIII.)

This is characteristic and unusually explicit: not only the 'circumstances darkly curtaining their very cradles' heads' but the converse 'could scarcely go astray, be they vicious as they would'. And then what is interesting is that while Dickens retains, into his maturity, the former emphasis, he on the whole changes the latter. Evil can nearly always be referred to its breeding places: typically the slums maintained by indifference and neglect. But the simple converse – 'good' homes produce 'good' people – is radically modified, or rather the goodness is seen not as a matter of class or affluence but of human spirit. It is in the later, darkening fiction that we see evil breeding in the fine houses of Dombey or Merdle. And this is of course the point of transition from the traditional view of 'good families', 'good stock'. In an exploiting and indifferent society, moral damage is a function of general relationships. As he puts it in *Dombey and Son*:

> some who have never looked out upon the world of human life

around them, to a knowledge of their own relation to it . . . a perversion of nature in their own contracted sympathies and estimates; as great, and yet as natural in its development when once begun, as the lowest degradation known. (Chap. XLVII.)

Degradation by environment is then as evident in the indifferent rich as in the neglected poor; and certain kinds of living, in greed and pride, breed vice and misery as directly as the pestilential slums.

Two problems then remain: the survival of virtue, and the agency of change. In the former Dickens is very unlike Owen but also unlike most contemporary religious interpretations. An indestructible goodness – *Little Dorrit* is only the most obvious of many examples – emerges, as it were miraculously, from conditions which in others breed vice. This is his main variation on the character-and-environment theme, and in the lineage of ideas is primarily related to a Romantic emphasis, found also in much popular Christianity, on the innocence, the positive innocence, of childhood. So many of Dickens's examples of positive goodness are related to this sense of a retained childlikeness that the point needs little emphasis. It is the qualifying factor in the otherwise dark and darkening vision of an ugly and evil society reproducing ugliness and evil.

But then, as a qualifying factor, it combines, sometimes uneasily, with the emphasis Dickens shares with Owen: that the chain of cause and effect could be quite quickly broken, if we made up our minds to break it. Owen was much hindered, in his early advocacy, by his explicit rejection of religion. He needed no supernatural sanctions but only social intervention, yet the latter without the former was seen as infidel and dangerous. Dickens, by contrast, uses the language of popular religion, often significantly associated with the innocence of childhood, when he makes his related plea for change:

> owing one duty to the Father of one family, and tending to one common end, to make the world a better place! (*Dombey and Son*, Chap. XLVII.)

Yet it is clear that what he has in mind is always human and social intervention, in the spirit of innocence. He rejects or seems not to know the alienated religious versions of redemption or salvation, which would occur *elsewhere*, and he certainly cuts through 'religious' rationalizations of the existing social order, which in Harriet Martineau and many others were commonplace. In this sense his vision – we must still, as always, call it that before we call it an idea – is a developed form of that Romantic humanism to which Owen's social thinking must also be related.

But there is another stress which makes him very like the early Owen: I mean as part of a common tradition, rather than from direct influence. For though the central agency of change, in Dickens, is innocence – indestructible innocence, which he repeatedly creates and makes survive, as a main bearing of his fiction – there is little doubt that in immediate terms he shares Owen's would-be-practical perspective:

> the application of proper means; which means are to a great extent at the command and under the control of those who have influence in the affairs of men.

Outside the novels this is how he worked, and inside the novels the perspective is often there, in the tone of his appeals to his readers. This is where a 'change of heart' and a 'change of system' come together, in practice: neither revolutionary change – the action of a new class; nor reformist change – the amendment of discrete wrongs. If we want a name for it, it is liberalism in its most general and heroic phase, itself directly related to romanticism: social liberalism, in which the general human condition will be generally transformed, by the action of the interested, the innocent and the humane. It was an action increasingly difficult and problematical in the real history of his times.

I have taken these examples of Dickens's central ideas both for clarification and for a more general purpose: their relation to his practice as a novelist. As I argued earlier, his novels are full of the first and second types of fictional idea: propagation and embodiment. But I think it is in the very difficult area I have just been discussing, of innocence and corruption, of systematic evil and of

97

transforming change, that he moves to the fifth and sixth types: of ideas dissolved into characters and actions, into fictional worlds. It is easy to show him, intellectually, as inconsistent, but my final point is that these deepest ideas and experiences tore at him, profoundly, in ways that make one see not inconsistency – the analytic abstraction – but disturbance – the creative source. It is in just this creative disturbance, in which significance is not given by systems but has to be found, under tension, in experiences, that he has the power to penetrate and illuminate his obscuring and shadow-filled world.

MICHAEL SLATER

DICKENS'S

TRACT

FOR

THE TIMES

Ten years after the passing of the Poor Law Amendment Act of 1834 and the trumpeted appearance, 'like Hyperion down the eastern steeps'[1] of the Poor Law Commissioners intended to set all to rights, the condition of the English working classes was still desperate. In the towns women struggled to feed their children and themselves – and, often, their unemployed husbands too – by working fifteen hours a day at shirt-sewing for a few farthings a shirt and in the country farm-labourers tried to maintain *their* families on a wage of seven or (if they were lucky) nine shillings a week. Escape from this harsh poverty lay only in crime, death or – for many the most terrible refuge of all – the workhouse. The newspapers were full of stories of crimes born of desperation – suicides, rick-burnings, infanticides: and there were plenty of social theories current which

---

[1] Carlyle, *Chartism*, 1840 (p. 129 of vol. xxix of the Centenary Edition of Carlyle's Works).

would incline the more prosperous readers of those papers to see such reports either as evidence of the natural viciousness of the poor or as the sad but inevitable result of over-population and the 'march of progress'. Some blamed the Corn Laws, some the New Poor Law, some the passing of the last vestiges of feudalism; but many blamed the poor themselves regarding their teeming existence itself almost as a troublesome impertinence.

Such was not Dickens's view, however. Speaking in Birmingham in February 1844, he declared, to loud applause, 'I do not myself believe that the working classes were ever the wanton or mischievous persons they have been so often and so long represented to be.'[1] Distressed and angered by what he saw and heard around him he determined, as he wrote to Macready later in the year, to strike a 'sledge-hammer blow' for the cause of the poor planting at the same time 'an indignant right-hander on the eye of certain wicked cant that makes my blood boil.'[2]

Possibly this idea first entered his head in March 1843 when he received a copy of the Second Report (Trades and Manufactures) of the Children's Employment Commission,[3] sent to him by one of the Commissioners, his friend Dr Southwood Smith. It was a horrifying document disclosing that parish orphans or the children of poor families were regularly sent out to work at the age of seven years and sometimes as early as three or four; that such wages as they earned invariably went entirely to their parents if they had any; and that their 'apprenticeships' (if any) gave them no real skill and were 'often passed under circumstances of great hardship and ill-usage.' In some industries children often worked fifteen, sixteen or eighteen hours a day 'without any intermission' in places 'very defective in drainage, ventilation, and the due regulation of temperature.' They had not 'good and sufficient food, nor warm and decent clothing.' When under the absolute control of adult work-

[1] *Speeches of Charles Dickens*, ed. K. J. Fielding, 1961, p. 63. Hereafter cited as *Speeches*.

[2] *Letters of Charles Dickens* (Nonesuch Edition), ed. W. Dexter, 1938, vol. i, p. 646. Hereafter cited as *Letters*.

[3] Presented to Parliament January 30, 1843. See: *Parliamentary Papers*, Session 1843, Vol. xiii. The Children's Employment Commission was appointed in October 1840 and the First Report (Mines) was presented to Parliament on April 21, 1842.

men, they were 'almost always roughly, very often harshly, and sometimes cruelly used.' In such leisure time as they had they were allowed to run completely wild; attempts to educate them were either non-existent or grossly incompetent; and, brutalized as they were by such a way of life, their moral condition was appalling.

Like another reader of this shameful catalogue – Elizabeth Barrett whom it moved to write her 'Cry of the Children' – Dickens felt stirred to do something. He wrote to Dr Smith on March 6,

> I am so perfectly stricken down by the blue-book you have sent me, that I think (as soon as I shall have done my month's work) of writing and bringing out a very cheap pamphlet called An Appeal to the People of England on behalf of the Poor Man's Child, with my name attached, of course.

Four days later, however, Dickens wrote again to Smith announcing a change of plan:

> Don't be frightened when I tell you that, since I wrote to you last, reasons have presented themselves for deferring the production of that pamphlet till the end of the year. I am not at liberty to explain them further just now; but rest assured that when you know them, and see what I do, and where, and how, you will certainly feel that a sledge-hammer blow has come down with twenty times the force – twenty thousand times the force I could exert by following out my first idea. Even so recently as when I wrote to you the other day I had not contemplated the means I shall now, please God, use. But they have been suggested to me; and I have girded myself for their seizure – as you shall see in due time.[1]

It has been argued that in these letters lies the origin of Dickens's second Christmas Book, *The Chimes*, but this is, I feel, to be too precise. The Commissioners' report seems not to give rise directly to anything we find in the characters, situations or incidents of the book. More probably, its appearance contributed, along with Carlyle's social criticism, newspaper reports of poverty and distress and other factors to be considered later towards the building up at this time in Dickens's mind of a conviction of the desperate wrong-

[1] *Letters*, vol. i, p. 512.

ness of the framework of contemporary society and of his duty as a popular writer to do something about it, to make some strikingly powerful plea for the poor and so shock the more comfortably-off classes at least into an awareness of the situation.

When modifying his first proposal to Smith, Dickens was no doubt reflecting that a story by him would make a far more potent appeal to the public than any pamphlet he might produce, and his deferment of the work 'till the end of the year' might well indicate that he had some notion of linking it to the traditional season of good will. His promise to Southwood Smith may have been in his mind when, at the end of 1843, he wrote the *Carol* – which because of Tiny Tim can be seen as an 'Appeal on behalf of the Poor Man's Child' as much as can *The Chimes* although it is a less precisely focussed one; and the Commissioners' Report was probably in his mind again a year later when he was working on *The Chimes* itself. But that the Report was the initial, and remained the chief, source of his inspiration for *The Chimes* does not seem to me to agree with such evidence as we have regarding the book's origins. It was undoubtedly undertaken in the first place in order to follow up the enormous commercial success of the *Carol*. But, certain of an audience at least as huge as for his full-length novels, Dickens surely also saw his second Christmas Book as a golden opportunity for his first overt entry as a novelist into the political arena. Certain contemporary events, public personalities and social theories had especially roused his anger during the course of the year 1843–44 and these rather than the Commissioners' Report alone were the matters which provided his imagination with a starting point for the story.

[2]

Early in 1844 Dickens, like many of his fellow-countrymen, had been outraged by the treatment of a poor woman called Mary Furley tried for infanticide at the Old Bailey on April 16. Her story was that she had left a workhouse because of the brutal ill-treatment suffered there by her infant child and had then tried to support herself by sewing shirts but, since the most she could earn in this way amounted to only 5¼d. a day, she had borrowed a few shillings to buy some ribbons to make up into dress-caps for sale. The money was either lost or stolen from her and, faced with the prospect of returning to the hated workhouse, she frantically resolved rather to drown herself and the baby. She was rescued from the Thames (crying, 'My child! My child!'), but the baby had slipped from her arms in the water and was dead. The jury, after hearing her evidence, at once found her guilty and the judge, pronouncing sentence of death, was reported in *The Times* as saying to her,

> You have been convicted of the crime of wilful murder, which crime is proved to have been committed under circumstances of evident premeditation. Your act, which would have been at any time cruel, is rendered more so by the fact of the crime being committed by you – the mother of the child.

There was an immediate public outcry. *The Times* proclaimed in a leading article on April 20 that the New Poor Law had 'brought this poor creature to the verge of madness'. Next day another leading article (headed 'A Threatened Deed of Blood'), in *Lloyd's Weekly London Newspaper*, urged, 'Let the first intimation . . . of the sentence being about to be carried into effect, carry hundreds of petitions to the throne'. The Home Secretary, Sir James Graham, granted a stay of execution on April 27 but gave no indication of what Mary's ultimate fate would be. Two days later *The Times* exhorted the public to petition on her behalf, maintaining, in words that Dickens must have echoed most heartily,

> Here the act was reconcileable with the deepest affection; it was the frantic impulse of a woman reduced to the abyss of want, and having no friend to rescue her or her child from the horrors of lingering starvation . . . [Middle-class readers] cannot realize to themselves the feelings with which a helpless mother regards the child of her love, whose cries for food she can only answer by unavailing sobs . . . It is in that moment of utter, hopeless, helpless desertion, when she sees that she is abandoned by all the world – that madness takes possession of the brain, and the purest affection which a mother's breast can know turns to desperation. No; the rich, the respectable, the comfortable members of society cannot imagine . . . a condition so deplorably miserable as to prompt a woman to infanticide.

Some three weeks later Graham announced that the sentence had been commuted to seven years' transportation – a 'Mockery of Mercy' *Lloyd's Newspaper* called it. 'They say he is a cold, hard man, bigoted to the New Poor Law,' Thomas Hood wrote of Graham[1] and his severity in this case caused widespread public indignation.

Dickens had himself been active during the furore. In an article he wrote for the May number of *Hood's Magazine* entitled 'A Threatening Letter to Thomas Hood from an Ancient Gentleman' appeared this fiercely ironic passage:

> There is only one judge who knows how to do his duty, now. He tried that revolutionary female the other day, who, though she was in full work (making shirts at three-halfpence a piece), had no pride in her country, but treasonably took it into her head, in the distraction of having been robbed of her easy earnings, to attempt to drown herself and her young child; and the glorious man went out of his way, sir – out of his way – to call her up for instant sentence of Death; and to tell her she had no hope of mercy in this world . . . He won't be supported, sir, I know he won't; but . . . no milk-and-water weakness on the part of the executive can ever blot them [his words] out.

Echoes of this *cause célèbre* were heard for months afterwards – Jerrold refers to it in a *Punch* article on October 5 – and there can be little doubt that it was again in Dickens's mind when he came to write of Meg's desperate flight to the river in *The Chimes*. The 'fierce and terrible expression mingling with her love' that Trotty fearfully notes in Meg's face when she looks at her child is Dickens's picture of 'that madness [taking] possession of the brain and the purest affection which a mother's breast can know [turning] to desperation' to which *The Times* leader-writer alludes. Certainly, many of the book's readers were reminded of Mary Furley by the scene; a reviewer in the Chartist organ, *The Northern Star*, wrote on December 28, 1844, 'At length, despair's complete victim, she [Meg] turns – proceeds down the dark street – and hastens to the river's brink: a true picture of MARY FURLEY, and too many hapless ones who, like her, have been driven to destruction.'

[1] *Memorials of Thomas Hood*, vol. ii, 1860, p. 234.

[3]

If the state of Mary Furley and her kind in the cities was one of intolerable wretchedness, so also was that of the agricultural labourers, especially those in the remoter Southern counties who could not easily seek work in a nearby manufacturing town. Enclosures by the big landowners had resulted in the virtual destruction of the yeoman class of smallholders and peasant farmers. A Select Committee on the Labouring Poor noted in 1843 that the labourers were being gradually shut out from 'all personal and direct interest in the produce of the soil.' No longer possessing any land of their own, they had to work on large farms and estates for whatever wages they could get. Their living conditions were often appalling. Another Commission of 1843 (appointed to examine into the employment of women and children in agriculture) reported that, 'in nine villages out of ten the cottage is still nothing but a slightly improved hovel'. One witness before the Commission remarked,

> I do assert of the agricultural labourers as a class, that they have found fewer friends of any weight to contend for their rights in high places, and more enemies to their moral and physical improvement at their own doors than any other class of society.

The Game Laws, for example, were strictly enforced and when Dickens makes Fern say to the assembled gentry, 'One of your keepers sees me in the broad day, near my own patch of garden, with a gun. To jail with [me]!' he was exaggerating very little. In October 1844 *Punch* had noted the case of a peasant found walking with a gun on the Earl of Jersey's estates. He denied a charge of poaching but was found guilty by the magistrate – 'a sportsman and a clergyman'. Being unable to pay the £10 fine, he was ordered to hard labour for two months.

The corrected proofs of *The Chimes* show that Dickens changed Fern's native country from Hertfordshire to Dorsetshire. This was undoubtedly because of the particular notoriety of Dorset at this time as a county where the peasantry existed in the utmost squalor and poverty. A Tory M.P. for Dorset, George Bankes, declared in 1844 that the local labourers often earned eleven shillings a week 'with cottages, fuel, and other advantages'; this was challenged in a letter from 'A Dorsetshire landlord' published in *Lloyd's Weekly Newspaper* on April 28. Seven or eight shillings week without a cottage was nearer the truth, the writer declared and the men, driven desperate, were resorting to robbery and violence. Another letter in the same paper on May 5 confirmed this. Able-bodied men in the county earned, the writer said,

> from 6s. to 9s. while [the weekly wages] of youths under 21, who, for the greater part, do the work of strong men, are from 3s. 6d. to 4s. 6d., out of which they have to find their working implements, and keep them in repair. The *Sherborne Journal* stated, that while getting in the harvest, last year, men received only 8s. a-week and many, who had large families to support, got only 7s. a-week.

Dorset was indeed becoming, as Lord Ashley warned a Sturminster Agricultural Dinner in 1843, 'a by-word in men's mouths'. An account of the deplorable state of the Dorsetshire peasantry by Richard Sheridan, apparently published that year, had caused something of a sensation and the Tolpuddle Martyrs of ten years earlier were not yet forgotten. By making Will Fern a labourer on a Dorsetshire estate, then, Dickens was sure to convey to any moderately informed reader a vivid impression of the man's desperate plight.

Moreover, just as he was concerned to show his readers how a Meg might be driven to infanticide or a Lilian to prostitution by social injustice, so Dickens wished to show how a decent labourer such as Fern might be driven to incendiarism – a wild revenge on the farmers who would not give him and his dependants the wherewithal to live. The *Annual Register* for 1844 shows that there had recently been a sharp rise in the number of cases of arson. The average figure for 1838 to 1842 was forty-nine; in 1843 it rose to one hundred and two, the highest figure since 1832. The authorities reacted by a strict invocation of the law. The spring of 1844 had seen the case of Gifford White, an eighteen-year-old Huntingdonshire labourer, who was transported *for life* merely for threatening arson if he and his fellows were not supplied with work; 'the offence,' remarked the judge, 'was of a most atrocious character'. White's case had already inspired Hood to write 'The Lay of the Labourer' which appeared in the November issue of *Hood's Magazine* while Dickens was actually working on *The Chimes* in Genoa.

[4]

Turning from the oppressed to the oppressors, we have depicted in *The Chimes* a whole gallery of mischievous characters; more fools than knaves, each is an eminently 'respectable' member of society and represents some attitude towards, or theory about, contemporary social problems especially favoured by certain sections of the upper and middle classes during the 1840s. Only in one case, as we shall see, did Dickens base such a character entirely upon an individual living person. The others, like the Parliamentary philanthropist, Sir Joseph Bowley, 'The Poor Man's Friend and Father,' were fictitious figures representative of whole groups of people. The traits attributed to Bowley were in one reviewer's opinion 'caustic hits at the pseudo-philanthropy of certain well-known politicians.'[1] A prominent example of this class was the Whig ex-Chancellor, Lord Brougham.

Brougham had been by turns a vociferous champion of Queen Caroline, the Reform Bill, education for the people and other popular causes. In 1844, during a speech in the Lords on the Factory Bill, he seemed to his critics to have given a signal demonstration of the superficial nature of his boasted philanthropy. Answering advocates of the Ten Hours' Bill who pointed out that women working long hours in the factories could not suckle their children, Brougham had asked their Lordships how many of their own wives 'voluntarily exempted themselves from following what *in this respect* was called the first law of nature . . . because *their various avocations interfered with it*'? Yet,

> they had never heard that any mischief resulted from the practice; but they were told that the children of women employed in factories

[1] *The Evening Sun*, December 18, 1844.

were swept down in scores in consequence of their mothers not being able to attend to them.

Punch promptly seized the chance to ridicule him (always one of its favourite sports) and in the number for April 6 appeared a bitterly sarcastic article by Jerrold entitled 'Lord Brougham on Wet-nurses':

> His lordship, giant as he is in intellect, could not conceive it possible that the factory women were unable, like the aforesaid Duchesses, to hire wet-nurses for their children, whilst they, the mothers, were engaged in their twelve-hour 'avocations' at the mill. And yet, wet-nurses they *do* hire, or rather buy, and their names are 'Opium', 'Godfrey's Cordial', and 'Gin'.

The image of the garrulous Peer that we are given in this article suggests strongly that he must later have been among the sitters for Dickens's Bowley. Jerrold makes great play with the phrase, 'the poor man's friend' and quotes Brougham's eulogy of his own philanthropy in which he stressed how he 'had endeavoured, through good report and evil report, to do whatsoever *he* could to serve [the people's] best interests.' With this compare Bowley's speechifying in *The Chimes*: 'What man can do, *I* do . . . I do my duty as the Poor Man's Friend and Father . . . ,' and his description of himself as one of those 'who are, through good and evil report, the Friends and Fathers of the Poor.'

Brougham's 'redundant richness of language' is mocked throughout by Jerrold and Dickens later makes this kind of oratory a feature of Bowley also. Jerrold fixes too on Brougham's Evangelical turn of phrase and in particular his attributing the plight of the poor to the 'mysterious decrees and inscrutible dispensations of Providence.' This complacent nonsense is echoed by Bowley who talks much of things being 'Ordained' and announces to the poor, 'I am your perpetual parent. Such is the dispensation of an all-wise Providence.'

Finally, the main point that Jerrold is making in the article is the crass ignorance that Brougham displays about the actual living conditions of the people whose champion he claims to be; it is beyond him even to imagine what things are really like for them. So it is with Bowley; when Fern admonishes him to 'hear the real Truth spoke for out once' he merely sneers.

Brougham and his fellow-politicians, however, were by no means Dickens's only target in his sketch of Bowley. He was doubtless also aiming at such great landowners as the Dukes of Buckingham and Richmond. The former, who gloried in his popular nickname of 'The Farmer's Friend', was a vigorous champion of the Corn Laws who ground his tenants hard for rent (in *Past and Present* Carlyle twice uses the term 'Chandos farm-labourers' – the Duke's title was Buckingham and Chandos – to denote the most oppressed kind of agricultural worker). There is surely an allusion to Dickens's Bowley in the following paragraph which appeared in *Punch* shortly after *The Chimes*'s publication:

> The Duke of Buckingham and Chandos, the Labourer's Friend and Farm-servant's Father, has lately been exercising a little wholesome fatherly severity upon his Irish tenants in Westmeath, where eighteen families have been turned adrift by the Duke's steward. Pleasant weather this for the wet bog, or the ditch-side! It appears that no rent was due from them. Doubtless, on the occasion of the next agricultural jubilee at Stowe, these eighteen families will form part of the pageant. . . .

'Every New Year's Day,' declared Bowley during Trotty's interview with him, 'myself and friends will drink his [the poor man's] health' and he appears performing this ritual in Trotty's vision of the fête at Bowley Hall. Here again Dickens was not departing very far from contemporary reality. 'The Health of the Labourer' was a traditional toast when farmers and landowners gathered together at agricultural dinners. The dichotomy between the sentiment of this toast and the practice of those who drank it so jovially was the subject of much comment. An article in the *Economist* for January 13, 1844, declared that English peasants fared worse even than the Poles under their foreign tyrants and added 'Consider the irony of the Duke of Richmond, and grandees, who have reduced the man to this state, drinking his health at agricultural dinners as the pride and main-stay of the country.'

The Duke of Richmond, however, continued unabashed either by the *Economist* or, indeed, by *The Chimes*. The New Year of 1845 found him again proposing 'The Health of the Labourer' at the Freemasons' Tavern banquet – and doing so while, as Jerrold acidly pointed out in *Punch*, the labourers themselves were starving in the streets.

Bowley's paternalistic attitude towards the poor and his condescension in playing skittles with his tenants caused many readers of *The Chimes* to identify him with a splinter group of Peel's Tories, led by Disraeli, who called themselves 'Young England' and whose romantic remedy for the distresses of the working classes – or 'Order of the Peasantry', as they preferred to call them – was the restoration of the Throne, the Church and the Aristocracy as the real governing institutions of the country. In the manuscript of *The Chimes* there appears, among Alderman Cute's cronies, 'a youngish sort of gentleman, in a white wasitcoat' who makes speeches in praise of the picturesque England of Tudor times. Contemplating Trotty Veck he exclaims,

> 'Restore . . . the Good Old Times, the Grand Old Times, the Great Old Times! Raise up this trodden worm into a man by the mysterious but certain agency (it always has been so) of Stained Glass Windows and Enormous Candlesticks . . . Then his Regeneration is accomplished. Until then, Behold him!'[1]

Nearly every word spoken by this character is a gibe at some aspect of 'Young England', a group with which Dickens, who viewed the Middle Ages (including Tudor times) as an era of wholesale superstition, brutality, disease and crushing social injustice, was totally out of sympathy. Even the character's white waistcoat is significant for this was, it seems, 'Young England's' uniform:

> 'Oh! the vests of Young England are perfectly white,
> And they're cut very neatly and sit very tight,
> And they serve to distinguish our Young Englishmen
> From the juvenile MANNERS to CONINGSBY BEN . . .'[2]

[1] Quotations from the manuscript of *The Chimes* are by courtesy of the Victoria and Albert Museum.

[2] *Punch*, September 28, 1844. Lord John Manners (born 1818) was a prominent Young Englander, author of the notorious lines,

In the passage from the *Chimes* manuscript just quoted Dickens is seizing on another detail, the affiliations of 'Young England' with the Oxford Movement, or the 'Puseyites'. Only the year before he had mocked the latter in an article published in *The Examiner* on June 3 and called 'A Report of the Commissioners Appointed to Inquire into the Condition of the Persons Variously Engaged in the University of Oxford':

> A vast number of witnesses being interrogated as to what they understood by the words Religion and Salvation, answered Lighted Candles. Some said water; some, bread; others, little boys; other mixed the water, lighted candles, bread and little boys all up together, and called the compound Faith.

Accurate as Dickens's observation of 'Young England' idiosyncrasies was, it nevertheless seems that Forster considered the satire either as too poor or too offensive to print and it was 'knocked out' (to use Dickens's phrase). The only bit to survive was Bowley's skittle-playing (eulogized in the manuscript by the 'youngish sort of gentleman') and this was widely recognized as a hit at 'Young England's' emphasis on 'manly sports and pastimes' as a way of bringing the nobility and peasantry into harmonious social contact. At this very time Disraeli, Manners and their followers were busily urging their aristocratic friends to found cricket-clubs for their employees and were themselves,

> [going] about from place to place engaging with great spirit and good nature in a variety of manly sports with the labouring population; until it almost seemed that we were about to witness the renewal of those scenes of mirth and jollity, which had earned for this country, in olden times, the enviable, but, alas! no longer applicable title of 'Merrie England'.[1]

Dickens replaced the Young England Gentleman with another

[1] *Lord John Manners. A Political and Literary Sketch. By a Non-Elector*, 1872, p. 55.

'Let wealth and commerce, laws and learning die
But leave us still our old Nobility!'
and *Coningsby; or The New Generation* (1844) was Disraeli's Young England manifesto in fictional form.

of his *bêtes noires*, 'a real good old city tory, in a blue coat and bright buttons and a white cravat, and with a tendency of blood to the head'.[1] Unnamed in the book, this character was appropriately called 'Choker' in the Adelphi's Theatre dramatization of the story. He too is a praiser of the 'good old days' and represents a type which had long infuriated Dickens who wrote to Jerrold in 1843,

> If ever I destroy myself, it will be in the bitterness of hearing those infernal and damnably good old times extolled. Once, in a fit of madness, after having been to a public dinner . . . I wrote the parody I send you enclosed, for Fonblanque . . . [2]

This parody appeared in the *Examiner*, which Fonblanque edited, on August 7, 1841. Entitled 'The Fine Old English Gentleman. New Version, To be said or sung at all Conservative Dinners', it contained eight verses of which this one is representative;

> The good old laws were garnished well with gibbets, whips, and chains,
> with fine old English penalties, and fine old English pains,
> With rebel heads, and seas of blood once hot in rebel veins;
> For all these things were requisite to guard the rich old gains
>   Of the fine old English Tory times;
>   Soon may they come again!

In the letter to Jerrold already quoted Dickens goes on to mention 'a little history of England' which he is compiling for his son written in 'the exact spirit of your paper' for, he says,

> I don't know what I should do if he were to get hold of any Conservative or High Church notions; and the best way of guarding against any such horrible result, is, I take it, to wring the parrots' necks in his very cradle.

Earlier in the letter he has said that he thinks 'the parrots of society are more intolerable and mischievous than its birds of prey.' He goes on to give an example of the 'parrots' who set up the cry about the 'good old days':

[1] Forster's *Life of Dickens*, ed. J. W. T. Ley, 1928, p. 355. Hereafter cited as Forster.
[2] *Letters*, vol. i, p. 517.

Oh Heaven, if you could have been with me at a hospital dinner last Monday! There were men there – your City aristocracy – who made such speeches and expressed such sentiments as any moderately intelligent dustman would have blushed through his cindery bloom to have thought of. Sleek, slobbering, bow-paunched, over-fed, apoplectic, snorting cattle, and the auditory leaping up in their delight. . . .

Writing to Jerrold again from Italy a few days after completing *The Chimes*, he describes the medieval instruments of torture he has seen and exclaims,

There are hundred of parrots, who will declaim to you in speech and print . . . on the degeneracy of the times in which a railroad is building across the water at Venice[1] . . . Before God, I could almost turn bloody-minded and shoot the parrots of our island with as little compunction as Robinson Crusoe shot the parrots in his.[2]

Indeed, he had lost few chances of stating his opinion about the 'good old days'. In *Martin Chuzzlewit*, for example, appears this acid aside; 'It [Tom Pinch's face] might have purified the air, though the Temple Bar had been, as in the golden days gone by, embellished with a row of rotting human heads'; and the way in which this particular species of parrot exposed its own folly was pointed out by him in a speech on February 28, 1844. In it he described an old gentleman he had met on a train who,

expressed himself most mournfully as to the ruinous effects and rapid spread of railways, and was most pathetic upon the virtues of the slow-going old stage coaches . . . he burst forth against such newfangled notions, and said that no good could come from them,

and yet, said Dickens, if ever the train was delayed, the old gentleman, 'was up in arms, and his watch was instantly out of his pocket, denouncing the slowness of our progress.'[3] This old gentleman is

---

[1] Or across the fells of the Lake District? It was only a few weeks before this that Wordsworth had published his sonnet attacking the projected Kendal and Windermere railway.

[2] *Letters*, vol. i, p. 639.

[3] *Speeches*, p. 62.

evidently the same type exactly as the diners at the hospital banquet or the 'Ancient Gentleman' whom Dickens feigns to be the author of the 'Threatening Letter' in *Hood's Magazine* and whose principle is, 'that no man ought to know anything about his own time, except that it [is] the worst time that ever was, or is ever likely to be.' And it was this type that Dickens was ridiculing in the figure of 'Choker'. Like the 'Young Englander' whom he replaces, the old Tory mourns for the 'good old days' but they would differ sharply in their view of the present; one would see it as a time of potential renaissance, the other simply as 'the worst time that ever was,' and there would be little sympathy between them. The 'Ancient Gentleman' is made to say contemptuously: 'England was Old England when I was young. I little thought it would ever come to be Young England when I was old.' Few reviewers of *The Chimes*, however, appreciated Dickens's distinction and 'Choker' was taken by nearly all of them who mention him to be a supporter of 'Young England.'

There could, however, be no doubt which breed of parrots Dickens was attacking when he drew Mr Filer. Filer stood for all the Malthusians and political economists, all the utilitarians and statisticians – the 'philosophers' of *Oliver Twist* – whom Dickens had always detested and on whom he was eventually to launch a full-scale attack in *Hard Times*. For him the work of such men as McCulloch or John Stuart Mill was a mere heaping-up of 'facts on figures, facts on figures, mountains high and dry' without the least notion what such facts and figures really meant in human terms. Scrooge's glib phrase about the 'surplus population' represented for Dickens an outrageously callous way of thinking,[1] and he has Malthus's theories again in mind when he makes Filer say of the poor, 'they have no earthly right or business to be born . . . we know they haven't. We reduced it to a mathematical certainty long ago!' He was very likely thinking of a particular notorious passage in the

---

[1] Jowett's testimony may show that Dickens was not exaggerating: 'I have always felt a certain horror of political economists since I heard one of them say that he feared the famine of 1848 in Ireland would not kill more than a million people, and that would scarcely be enough to do much good.' Quoted by C. Woodham-Smith in *The Great Hunger*, 1962, p. 375.

second edition of Malthus's *Essay on the Principle of Population* (1803) which ran,

> A man who is born into a world already possessed, if he cannot get subsistence from his parents, on whom he has a just demand, and if society do not want his labour, has no claim or *right* to the smallest portion of food, and, in fact, has no business to be where he is. At nature's mighty feast there is no vacant cover for him. She tells him to be gone . . .

This horrifying passage was withdrawn in subsequent editions but it was long remembered by Malthus's opponents; on August 6, 1844 it was quoted by the Bishop of Exeter during a Lords debate on the Poor Law Amendment Bill the *Times* report of which was probably read by Dickens in Genoa only a few weeks before he began work on *The Chimes*. It may indeed have been this very passage which gave him the idea for the central theme of the book – Trotty's reluctant belief that the poor really have no business to be alive at all. The *Northern Star* reviewer (December 21, 1844) certainly saw the connection: 'Probably Trotty had been led to reflect on the possibility of there really being "no seat for him at Nature's board," from the fact that he was too often without a dinner.'

Dickens had, moreover, a particular grievance against the political economists which derived from a mention of the *Christmas Carol* in the *Westminster Review*'s notice of Horne's *New Spirit of the Age* (June 1844). The reviewer had remarked, 'Who went without turkey and punch in order that Bob Cratchit might get them . . . is a disagreeable reflection kept wholly out of sight [by Dickens].' That this foolish criticism rankled we can see from a letter to Forster dealing with the latter's objections to Filer;

> File away at Filer, as you please; but bear in mind that the *Westminster Review* considered Scrooge's presentation of the turkey to Bob Cratchit as grossly incompatible with political economy.[1]

It was doubtless in Dickens's mind when he composed the absurd speech in which Filer 'proves' statistically that Trotty has snatched

[1] Forster, p. 355.

his tripe 'out of the mouths of widows and orphans'. The same joke against the political economists appears at other points in the story, too, e.g., when Trotty meditates on Meg's beauty: 'Even her good looks are stolen from somebody or other, I suppose . . . She's been and robbed five hundred ladies of a bloom a-piece, I shouldn't wonder.'

[5]

With Filer, as with Bowley, the Young England Gentleman and 'Choker', Dickens was satirizing various groups of 'the parrots of society' rather than individuals, but, in creating Alderman Cute, he set out to attack a particular contemporary figure as well as the group-opinion which that figure represented. The man was Sir Peter Laurie, a wealthy saddler and former Lord Mayor of London, and in 1844 a noted Middlesex Magistrate.

In common with most Liberal or Radical writers, Dickens had always considered the Bench fair game but Sir Peter had rendered himself particularly obnoxious to humanitarian opinion by his campaign, begun in 1841, to 'put down' suicide and it is on this that Dickens concentrates in his sketch of 'Alderman Cute'. But there was much more to identify Dickens's character with his original than this anti-suicide hobby-horse, and a comparison of favourable contemporary descriptions of Sir Peter with the figure we meet in *The Chimes* shows us that those aspects of his character and activities most praised by his admirers were the very ones which Dickens satirises most severely. James Grant's *Portraits of Public Characters* (1841), for example, includes a eulogistic sketch of the magistrate in which his 'facetious disposition' is emphasised:

> He devotedly loves his jokes . . . he is essentially a jocular man. It requires of him a positive effort to put on a grave countenance . . . He smiles at everybody and everything . . .

Such joviality in the face of all the misery and desperation which Laurie saw every day from his magistrate's bench particularly incensed men like Jerrold and Dickens, and the latter makes it a prominent feature of Alderman Cute: 'The Alderman laughed and winked; for he was a merry fellow, Alderman Cute. Oh, and a sly fellow too!' He is 'mightily diverted' by the rival views of Filer and 'Choker,' and banters Trotty about his dead wife 'pleasantly'.

Moreover, according to Grant,

> ever since he [Laurie] began to act a prominent part in public life, [he has] had the reputation of being a man of unusual shrewdness . . . his knowledge of character was proved to be singularly accurate during the period of his mayoralty . . . There is a story, which is just now going the round of the journals, under the appropriate head of a 'Jonathanism,' to the effect, that there is a Yankee down east, who is so remarkably quick-sighted, that he can see fairly through a man in a few seconds . . . Sir Peter has, times without number . . . brought out in all their fulness and freshness the oddities of persons examined before him . . . The Mansion House . . . was daily thronged with strangers, anxious to witness the rich scenes which . . . were exhibited by Sir Peter's manner of examining witnesses . . .

The aptness of Dickens's nomenclature is clear for Cute is not only a 'merry fellow', but also, 'A knowing fellow. Not to be imposed upon. Deep in the people's hearts! He knew them, Cute did.' During Fern's impassioned speech at Bowley Hall,

> Alderman Cute stuck his thumbs in his waistcoat-pockets, and leaning back in his chair, and smiling, winked at a neighbouring chandelier. As much as to say, 'Of course! I told you so. The common cry! Lord bless you, we are up to all this sort of thing – myself and human nature.'

Laurie was celebrated, too, for his directness in dealing with offenders brought before him and his ability to talk to them in their own language. Dickens plays on this also. 'You can't "chaff" me,' says Cute to Trotty,

> 'You understand what "chaff" means, eh? That's the right word, isn't it? Ha, ha, ha! Lord bless you,' said the Alderman, turning to his friends again, 'it's the easiest thing on earth to deal with this sort of people, if you understand 'em.'

Sir Peter's speeches were full of what his admirers thought to be sturdy common-sense – and it is this that Dickens is mocking when he says of Cute, '*he* was a philosopher, too – practical, though! Oh, very practical.' One of *Punch's* nicknames for Laurie was 'the City Solon.'

Grant comments, too, on the magistrate's multifarious activities:

> Sir Peter is a perfect pluralist as regards the number of offices he fills. I can only name a few of them ... President of Bridewell and Bethlehem ... Chairman of the Marylebone Petty Sessions, and Governor of the Union Bank of London ...

and Dickens does not fail to make a point of this either: 'But everybody knew Alderman Cute was a Justice! O dear, so active a Justice always! Who such a mote of brightness in the public eye as Cute!'

In fact, Dickens produced a hostile but unmistakeable sketch of his eminent acquaintance and there was scarcely need for Leech to underline the fact by drawing Cute as a recognizable caricature of the real-life original.

As I have indicated earlier, it was Laurie's attitude towards attempted suicide on the part of those driven to despair by unemployment and poverty that chiefly outraged Dickens. The case of Elizabeth Morris (to which I shall return) in October 1844 ensured that Laurie's somewhat arbitrary campaign was fresh in the public's mind when they came to read *The Chimes* but Laurie's first victim had been William Simmons, an unemployed tailor, brought before him three years earlier. Simmons who, according to his own account, was 'in a perishing condition, and could get nothing to do' had tried to cut his throat (he did not cut very deep, the police said). Passing sentence Laurie observed,

> Suicides and attempts, or apparent attempts, to commit suicide very much increase, I regret to say. I know that a morbid humanity exists, and does much mischief, as regards the practice. I shall not encourage attempts of the kind, but shall punish them; and I sentence you to the treadmill for a month, as a rogue and vagabond. I shall look very narrowly at the cases of persons brought before me on such charges.[1]

[1] *The Times*, October 23, 1841.

Two days later Laurie dealt equally briskly with a young woman who had travelled in from Kennington to throw herself off Blackfriars Bridge. He

> asked if she had not been told by some person that this bridge had become the fashionable place to commit suicide, and that three or four persons were apprehended every week for it?

At this point a police sergeant stated,

> the attempts were more frequent than the magistrate had mentioned. One or two occurred every night, and the police kept them off as well as they could, and persuaded them to return.

The prisoner was then committed for trial at the Old Bailey. Laurie recalled that he had noticed when he was sheriff that,

> when any particular species of crime ... became more prevalent than usual, the judges ... used to say, 'We must stop this by treating it with severity.' This was the course he should adopt to check the passion for being drowned at Blackfriars-bridge.[1]

His procedure was commended in some quarters; the Guildhall Clerk commented a few days later that,

> There was no question than an attempt to commit self-murder was a misdemeanour in law, and nothing was so likely [as Laurie's method] to put a stop to the mania. In some cases there was no intention to complete the offence, but they wished to excite sympathy. The story got into the newspapers, and then some charitable persons sent money.[2]

On December 15, 1841, Laurie preened himself on the results of his actions. He remarked that,

> The effect of this mode of treating [would-be suicides] was admirable. From the moment the magistrates showed a determination to punish

[1] *The Times*, November 5, 1841.
[2] *The Times*, November 9, 1841.

attempts to commit suicide as other felons were punished the mania ceased altogether, and not one charge had been made in the city during the gloomy month of November and the miserable days of December which had already passed away.

The Clerk of the Court,

> observed that several desperate imposters had made money by the experiment of tumbling into the Thames. The infliction of imprisonment and hard labour for the offence would certainly check the practice as far as pretenders were concerned, whatever effect it might have on those who seriously wished to get rid of life. The result for the last five or six weeks certainly showed that the great majority of those who were charged were imposters,

and Laurie announced that he would certainly follow his plan through;

> Every man and woman brought before me for jumping or trying to jump into the river shall most positively walk off to Newgate, and I am very much mistaken if the judges do not henceforward inflict upon such offenders very heavy punishments.

During the course of the next three years he neglected few opportunities of carrying out his plan, doubtless encouraged by such praises as those bestowed on him by the *Illustrated London News* on January 21, 1843 for 'boldly encountering the risk of being rated for a want of feeling' in using 'the dread of exposure at the Old Bailey [to] put an end to the drowning mania.' On June 6, 1843, for example, he sent for trial another woman who had jumped from the inevitable Blackfriars Bridge. She said that

> she made the attempt through distress. Her husband had been out of work a long time ... SIR P. LAURIE said, he would endeavour to check these frequent attempts at self-destruction, which were stopped for about two years, by sending the offenders to be tried at the Old Bailey for the misdemeanor [*sic*]. He should now take the same course with the prisoner, and commit her to Newgate.
> The prisoner implored him for God's sake not to do that, and protested solemnly she would never do such a thing again.

SIR P. LAURIE replied, he was determined to send all such persons to trial; and she was committed.[1]

And in the autumn of 1844 there occurred the case of Elizabeth Morris, brought before Laurie accused of trying to poison herself. The magistrate,

said he should send her to the Old Bailey ... It was a fit case for trial, and he had no doubt she would be transported. He had put an end to persons attempting to drown themselves; he would now try the same cure for attempted poisoning. He had no doubt that those who took poison did not do so for the purpose of self-destruction, but for the purpose of exciting sympathy; and such morbid charity was more calculated to do injury than anything else[2]

And only a month before *The Chimes* appeared, Laurie took the opportunity afforded by another case to sum up his activities and their results:

SIR P. LAURIE said, during the year 1841 the offence of attempting to commit suicide seemed to be on the increase, and to check it he and another alderman each committed one person for trial ... The effect might be seen from the following return, the commitment taking place in October:—

'Number of persons brought before the magistrates at Guildhall for attempting to drown themselves –
Between the 1st of September and the
   31st of October, 1841 23
Between the 1st of November, 1841 and the
   20th December, same year 2
         J. A. NEWMAN, Assistant Clerk.'

The persons tried at the Old Bailey were imprisoned for a few days only and given up to their friends. What a theorist might call cruelty was in fact an act of humanity; for the dread of exposure and punishment prevented persons from making attempts to drown themselves, in which unhappily they might have succeeded. There

---

[1] *The Times*, June 7, 1843.

[2] Report quoted by Jerrold in *Punch* (in an article bitterly attacking Laurie over the Morris case) October 5, 1844.

was no satisfaction in punishing, except what arose from the terror of exposure and punishment deterring others from repeating the offence.[1]

I have gone into the facts of the situation at some length because I believe that a comparison of them with the impression of Laurie and his magisterial activities that we derive from *The Chimes* sheds some interesting light on Dickens as a satirist. Although there clearly was something to be said for Laurie (and he said it himself, frequently) Dickens totally ignores this and presents the at least well-meaning magistrate as a monster of deliberate callousness and brutal insensitivity. It certainly appears that Laurie was somewhat arbitrary and often made examples of genuine cases of distress but, from the figures quoted, there can be little doubt that he did succeed in 'putting down' those 'desperate imposters' who traded on the public's sympathies.[2] But Dickens, out to strike a 'sledge-hammer blow' for the poor, could allow no quarter to any of those who believed, however sincerely, that such widespread and grinding human misery could be dealt with by Cute's 'practical' rules-of-thumb any more than by Filer's cut-and-dried theories, the 'Young England' gentleman's romantic regression to the 'glorious and Feudal times' or Sir Joseph Bowley's patronising despotism.

For *The Chimes* was, above all, a tract for the times, of intensely topical reference. 'If my design by anything at all', Dickens wrote to Forster, 'it has a grip upon the very throat of the time'.[3] So topical was it that a reviewer in the *New Monthly Belle Assemblée* (February 1845) questioned whether Dickens had not 'injured the general interest of his story by making so much of it unintelligible, save to the "constant readers" of the police report in *The Times*.' The book is indeed full of echoes of the sad events recorded in those annals. When Lilian says to her 'adopted sister', Meg, as they toil over their sewing in a garret, 'you look so anxious and so doubtful

---

[1] *The Times*, November 13, 1844.

[2] At least he was never so crass as a certain Liverpool magistrate in 1939 who sentenced a man to one month's hard labour for attempted suicide with the words, 'If you are fool enough to pour poison down your throat, you deserve to suffer' (see *The Dickensian*, vol. xlii, 1946, p. 158).

[3] Forster, p. 346.

... There is little cause for smiling in this hard and toilsome life, but you were once so cheerful', Dickens even seems to be verbally echoing a moving case reported in *The Times* on August 23 and 27, 1844 – probably read by him only a few weeks before he began work on *The Chimes*. Two young sisters, rendered desperate by poverty, had tried to drown themselves after attempting to subsist on 6d. a day each, the most that they could earn by shirt-sewing. One was rescued and said of her drowned sister, 'Formerly she was very cheerful and had an overflow of spirits, but the toil and privation she had recently undergone had worked a complete change.'

The last word on this scorchingly contemporary little book, as indeed on all Dickens's social criticism, should perhaps go to Ruskin who remarks in *Unto This Last* that in this aspect of Dickens's work readers

> will find much that is partial, and, because partial, apparently unjust; but if they examine all the evidence on the other side, which Dickens seems to overlook, it will appear, after all their trouble, that his view was the finally right one, grossly and sharply told.

DICKENS AND THE PUBLIC SERVICE

Dickens's creation of the Circumlocution Office, and his use of it as one of the emblematic threads throughout *Little Dorrit*, was very well recognized in his own time and has been since. But he was not the only eminent nineteenth-century novelist to become interested in public administration as a fictional background or subject. Balzac in *Les Employés*, published in 1836, over twenty years before *Little Dorrit* (1857), devoted a whole novel to government service; so, in a different fashion, did Trollope in *The Three Clerks* (1858).

I shall refer to Trollope's book again, since it has a relation – a relation of opposites – to *Little Dorrit*. Balzac's is not so directly relevant. There is no evidence that Dickens read it; in fact, that is unlikely, for it is one of the least-known volumes in the *Comédie Humaine*. No one could call it a good novel: as far as that goes, it is scarcely a novel at all, so much as a treatise on the way to reform the French civil service, period 1820–30. A good slice of the book actually consists of a kind of memorandum on that topic, conceived by Balzac's ideal civil servant, Rabourdin. This has its own interest, and so has the book itself. Rabourdin is intellectually in a quite different class from any of the functionaries in Dickens and Trollope, just as Balzac's constructive imagination – not as an artist, but as a thinker about his world – was in a different class from theirs. Several of Rabourdin's proposals have actually been re-invented in both the French and British civil services, but not until over a hundred years later, after the second world war.

Nevertheless, that is a somewhat esoteric recommendation. I have mentioned *Les Employés* for a different reason: it is worth reminding ourselves that Balzac and Dickens (two of the greatest novelists, along with Tolstoy and Dostoievsky and perhaps Proust, who have ever lived) and also Trollope, more naturally gifted as a psychologist than any other English novelist, thought it valuable to write novels about this special aspect or component of the public life. It is true, of course, that all three of them lived in close contact with the workaday world; they were engaged with it in a way which would have been impossible for, say, Henry James or Joyce. It is also true that reflective men of their period were becoming conscious of the increase in social complexity and articulation, and were noticing the public service as something like a symptom of change. Still, with all that said, it is hard to imagine so many writers of such gifts doing anything comparable nowadays. We have to remember how much the scope of the novel – despite or because of its verbal developments – has shrunk.

All three of them, I have just said, were engaged with the workaday world. But here Dickens was quite different from the other two. He was engaged in a fashion peculiarly his own, ambiguous, often contradictory, full of passion but sometimes perverse. To say that he saw it as an outsider, or that he was, in our contemporary jargon, alienated, is partly true, but like all straightforward statements about him misleading. He actually lived inside his society, in its clubs, in its committees, in friendships with the influential, to a far greater extent than Balzac did in his. Few people had a more intense, and often frenetic, social life. To say that he saw the world as a radical (which he himself believed) is again partly true, and also equally misleading. In many ways he reminds one, at the time when he was writing the dark novels of his last period, of a middle-aged American liberal of the present day: who has had great hopes and found them eroded: who doesn't like what he sees round him and can't find a place to stand: who is nevertheless unbreakably bound to the society in which he grew up.

One doesn't have to be abnormally attentive, or to know the circumstances in which the book was written, to read those qualities in *Little Dorrit*. They give it its special mixture of sadness and violence. They leap out of his famous attack on the Circumlocution Office, which begins as his image of the British public service, and ends as something cloudier but more menacing.

It is probably sensible, at any rate it may clear up some misconceptions, first of all to treat this attack, as his contemporaries did, on the plane of fact. What was the public service in 1857 really like (for though *Little Dorrit* is set in the 1820s, the references to the Circumlocution Office are almost entirely contemporary)? How far was this an exercise in critical realism? How much are we to trust it, if we are thinking of Victorian history?

I shall shortly be making some detailed comments which may sound niggling or ungenerous. So, at the beginning, I should like to say that, to my mind, *Little Dorrit* as a whole is one of Dickens's two or three best novels, and therefore one of the best novels in the language. It isn't my job here, though, to speak of its beautiful architecture and its overwhelming cumulative effects. I have to confine myself to the Circumlocution Office, and it is time to consider what he actually wrote.

Chapter x of Book I, in which the Office is introduced for the first time, has been famous since it was written (before it was published, Dickens was already saying 'I have relieved my soul with a scarifier'), and sets the tone for the rest of his treatment of English public life. We ought to have some extracts in front of our eyes. It begins and ends, and the device is deliberate, with the words 'the Circumlocution Office'.

CHAPTER X

CONTAINING THE WHOLE SCIENCE OF GOVERNMENT

The Circumlocution Office was (as everybody knows without being told) the most important Department under Government. No public business of any kind could possibly be done at any time, without the acquiescence of the Circumlocution Office. Its finger was in the largest public pie, and in the smallest public tart. It was equally impossible to do the plainest right and to undo the plainest wrong, without the express authority of the Circumlocution Office. If another Gunpowder Plot had been discovered half an hour before the lighting of the match, nobody would have been justified in saving the parliament until there had been half a score of boards, half a bushel of minutes, several sacks of official memoranda, and a family-vault full of ungrammatical correspondence, on the part of the Circumlocution Office.

This glorious establishment had been early in the field, when the one sublime principle involving the difficult art of governing a country, was first distinctly revealed to statesmen. It had been foremost to study that bright revelation, and to carry its shining influence through the whole of the official proceedings. Whatever was required to be done, the Circumlocution Office was beforehand with all the public departments in the art of perceiving – How Not To Do It.

Through this delicate perception, through the tact with which it invariably seized it, and through the genius with which it always acted on it, the Circumlocution Office had risen to overlap all the public departments; and the public condition had risen to be – what it was.

It is true that How not to do it was the great study and object of all public departments and professional politicians all round the Circumlocution Office. It is true that every new premier and every new government, coming in because they had upheld a certain thing as necessary to be done, were no sooner come in than they applied their utmost faculties to discovering How not to do it. It is true that from the moment when a general election was over, every returned man who had been raving on hustings because it hadn't been done, and who had been asking the friends of the honorable gentleman in the opposite interest on pain of impeachment to tell him why it hadn't been done, and who had been asserting that it must be done, and who had been pledging himself that it should be done, began to devise, How it was not to be done. It is true that the debates of both Houses of Parliament the whole session through, uniformly tended to the protracted deliberation, How not to do it. It is true that the royal speech at the opening of such session virtually said, My lords and gentlemen, you have a considerable stroke of work to do, and you will please to retire to your respective chambers, and discuss, How not to do it. It is true that the royal speech, at the close of such session, virtually said, My lords and gentlemen, you have through several laborious months been considering with great loyalty and patriotism, How not to do it, and you have found out; and with the blessing of Providence upon the harvest (natural, not political), I now dismiss you. All this is true, but the Circumlocution Office went beyond it.

Because the Circumlocution Office went on mechanically, every day, keeping this wonderful, all-sufficient wheel of statesmanship, How not to do it, in motion. Because the Circumlocution Office was down upon any ill-advised public servant who was going to do it, or who appeared to be by any surprising accident in remote danger of doing it, with a minute, and a memorandum, and a letter of instructions, that extinguished him. It was this spirit of national efficiency in the Circumlocution Office that had gradually led to its having something to do with everything. Mechanicians, natural philosophers, soldiers, sailors, petitioners, memorialists, people with grievances, people who wanted to prevent grievances, people who wanted to redress grievances, jobbing people, jobbed people, people who couldn't get rewarded for merit, and people who couldn't get punished for demerit, were all indiscriminately tucked up under the foolscap paper of the Circumlocution Office.

Numbers of people were lost in the Circumlocution Office. Unfortunates with wrongs, or with projects for the general welfare (and they had better have had wrongs at first, than have taken that bitter English recipe for certainly getting them), who in slow lapse of time and agony had passed safely through other public departments; who, according to rule, had been bullied in this, over-reached by that, and evaded by the other; got referred at last to the Circumlocution Office, and never reappeared in the light of day. Boards sat upon them, secretaries minuted upon them, commissioners gabbled about them, clerks registered, entered, checked, and ticked them off, and they melted away. In short, all the business of the country went through the Circumlocution Office, except the business that never came out of it; and *its* name was Legion.

Sometimes, angry spirits attacked the Circumlocution Office. Sometimes, parliamentary questions were asked about it, and even parliamentary motions made or threatened about it, by demagogues so low and ignorant as to hold that the real recipe of government was, How to do it. Then would the noble lord, or right honorable gentleman, in whose department it was to defend the Circumlocution Office, put an orange in his pocket, and make a regular field-day of the occasion. Then would he come down to that house with a slap upon the table, and meet the honorable gentleman foot to foot. Then would he be there to tell that honorable gentleman that the Circumlocution Office not only was blameless in this matter, but was commendable in this matter, was extollable to the skies in this matter. Then would he be there to tell that honorable gentleman, that, although the Circumlocution Office was invariably right and wholly right, it never was so right as in this matter. Then would he be there to tell that honorable gentleman that it would have been more to his honour, more to his credit, more to his good taste, more to his good sense, more to half the dictionary of commonplaces, if he had left the Circumlocution Office alone, and never approached this matter. Then would he keep one eye upon a coach or crammer from the Circumlocution Office sitting below the bar, and smash the honorable gentleman with the Circumlocution Office account of this matter. And although one of two things always happened; namely, either that the Circumlocution Office had nothing to say and said it, or that it had something to say of which the noble lord, or right honorable gentleman, blundered one half and forgot the other; the Circumlocution Office was always voted immaculate, by an accommodating majority.

Such a nursery of statesmen had the Department become in virtue of a long career of this nature, that several solemn lords had attained the reputation of being quite unearthly prodigies of business, solely from having practised, How not to do it, at the head of the Circumlocution Office. As to the minor priests and acolytes of that temple, the result of all this was that they stood divided into two classes, and, down to the junior messenger, either believed in the Circumlocution Office as a heaven-born institution, that had an absolute right to do whatever it liked; or took refuge in total infidelity, and considered it a flagrant nuisance.

The Barnacle family had for some time helped to administer the Circumlocution Office. The Tite Barnacle Branch, indeed, considered themselves in a general way as having vested rights in that direction, and took it ill if any other family had much to say to it. The Barnacles were a very high family, and a very large family. They were dispersed all over the public offices, and held all sorts of public places. Either the nation was under a load of obligation to the Barnacles, or the Barnacles were under a load of obligation to the nation. It was not quite unanimously settled which; the Barnacles having their opinion, the nation theirs.

The Mr. Tite Barnacle who at the period now in question usually coached or crammed the statesman at the head of the Circumlocution Office, when that noble or right honorable individual sat a little uneasily in his saddle, by reason of some vagabond making a tilt at him in a newspaper, was more flush of blood than money. As a Barnacle he had his place, which was a snug thing enough; and as a Barnacle he had of course put in his son Barnacle Junior, in the office. But he had intermarried with a branch of the Stiltstalkings, who were also better endowed in a sanguineous point of view than with real or personal property, and of this marriage there had been issue, Barnacle Junior, and three young ladies. What with the patrician requirements of Barnacle Junior, the three young ladies, Mrs. Tite Barnacle née Stiltstalking, and himself, Mr. Tite Barnacle found the intervals between quarter day and quarter day rather longer than he could have desired; a circumstance which he always attributed to the country's parsimony.

Those are the first ten paragraphs. The chapter is a long one (about 8,000 words) and develops into some good particularized scenes with Barnacle Junior and Tite Barnacle.

Some of the inferences which we can draw, reading that introduction, are obvious enough. First of all, Dickens had had a stroke of genius, journalistic genius if you like, in hitting on the name for his office. He was well aware of it, and consequently overdid it. In fact, he went on overdoing it, not only throughout *Little Dorrit* but in later publications. He inserted it with proprietary pride, as though unnecessary to explain, in essays in *The Uncommercial Traveller*. It became immediately a cliché of his time. Trollope used it (at the same time indicating that he was going to take a different view of the government service) in the second paragraph of *The Three Clerks*, published in the following year. It is quite possible that, without this brilliant catchphrase, the entire treatment of government in the novel would have passed with far less notice. But catchphrases are not to be despised. Dickens, as well as being various sorts of a writer of genius, was a journalist of genius. Balzac happened on only one such phrase (the title of his oeuvre) in his whole career: Trollope on none at all.

What also can we infer? It seems to me equally obvious that, in that opening, Dickens was writing in one of those moods of manic incantatory rhetoric which came upon him when he had something simple to say upon a public issue. Compare the passages on revolution in *The Tale of Two Cities*. In fact, he was doing just what many people do when they make a public speech. He had become convinced of, or obsessed with, or had acquired[1] a simple black-and-white conception. He didn't wish to qualify the conception, but he did want to rub it in. Many of us have done the same thing in a public speech, and have fallen into the same tricks of reiteration. Listen to the stresses in paragraph 4. '*It is true . . .How not to do it . . . It is true . . .How not to do it. It is true . . .How it was not to be done. It is true . . .How not to do it. It is true . . .How not to do it. It is true . . .How not to do it* and you have *found out*.'

This is a standard oratorical repetition: though, in our own day, a speaker would have lost his audience if he had repeated the key phrases so many times. In paragraph seven, of course, Dickens is himself parodying the repetitive rhetoric of a parliamentary spokesman. '. . . not only was *blameless in this matter*, but was *commendable in this matter*, was *extollable to the skies in this matter* . . . it never was *so right as in this matter* . . . never approached *this matter*'. Dickens drops into his own rhetorical stresses and devices whenever the concept of the Circumlocution Office enters the novel. See, for instance, Book I, Chap. XXXIV (which has the picturesque title of 'A Shoal of Barnacles') for the utterances of Lord Decimus Tite Barnacle. This mechanical tom-tom prose jars even more, because in the rest of the book, as in *Great Expectations* or *Drood*, Dickens was writing with a brilliance, variety and control that – although we know that the words came with more difficulty – he had never equalled in his marvellous youth.

What impression ought this rhetoric to leave on us? Not that he was insincere or merely playful. That is to misjudge the nature of rhetoric, and particularly his. No, he was in dead earnest: such dead earnest that he just wanted to shout the slogan and not listen to any doubt either from himself or anyone else. Yet, if we have

---

[1] Some of Dickens's views on government were fairly certainly learnt from Carlyle, who had great influence on him. Cf. both the substance of and manner of the third of Carlyle's *Latter-Day Pamphlets*, called 'Downing Street', published 1st April 1850.

listened to slogans before, we have learned (usually, though not quite always, correctly) to think that nothing can be as simple as all that. Our immediate impression, as we keep having the Circumlocution Office drummed into our ears, is that this is altogether too black-and-white. Which is precisely what Dickens's sophisticated contemporaries thought.

The most interesting criticism of *Little Dorrit* in its year of publication appeared in *The Edinburgh Review* under the title of 'The License of Modern Novelists': the article dealt, first with Dickens, and then with Charles Reade's *It is never too late to mend* and Mrs Gaskell's *Life of Charlotte Brontë*, and was written, according to *Edinburgh* custom, anonymously. The writer was actually James Fitzjames Stephen, and it is just as well to remember that he wasn't impartial. He was the son of Sir James Stephen, one of the great civil servants of the century: Sir James was Permanent Under-Secretary at the Colonial Office from 1835 to 1847 and, for years during that period and before, effectively rules the Colonial Empire. Ruled it, incidentally, with exceptional imagination and humanity: he wasn't the nephew of Wilberforce for nothing, and the ending of slavery owed as much to him as to any single man. On the other hand, the whole Stephen family, including his third son, Leslie Stephen, the father of Virginia Woolf, long after Sir James's death, believed that he was the original of Tite Barnacle. (The fact that the Barnacles were an aristocratic clan, and the Stephens quintessentially haute bourgeoisie, seems to have distracted no one: they probably assumed that Dickens wasn't sensitive about those distinctions, thinking, as he appears to have done, for example, that Lord Decimus Tite Barnacle could be the style of a member of the House of Lords. So Fitzjames Stephen had no reason to love Dickens: but he was very well-informed about the official life, and on the whole a fairminded man. If we allow for a certain animus, his reaction to the Circumlocution Office was pretty representative of professional England's. A few quotations:

> They [Dickens and Reade] tend to beget hasty generalisations and false conclusions. They address themselves almost entirely to the imagination upon subjects which properly belong to the intellect.

We wish he [Dickens] had dealt as fairly and kindly with the upper classes of society as he has with the lower . . . Acute observer as he is, it is to be regretted that he should have mistaken a Lord Decimus for the type of an English statesman, or Mr. Tite Barnacle for a fair specimen of a public servant. But in truth we cannot recall any single character in his novels, intended to belong to the higher ranks of English life, who is drawn with the slightest approach to truth or probability. His injustice to the institutions of English society is, however, even more flagrant than his animosity to particular classes in that society.

In Mr. Dickens's voluminous works, we do not remember to have found many traces of these solid acquirements; [i.e. actual knowledge of the professions]; and we must be permitted to say, for it is no reflection on any man out of the legal profession, that his notions of law, which occupy so large a space in his books, are precisely those of an attorney's clerk.

[Fitzjames Stephen, like his father, had been called to the Bar. Later he had a distinguished legal career and became a High Court judge.[1] His attitude and Dickens's were in antagonism on one other occasion, when in 1867 Fitzjames Stephen acted for the Jamaica Committee, which attempted to get Governor Eyre tried for his severity in putting down a rebellion. Dickens and Carlyle, behaving like members of the ultra-right, strongly opposed the Committee.]

'. . . that universal system of jobbing and favouritism, which was introduced into the public service by Sir Charles Trevelyan and Sir Stafford Northcote, shortly before the time when Mr. Dickens began his novel.'

[This is savage, but justified, sarcasm. The Northcote-Trevelyan report, which recommended open competition for the civil service, appeared in 1853, and was already beginning to be acted on. Dickens must have known this.]

. . . any careful observer of his method might have predicted with confidence that he would begin a novel on that subject within a very few months after the establishment of a system of competitive examinations for admission into the Civil Service. He seems, as a

---

[1] In something like senility, he was the judge in the Maybrick case. But, before his stroke, his judicial reputation was very high.

general rule, to get his first notions of an abuse from the discussions which accompany its removal, and begins to open his trenches and mount his batteries as soon as the place to be attacked has surrendered. This was his course with respect both to imprisonment for debt and the Chancery reform.

[This point was made frequently during Dickens's life-time.]

A large proportion of the higher permanent offices of state have always been filled by men of great talent, whose promotion was owing to their talent. Did Mr. Dickens ever hear that Mr. Hallam, Mr. William Hamilton, Mr. Phillips, Sir George Barrow, Sir A. Spearman, Sir James Stephen, Sir C. Trevelyan, Mr. Merivale, Mr. Henry Taylor, or Mr. Greg are, or have been, members of the permanent Civil Service? Will he assert that these gentlemen were promoted simply from family motives, or that they are fairly represented by such a lump of folly and conceit as the Mr. Stiltstalking of his story?

[Fair comment. Nearly all those men were able administrators, who would have been successful civil servants at any later period. They were all from middle class families, some relatively humble. Cf. my comments on the social composition of the unreformed civil service below.]

Or, to take a single and well-known example, how does he account for the career of Mr. Rowland Hill? A gentleman in a private and not very conspicuous position, ... Did the Circumlocution Office neglect him, traduce him, break his heart and ruin his fortune?

It was this last comment to which Dickens directed almost all of his reply. Fitzjames Stephen's criticism had attacked the book on the plane of fact, as though it were written for the historical record: Dickens answered on precisely the same plane of fact, as though he too assumed that he was writing history and was to be judged by its accuracy. We oughtn't to smudge this over. Dickens, at least in his later years, was a highly conscious and deliberate artist, fully aware of what he called his 'emblems' and the use he made of them. Nevertheless he, like Dostoievsky, spoke and thought of his books as exercises in realism in the most simple of senses. It is singularly condescending of us, and a token of our superior wisdom and

literary insight, to assume that he hadn't really very much idea what
he was doing or what he really meant.

Dickens sometimes wrote prefaces to his hardback editions, after
a novel's serial publication, in which he answered criticisms, such
as Thackeray's gibes at Nancy in *Oliver Twist* or G. H. Lewes's not
unreasonable objections to the spontaneous combustion in *Bleak
House*. But it was rare for Dickens to do anything of the kind in a
journal, whether it was edited by himself or anyone else. However,
Fitzjames Stephen had wounded him, and in *Household Words* on
August 1, 1857 he set to work. He was irritated: and when he was
irritated in controversy he tended to become arch. He quoted the
passage in the *Edinburgh Review* about Rowland Hill, and then:

> The curious misprint, here, is the name of Mr. Rowland Hill.
> Some other and perfectly different name must have been sent to the
> printer. Mr Rowland Hill! ! Why, if Mr Rowland Hill were not, in
> toughness, a man of a hundred thousand; if he had not had in the
> struggles of his career a stedfastness of purpose overriding all
> sensitiveness, and steadily staring grim despair out of countenance,
> the Circumlocution Office would have made a dead man of him long
> ago. Mr Dickens, among his other darings, dares to state, that the
> Circumlocution Office most heartily hated Mr Rowland Hill: that the
> Circumlocution Office most characteristically opposed him as long as
> opposition was in any way possible; that the Circumlocution Office
> would have been most devoutly glad if it could have harried Mr
> Rowland Hill's soul out of his body, and consigned him and his
> troublesome penny project to the grave together.

[In the next paragraphs, which deal with the introduction of the
penny post, 'the Circumlocution Office' is reiterated seventeen
times.]

> If the Edinburgh Review could seriously want to know 'how Mr.
> Dickens accounts for the career of Mr. Rowland Hill,' Mr. Dickens
> would account for it by his being a Birmingham man of such
> imperturbable steadiness and strength of purpose, that the Circum-
> locution Office, by its utmost endeavours, very freely tried, could not
> weaken his determination, sharpen his razor, or break his heart. By
> his being a man in whose behalf the public gallantry was roused, and
> the public spirit awakened. By his having a project, in its nature so
> plainly and directly tending to the immediate benefit of every man,

woman, and child in the State, that the Circumlocution Office could not blind them, though it could for a time cripple it. By his having thus, from the first to the last, made his way in spite of the Circumlocution Office, and dead against it as his natural enemy.

But the name is evidently a curious misprint and an unfortunate mistake. The Novelist will await the Reviewer's correction of the press, and substitution of the right name.

On this specific issue Dickens was probably in the right. Stephen had been, for once, rash and had overstated his case. It is true that Rowland Hill was more than a bit of an egomaniac (Trollope, who was a colleague for years, detested him, and Trollope wasn't given to easy detestation) and would have run into opposition from any administration on earth. But Dickens would have been able to reply that administrations should and must be capable of coping with egomaniacs, if they come up with first-class ideas.

In general, though, contemporary opinion felt that Dickens, by concentrating his answer on what was after all a very minor point, exposed the weakness of the rest of the Circumlocution Office attack. Fitzjames Stephen, so the professional world thought at the time, had had very much the better of it.[1] The professional world was not unbiassed: it wanted to believe that Dickens was wrong. But even now, after more than a hundred years, it is difficult not to conclude that, on the plane of fact where he had argued with Fitzjames Stephen, he was much more wrong than right.

One or two modern commentators have thought the opposite: but one can't help thinking that they hadn't the opportunity to examine the evidence, which is tangled and even now not at all well-known. Humphry House remarked in Chapter VII of *The*

---

[1] Here I have to rely on oral tradition which may not be reliable. Men such as G. M. Trevelyan, Desmond MacCarthy, G. H. Hardy, who were all speaking of a generation before their own, used to talk of the general pleasure in Fitzjames Stephen's triumph. I have not been able to find any written evidence but there is no inherent improbability in this account. It is well-known that the Stephen family kept up the hostility (v. Leslie Stephens's entry on Dickens in the *DNB*), and echoes of it still survived in Cambridge in the 1920s. Personally, I do not remember hearing one genuinely favourable comment on Dickens as a writer. As a rule, he was passed over as not suitable for serious literary discussion. Quiller-Couch's 1925 lectures on Dickens were a notable exception and then, as he wryly observed, the newspapers upbraided him for treating Dickens as 'a genius of the first class' (*Charles Dickens and Other Victorians*, 1927, p. 59).

Dickens World: 'It was, of course, the Crimean campaign that made the Circumlocution Office parts of *Little Dorrit* peculiarly topical, and they were substantially fair.' He doesn't seem to have had much basis for his 'substantially fair' except for the military mess in the Crimea. In fact, military administration was unspeakably bad in every country in Europe throughout the nineteenth century, with the single exception of Prussia: you have to think systematically about war to prepare for war, and only Prussia was equipped for that. It required two administrators of extraordinary talent, Cardwell and Haldane, to get England into some sort of condition for the 1914 war. But military administration often, and perhaps usually, doesn't have much relation to civil administration. The English colonial administration, to take one example, was of a high standard through most of Dickens's life-time.

Other commentators have praised the fidelity of such portraits as that of Young Barnacle. True: he has the Wodehousian vacuity and rudeness of some upper-class Englishmen at their worst, and his conversation is admirably parodied. Dickens met him somewhere. But (this I would guess but cannot, of course, prove) he is much more likely to have been an ADC or someone encountered in a club than a Treasury civil servant, even in the unreformed civil service of the 1850s.

In two of the best books ever written on Dickens, Edgar Johnson and Jack Lindsay have said the Circumlocution Office is a correct exposure of the evils of capitalist administration. That, too, won't wash. We now know something of the features of non-capitalist administration. I will return to this point later. I need only mention here that the misadventures of the unfortunate Mr Doyce in the labyrinth of the Circumlocution Office are quite remarkably similar to those of Dudintsev's hero in *Not by Bread Alone*, published in the Soviet Union in the 1950s.

No: there is a cumulative mass of evidence, though it takes a little patience to discover, about the condition of the English civil service in Dickens's period. It was not much like what he imagined.

The evidence can be found in various types of source. The biographical entries of civil servants in the *DNB*: there are quite a number, and give a good deal of sociological information. There is

the Northcote-Trevelyan report itself, and, even more, the correspondence and comments which preceded and followed it. Personal
reminiscences, of which Trollope's *Autobiography* and the novel
The Three Clerks are the best known. *The Three Clerks* is actually
more informative than the *Autobiography*. It was a novel for which
Trollope always had a soft spot, for it preserved – and he thought
faithfully – his difficult and unsatisfactory youth. We learn (there
is no reason to doubt the factual verisimilitude) how he got
appointed to the Post Office, the kind of colleagues he worked with,
the dimness of the routine, the life of young civil servants inside
the office and out of it.

There is another autobiographical account,[1] which complements
Trollope's but has not for a long time had much attention. It was
written by Sir Henry Taylor, who was a high official at the Colonial
Office for very nearly fifty years. His origins were rather more
obscure than Trollope's, whose father was an unsuccessful barrister.
Taylor said himself that he was the son of a younger son of an
insignificant squire. He hadn't been either to a public school or a
university (those weren't prerequisites in the civil service of the
1820s, when he entered). Still, he was appointed to the Colonial
Office at the age of twenty-three at a salary of £350, rising to £600
a year. This was real money in the early nineteenth century.
Compare Trollope's £90 p.a. in the Post Office, a far less glamorous
department. Taylor became a much more eminent civil servant
than Trollope ever could have done. He was offered the top job in
the Colonial Office when James Stephen retired, and refused it,
apparently on the grounds that he didn't want to be too much tied.
He preferred to remain a kind of exalted and anomalous No. 3,
stayed in that position until he was seventy-two, and found it con-
venient for the final twelve years of his tenure to discharge his
duties not from Whitehall but from Bournemouth. (Though his
career shows that some abuses existed only in Dickens's imagination,
it shows also that there were abuses which Dickens hadn't imagined
at all.) He received many honours, including a KCMG and an
honorary degree from Oxford: if life peerages had been created,

[1] *Autobiography of Henry Taylor* (2 vols.) 1885.

which was seriously contemplated in the early 1870s, he would have been one of the first recipients.

It may seem a little mysterious that he should have been so handsomely treated. It is true that his state papers were unusually well-written; he was a percipient and liberal man of very steady judgment. But the real secret was quite different. He had a minor literary talent, and like other Victorian men of letters, had a passion for writing verse dramas. The best known was *Philip van Artevelde*. This was actually put on the stage by Macready, and flopped. Not undeservedly: it was pretty bad, though no worse than most other nineteenth-century verse dramas. But this and his other literary productions gave him a reputation with his colleagues and political acquaintances, in fact with much of serious-minded London. Mid-Victorians made a fuss of culture when they saw it, although they often saw it wrong. So they did their best for Sir Henry Taylor. Well – one can think of more unamiable transactions.

All these various sources give us aspects of how government was carried on, and what insiders thought of it. Broadly, there aren't many contradictions, and the stories converge on what seems to be something like the objective state of affairs.

To begin with, the civil service, that is, the working officials of the government departments (the term had not entirely crystallized until just before the time of *Little Dorrit*), was not in the least an appanage of the aristocracy.[1] The numbers of Barnacles and Stiltstalkings in the departments were tiny: and the one or two who did get there went into politics proper, the House of Commons, at the first opportunity. It is true that there were jobs, some lucrative and some sinecures, and a few which were both, at the disposal of the Prime Minister. But this patronage was much more limited than we tend to think: Prime Ministers often complained how limited it was.[2] Such as it was, most of it did go to members of the aristocracy, or their connections, since parliament was still largely aristocratic. There is nothing at all improbable about the

---

[1] Except perhaps for the Diplomatic Service. Even here, though, the conventional idea of an aristocratic preserve may be an over-simplification.

[2] Edward Hughes, 'Civil Service Reform, 1853-55' (*Public Administration*, Spring 1954).

career of Lord Lancaster Stiltstalking, except that Dickens may, as usual, have got his title wrong.

But those appointments had almost no connection with the working civil service. This was organized and staffed department by department (to an extent which later proved hard to break down). Let us take for a moment the Circumlocution Office in its most re-stricted meaning, which is clearly the Treasury. The appointments in the department were in the gift of the permanent head – Tite Barnacle in Dickens's novel, though the actual permanent head wouldn't have been an aristocrat, but someone much more like one of the civil servants enumerated by Fitzjames Stephen. The permanent head received requests for nominations from all sorts of acquaintances – political, social, official. Much more often than not, aristocratic politicians wanted nominations, not for their relatives, but for the sons of neighbours and dependents. The doctor's son, the parson's son, the son of a local squire. The characters in Trollope's novels, Johnny Eames, the Tudors, Graham, represent precisely this kind of nomination: so did Trollope himself and Henry Taylor. So did James Spedding, Merivale, Greg, Hamilton and the majority of the eminent civil servants of the time. Not all, of course. Some, like the Stephens and H. E. Manning, who if it hadn't been for other attractions might have had a prosperous career in the Colonial Office, came from a more affluent upper-middle-class. A few, but only a very few, came from strata higher than that.

When a young man had been nominated, in most departments he was made – years before the Northcote-Trevelyan report – to sit for an examination. In the Treasury this was quite an arduous test, involving some genuine mathematics: in the Post Office, to judge by Trollope's account, something much more rough-and-ready. Northcote-Trevelyan implied that not much notice was taken of this test. Indignant heads of departments, after the report came out, denied the implication. Anyway, it wasn't a real competitive exami-nation: but, certainly in good departments,[1] there was some attempt to set a standard.

---

[1] Departments varied very much in standard. The G.P.O. was known as an 'inferior' department, the Treasury as a 'superior' one.

When the young man finally got his place, he was, if unlucky, fated to spend years in what one might call underworked drudgery. This was an abuse which escaped Dickens's attention: but in fact, in terms of efficiency, it may have been much more of an abuse than patronage, and one of the major results of Northcote-Trevelyan was to wipe it out. It seems incredible today – much more incredible than human venality – that there was no distinction between what Northcote-Trevelyan called 'mechanical' and 'intellectual' functions. Thus Trollope spent years copying by hand official documents, as his main and often his only job. In some departments there wasn't much even of this: the young men were left idle, waiting to be moved up by seniority.

There was very little financial corruption. By the middle of the century the standard of that kind of probity was already taking form, the very rigid and valuable form which was one of the English nineteenth-century inventions. One can trace the process in Trollope's novels: the story of Alaric Tudor is a cautionary one. When the Civil Service Commissioners were first instituted in 1855, they were deeply preoccupied with the problem of what they referred to as 'personation', i.e. someone taking a competitive examination in place of another. But they soon got less alarmed. Commonplace honesty, or the ability to take it for granted, is of course a late intervention in human affairs.

Ordinary promotion went by seniority, but the top jobs were filled by the political minister, at least in form, though probably the real choice was affected, and sometimes made, by permanent officials. When one thinks of the tedium of the young civil servant's initial years, it is surprising that many turned out to be so competent. The first half-dozen civil servants of 1857, the time of *Little Dorrit*, were very able men, and Dickens could have had no answer to Fitzjames Stephen's roll-call. Further, he could have had no answer to a deeper criticism. As we have seen, he was quite wrong in imagining that the civil service was a homogeneous aristocratic enclave. This is obvious, when one examines the kind of young man who was nominated. It is even more obvious, when one reads Trollope and Taylor describing their colleagues. Each of them happened to possess a very delicate sense for the minute English social gradations. No English novelist ever had this sense more subtly attuned than Trollope. Think of the interplay between the Greshams and the Courcys, or the Pallisers and Frank Tregear. There wasn't a step between the lower-middle class and the highest aristocracy that he didn't know by instinct.

For an Englishman, Dickens was unusually deficient in this social sense. He would have found it hard to feel his way round the Circumlocution Office and realize that, far from being homogeneous, they actually came from a widish spectrum (exactly Trollope's spectrum) of English society. He hadn't the antennae for that. He might have found it even harder to realize that once in, once having penetrated towards the centre of the English official life, nearly all of them were at ease, accepting and accepted.

There is a curiously revealing passage in Taylor's autobiography. In terms of precise social notation, it tells one more of early Victorian governmental England than the whole of *Little Dorrit*. Taylor is describing his position at the age of thirty-eight. His father was urging him to whip up all personal influence in order to get the permanent headship of the Department (which was in fact, as I have mentioned, offered to him nine years later and which he finally refused).

> My father was anxious that I should take into account the preference to be given to £2,000 a year over £1,000, in addition to the superior official rank, as enabling me to marry: or rather enabling me to have a wider field of choice in marriage. I agreed that the appointment would be a facility in that way.

He then quotes from a letter to his father.

> The official rank would go for a good deal with the middle classes, the country gentlemen, and the humdrum aristocracy. Amongst the fashionable aristocracy it would not go for much: because my position in that society would hardly be more improved by being Under-Secretary of State than Sir Walter Scott's was – elsewhere than at Selkirk – by being 'the Shirra' ... As to applications and claims, I am satisfied that my best course is to have nothing to do with them. I know by experience that the parts of candidate and claimant are parts which I cannot perform, and it is vain for me to

undertake them. I know also what Her Majesty's Ministers are made of. I am personally acquainted with almost all the members of the present Cabinet, and am on terms of rather friendly acquaintanceship with some of them.

That was written in 1838. Remember Taylor had started as an entirely obscure young man. No one of his age or civil service position would have been able to write with that confident intimacy a hundred years later.

It was this comfortable, heterogeneous, predominantly middle-class world – the Trollopian spectrum – which felt itself threatened by the Northcote-Trevelyan report. Open competition? Skilful examiners from Heaven knows where? The prospect appears to have been equally displeasing to Queen Victoria, Sir James Stephen, and Trollope (who in *The Three Clerks* heavyfootedly satirized the first efforts of the Civil Service Commission and the personalities of Northcote and Trevelyan. Trollope, though he could see plenty wrong with the world he lived in, nevertheless liked it as it was). One might have thought that Dickens would have been an advocate for the other side. Not a bit of it. There is not a word about any possibility of civil service reform in *Little Dorrit*: nor, so far as I have been able to find, in his polemics in *Household Words* or Forster's *Examiner*. This might suggest that he didn't know what had happened under his eyes. But Dickens, in all his public campaigns, was neither naive nor ignorant. He belonged to that same world which Taylor was describing, to an extent which would be unusual for a twentieth-century writer. He was a public figure and a public force, and had all the information at his disposal. In fact, this particular information was openly at his disposal: for he was a member of the Administrative Reform Association, started by his friend Layard in 1855, and made a speech to it that same year, two years *after* the publication of the report. It was a witty and eloquent speech, but again gave no sign that the Circumlocution Office, if it had ever existed, was being torn up from inside.

That is a picturesque irony. But there is an irony even more picturesque. For, when the Northcote-Trevelyan report was fully in action (i.e. when all nomination to the senior class of the civil service was abolished – about 1870), there was a result which would have been astonishing equally to Queen Victoria, Sir James Stephen, Trollope, and presumably Dickens. This result was a very simple one: just that the social composition of the civil service remained remarkably unchanged. It was still drawn, and continued to be drawn until the second world war, from the Trollope-Taylor middle class. The chief difference being that now it drew exclusively from the intellectual élite of that class, the cleverest and academically best trained. The Stephens, Trevelyans, T. H. Farrers, Algernon Wests, continued to get in: the Trollopes probably didn't. It is fair to say that this result wouldn't have surprised Northcote and Trevelyan themselves, nor their academic advisers such as Benjamin Jowett. It was precisely what they were aiming at. They wanted a meritocracy, not a democracy. None of them was an egalitarian: what they were searching for was efficiency. Which, incidentally, was what Dickens was searching for in most of his particularized administrative campaigns.[1]

So there doesn't seem much left of the Circumlocution Office. Yet there is something.

One mustn't be too ingenious. A writer as complex, and often as ambivalent, as Dickens, offers too many temptations. It would be possible to produce an interpretation something like this. Yes, he ignored what was already happening in English administration. But, after all, didn't he show a prophetic sense? The civil service was reformed, that is granted. It became the most intellectually powerful (except perhaps for the French), the most competent and honest that the world has ever known. Still, in the most fundamental things it failed. The date of publication of *Little Dorrit* coincides almost exactly with England's peak of power. By the time of Dickens's death in 1870 that power was already in decline. In another generation it had been quite surpassed – far more than those living realized – by the United States and Germany. The civil service might have become superlatively competent, but it showed no foresight: the whole government apparatus gave thought to superficialities, like the Empire, and very little to the industry and

---

[1] In my comments on the unreformed civil service, I am grateful for much advice from the late Lord Bridges and Mrs Jenifer Hart (St Anne's College, Oxford). I must, of course, take responsibility for the conclusions I have reached.

talent that should have made the wealth. It didn't educate enough: it didn't break down enclaves: it lived, even though with considerable efficiency, in the past.

All those statements are true, or at least arguable. But to credit Dickens with that kind of prophetic vision is, I should have thought, to misunderstand completely the nature of his social protests. This would have been too long-range and abstract for him: it would have needed a mind much more of the nature of T. H. Huxley's, and even he, though he had intuitions, was too much a child of his time.

We can try again. There *is* something in the Circumlocution Office. Isn't it better to get all the details wrong, and yet lash out, feeling that the collective life isn't good enough – than to respond like Trollope, knowing all the details like his own hand-writing, and still content with the life round him which he understood so well?

Here perhaps we are getting nearer. But we still have to remember that feeling such discontent with the collective life doesn't help anyone much. It isn't in itself a prescript for action. There is nothing in the attack on the Circumlocution Office which is in fact a prescript for action. (Cf. Balzac's prospectus for reform in *Les Employés*). It is much too generalized for that. In that respect, and it is a primary respect, this attack is different in kind from almost all the other social attacks which Dickens made, either in his fiction or outside it. They are nearly all specific and particular: and the more particular they are, the closer they are to action. Take, for example, his articles in the *Examiner* – anonymous, like all the social polemics he wrote for the paper – on the Tooting disaster[1], where a hundred and fifty children in a baby farm died of cholera. On this – it was a case of Belsen-like neglect – Dickens, as can be imagined, wrote as a journalist at his savage best. But, perhaps what won't be so easily imagined, he was entirely practical and precise in tracing where the administrative responsibility lay and how both the law and governmental practice could be made more brute-proof. Very much the same is true of so many of his social causes: he knew and said (though not in fiction) a great deal about administrative re-

---

[1] A. W. C. Brice and K. J. Fielding, *Victorian Studies*, vol. xii, No. 2, pp. 228-44.

sponsibility. He was, after all, a very businesslike man in his working life.

But those were particularities: about the Circumlocution Office he was generalizing, there aren't many particularities, and such as there are fritter away under inspection. Some have thought – at times he seems to have done so himself – that he was attacking the condition of England. But the English particularities, the fine structure of the social picture, are nowhere near the truth: and when those are stripped away he might as well have been writing about the condition of France or Prussia or America.

Yet there is still a residue left. Not a prescript for action: not a diagnosis of English sickness or any other sickness. He might as well have been writing about France, etc., and *that* is the residue which has power for us today. Inaccurate, unhistorical – under it there is a cry against all administrative systems anywhere. It isn't useful. One doesn't make a more tolerable world like that. But we all at times feel it. When everything else has been disposed of, that is his strength.

The nightmare oppressions – the Kafka-like anxieties, if you like – of all administrative systems anywhere. That was the simple undiluted conception which set the tom-tom of his rhetoric beating. We should like to think that we are superior to, not hypnotized by, simple undiluted conceptions and the tom-tom of rhetoric. If we do think that, we have a singularly high opinion of ourselves.

All administrative systems anywhere. In our blander optimisms, people have believed that in a fairer, transformed society adminis-tration will itself be transformed. That is a cardinal, and by this time an impermissible mistake. It was made by Shaw, and, as I have already mentioned, by men of good will after him, such as Jack Lindsay and Edgar Johnson. Sixty years have passed since Shaw wrote about *Little Dorrit*, and they have given us the chance to compare administrative systems under all the varieties of govern-ment that we have so far been exposed to – industrial capitalist (Victorian England), modified capitalist (present-day England), technological capitalist (present day U.S.), sophisticated com-promise capitalist (Sweden): primitive socialist (China), techno-logical socialist (U.S.S.R.), compromise socialist (Yugoslavia): and so on. Obviously those administrative systems are, in some respects, different: but considered purely as systems – without respect to what they are trying to do – they are formally much more alike than different. Morphologically they describe the same patterns. To take one obvious example – all administrative systems, irrespective of politics, develop a kind of internal coherence or solidarity. The individuals who compose the system may dislike or distrust each other: but inside the machine they form a collective self-protective system. Any individual within it might in private life admit without a second thought that he had been wrong: for himself and the fellow-members of the system, speaking as a collective whole, it becomes almost pathologically difficult. That is true of any administration under any government which has so far existed.

That was one of the characteristics of the Circumlocution Office. There are features of the most humane administrations on earth which oppress us, as private citizens, as the Circumlocution Office might have done. It is 'nobody's fault', to quote Dickens's first title for *Little Dorrit* but with a different stress. It is a consequence of highly articulated large-scale systems. We ought to be able to ameliorate them. But most private citizens will never be at home with them. It is to that strain in us that the Circumlocution Office still speaks.

It is, of course, partially for that reason that a new generation of protesters have taken to denouncing 'structures' wherever they exist. In doing so, they are following Dickens. The Circumlocution Office was the image of all 'structures'. And the new protesters are somewhere near the same danger as he fell into. For that kind of anarchic protest is in the end self-destructive: society can't live without structures, like them or not, and man can't live without society: if he tries (and Dickens was a more passionate malcontent than most men), he ends up in the harsh fits of reaction that afflicted Dickens in his later years.

Finally, if the Circumlocution Office were not imbedded in a great novel, which is a representation of all the imprisoning oppressions that we can feel afflicted by, would it still have struck home? Imagine it was just an essay, with fictional illustrations, on its own. Would it seem crude, cruder than it does now, relieved by its superb accompaniments? I don't know the answer. But I suspect that we are all simpler than we like to believe, and that Dickens's rhetoric, even against our will, even at its most brassy, manages to make our imaginations respond just as forcibly as passages such as the history of Miss Wade, which don't leave us with any comparable doubts, because there we know that we can conscientiously admire.

PART THREE

THE
FELLOW-MAN

DICKENS
ON THE
HEARTH

At the beginning of his career as a writer, Dickens developed a descriptive speciality which was quickly accepted as a personal trademark: the cosy, contented, cheerful, sheltering middle-class home. This vision, of a highly moral and unpretentious domestic happiness which is both a goal in life and a cure for all its ills, appears fleetingly even in the early *Sketches by Boz*, where we are treated to a Christmas dinner at which 'Uncle George tells stories, and carves poultry, and takes wine, and jokes with the children at the side-table, and . . . there is such a laughing, and shouting, and clapping of little chubby hands, and kicking up of fat dumpy legs, as can only be equalled by the applause with which the astonishing feat of pouring lighted brandy into mince-pies is received by the younger visitors.' The happy home in a state of festivity (a wedding this time, not a Christmas) is one of the highlights of *Pickwick Papers*, published two years later than the *Sketches*, in 1837, and from this point there is not, I think, a novel in which the domestic hearth is not presented in one way or another as a shrine of happiness, the kind-hearted man's ideal.

Such a rosy presentation of ordinary domesticity, available to everyone whose heart is in the right place, was a potent element of Dickens's attraction in those very homes in which his serial instalments were most eagerly devoured. In those homes his great popular unsophisticated and largely uncritical public passed their lives, and his tender, not to say sentimental, presentation of the domestic dream brought about an unlooked-for canonization. Dickens was elevated into a humorous but Puritan god of the domestic hearth.

> If this climate of ours [said *The Morning Chronicle*, reviewing *The Battle of Life* on Christmas Eve 1846] had only been sunny and dry, instead of cold and rainy, we very much doubt whether Mr. Dickens would ever have achieved the high position in literature which he now enjoys. He is so peculiarly a writer of home life, a delineator of household gods, and a painter of domestic scenes, that we feel convinced, had Italy, or Spain, or any country nearer the tropics than ours produced him, instead of describing lazzaroni, and maccaroni, and water melons, or Andalusian young ladies, and cigaritos, and chocolate, and mantillas, he would have migrated to our more northern shores for the sake of firesides, purring cats, boiling kettles, Dutch clocks and chirping crickets.

This image has been largely responsible both for his popular success and for the long critical neglect from which his work, until comparatively recently, has suffered among scholars and other fastidious persons. Which is rather strange when you come to think of it, for an attentive reading of the novels, or indeed of almost anything that Dickens wrote, letters included, discovers a wry observation of domestic life in general and of connubial happiness in particular, a long way removed from the coy relish of the celebrated domestic set-pieces.

The truth, in fact, seems to be that on this subject Dickens's desires and imaginings were often quite sharply at variance with his experience. He passionately desired the domestic ideal, as his emotional need and his imagination conceived it. Again and again he anatomized it in his novels, with the minuteness of a painter re-working an obsessive theme. But quite as often, indeed I believe more frequently, his fictional marriages are bleak and disillusioned, his women shrewish or otherwise disagreeable, his domestic backgrounds cold, arid, comfortless. The dream refused to identify with reality, as he eventually and disastrously proved in his own life.

What that dream was, in outline and also in lingering detail, we can make out from at least one manifestation in each of the novels, with the intentionally grim exception of *Hard Times*. It is of an essentially modest home, not rich or ostentatious (as Dickens's own homes had a slight tendency to be as soon as he had means enough to indulge his taste for comfort and display), but warm, bright, clean, a pattern of good management and homely virtues. Cleanliness is repeatedly insisted upon, as it was in Dickens's own domestic arrangements at all periods of his life. Clearly it is impossible for him to imagine any right-minded person being happy in a squalid or a careless home, or even in one that is not punctiliously kept. Our glimpse into the home of Mr Toodles the railway stoker, for instance, shows us 'a clean parlour full of children,' though he himself is 'abundantly besmeared with coal-dust and oil, and had cinders in his whiskers, and a smell of half-slaked ashes all over him.' The lodgings in which Tom Pinch and his sister Ruth set up house together – 'the triangular parlour and two small bedrooms' – are transformed in a flash into a domestic haven by Ruth's playful housewifery, in spite of 'two little damp cupboards down by the fire-place' and the presence of blackbeetles. David Copperfield's first marriage, on the other hand, is doomed from the start since Dora is quite incapable of housekeeping, the food is ill-cooked and nothing is ever where it should be. Domestic skill, in short, is one of the essential virtues of a Dickens heroine. (In his own home he was something of a martinet, carrying out periodic inspections of the rooms, and making it a point during at least one of his absences that articles of furniture and ornaments should not be moved from their places, so that he might envisage the scene with confidence.)

The perfect home, then, is clean, neat and snug, with 'a nice little dumpling of a wife' in it, and a varying number of well-behaved well-washed children. Dickens himself was enormously fond of children and emotionally responsive to them. Even small babies interested him; he had none of the average man's distaste for the details of their lives and habits, and observed them – Mrs Peerybingle's baby under Tilly Slowboy's management, and the 'very Moloch of a baby' in the Tetterby family are prime examples – with the same delighted attention that he gave to the mature and the articulate.

The extreme of the domestic fantasy is found in the *Christmas Books*, which were designed to appeal to exactly that sentimental and uncritical audience which most readily responded to deliberately seasonable offerings. They are difficult to accept today, our response to the 'Christmas number' type of confection being so radically altered; but this is not to say that they were cynically conceived as ready-made best-sellers, which is the impression they inevitably make on the modern reader. Dickens, ever anxious for big sales, took pains to supply his public with what it wanted; emotional reciprocity was fully as important as profits; but because for the most part he entirely shared its views and tastes, no cynicism was involved. He was not required to do violence to his own feelings. So the Cratchits' home in *A Christmas Carol* (a much poorer one than Dickens himself had ever known, even as a child) is made warm and wonderful with all the essential ingredients – hot fire, good homely food, bustling little woman in charge, 'brave in ribbons, which are cheap and make a goodly show for sixpence', given added emotional weight by the pathos of Tiny Tim. It is an appealing picture when one first encounters it, and the simple moral, that the world would be a better place, especially at Christmas, if rich employers were both generous and kind, was congenial and obvious to readers who would have shied away from more basic or more organized social reforms.

In *The Cricket on the Hearth*, in more concentrated form even than in Ruth Pinch, or in Bella Wilfer after her marriage, we find the 'little woman', that piece of ideal-home furniture which is as important as a good brisk fire and an ample meal with 'something hot' after it. Mrs Peerybingle is worth examining, for since she appears in one guise or another whenever Dickens is furnishing a happy hearth, we may reasonably take her as representing his own preference. She is not exactly a child-wife in the Dora Copperfield sense, since she is sensible and domestically capable, but she is certainly very young; her husband the carrier is 'a sturdy figure of a man, much taller and much older than herself, who had to stoop a long way down to kiss her', and she herself speaks of 'being such a child, and you more like my guardian than my husband.' She is small and childish in appearance, with 'chubby little hands', a type of that 'nice little dumpling of a wife' whom Walter Gay envisages in *Dombey*; 'something of what is called the dumpling shape,' Dickens describes her, adding, 'but I don't myself object to that.' She is, in fact, very much to the taste of the 1840s, as we can confirm by a glance at the fashion-plates and album beauties of the time. Rounded arms, rounded cheeks, voluptuous heavy-lidded eyes and rosebud mouths, these were the contemporary symbols of sex appeal, to which Dickens himself delightedly responded, however much he might laugh at the stereotyped pin-ups of the albums and annuals, all with 'that compound expression of simpering and sleepiness which, being common to all such portraits, is perhaps one reason why they are always so charming and agreeable.' There is no better description, after all, of Catherine Dickens in that charming early portrait by Maclise, in which she is seen between her young husband and Georgina Hogarth. (Simpering was easy to put up with in pretty young women, but sleepiness augured less well, as he was to discover later.)

Mrs Peerybingle, at least, is wide awake and perfectly capable of looking after things, against a backdrop of 'the small snug home and the crisp fire', with kettle singing, cradle rocking, hot tea and crusty loaf on the table, the candle lit, to say nothing of a cricket on the hearth and a cat purring by the fender. All are ready and waiting for the carrier's return. And when the knuckle of ham and the bread and butter are consumed, there is John Peerybingle's pipe to be prepared, a performance which sends Dickens into an ecstasy.

> She was, out and out, the very best filler of a pipe, I should say, in the four quarters of the globe. To see her put that chubby little finger in the bowl, and then blow down the pipe to clear the tube,

157

and, when she had done so, affect to think that there was really something in the tube, and blow a dozen times, and hold it to her eye like a telescope, with a most provoking twist in her capital little face, as she looked down it, was quite a brilliant thing . . .

It is quite a feat in its way, introducing such an erotic note into an everyday practical detail. The trick is repeated with even greater success in *Martin Chuzzlewit*, when Ruth Pinch makes her first beefsteak pudding:

> And being one of those little women to whom an apron is a most becoming little vanity, it took an immense time to arrange; having to be carefully smoothed down beneath – Oh, heaven, what a wicked little stomacher! . . . And then, there were her cuffs to be tucked up, for fear of flour; and she had a little ring to pull off her finger, which wouldn't come off (foolish little ring!); and during the whole of these preparations she looked demurely every now and then at Tom, from under her dark eye-lashes, as if they were all a part of the pudding and indispensable to its composition.

This is the way that little women behave, and it can be very fetching. A marked insistence, however, on the little-woman image, though it endeared Dickens to his contemporaries, is one of the barriers – an accident of time, taste, fashion – between him and the modern reader. Bella Wilfer is one of his most delightful heroines, for the very reason that she is far from perfect, being selfish, mercenary and self-willed as well as lively, attractive and affectionate. But as soon as she is married to John Rokesmith, all the familiar Peerybingle symptoms appear, and she develops 'a perfect genius for home.' No sooner has her husband left in the morning, it seems, than

> the dress would be lain aside, trim little wrappers and aprons would be substituted, and Bella, putting back her hair with both hands . . . would enter on the household affairs of the day. Such weighing and mixing and chopping and grating, such dusting and washing and polishing, such snipping and weeding and trowelling and other small gardening, such making and mending and folding and airing . . .

and so on, until we find Bella studiously immersed in *The Complete British Family Housewife*, 'with all her dimples screwed into an expression of profound research.' We are in no doubt about her complete success; if she were not a perfect (little) housewife she would never have been allowed the status of heroine. When her baby is born (and a playful little woman with a speckle-fisted baby to punctuate her remarks is something from which Dickens does not shrink) the image of the happy home is made complete. No doubt some Victorian husbands *did* address their wives in every other breath as 'my love . . . my life . . . my own,' as John Rokesmith does, or Dickens could never have made such a joke of the habit in Mr Mantalini: but between John Rokesmith-Harmon and his Bella the atmosphere becomes uncomfortably cloying.

> What had he done to deserve the blessing of this dear confiding creature's heart! Again she put her hand upon his lips, saying 'Hush!' and then told him, in her own little natural pathetic way, that if all the world were against him, she would be for him; that if all the world repudiated him, she would believe him,

and so on. The domestic hearth has been turned into an altar – the very word for it that Dickens employs in *The Cricket on the Hearth* – but fortunately for our enjoyment of the once-imperfect Bella, she has still too much spirit and character to become altogether nauseating.

There are, of course, other 'approved' types of young women in Dickens's novels, but the merry, cosy, childish little creature is the favourite. A sort of arrested pre-adolescent, happily and earnestly playing at keeping house, and very engaging and seductive to come home to. 'Really,' as George Orwell said of the novels, 'there is no objective except to marry the heroine, settle down, live solvently and be kind.'[1] This is an absurdly sweeping judgement, in the carping vein of much of Orwell's Dickens criticism, but there is a grain of truth in it. 'Home life,' Orwell concluded, probing as usual for the 'message', 'is always enough. And, after all, it was the general assumption of the age.'[2]

True, Dickens was not the inventor of the Victorian hearth, which

[1] Orwell, *The Decline of the English Murder*, Penguin Books, 1968, p. 122.
[2] *Ibid.*, p. 123.

was the creation of the young Queen herself if it belonged to anybody. (Hardly an annual, *Forget-me-not* or *Keespake* of the 1840s fails to present a romantic royal family group, handsome consort, adoring royal wife and mother, assorted pretty children of all ages, down to the latest princeling in long clothes and bonnet.) But undoubtedly he made himself its prophet, with perfect sincerity writing himself into a position which was to jeopardise his whole reputation in 1858, the year of the public breakdown of his marriage.

Before we try to see down to the roots of Dickens's 'happy home' vision, there are some surface details which are worth examining, since they are used over and over again with great skill and effect, whenever he wishes to evoke the magical atmosphere. Cleanliness, domestic order and efficiency, the little woman, a troop of happy and untroublesome children – one, perhaps, a particularly saintly one, allowed to be ailing or a cripple for greater effect – these are the essential scenery; the focus of the well-set stage is invariably the fire, ('the crisp fire,' 'the brisk sea-coal fire', the hearth in symbol and in fact); comfort and security are represented by food and drink. Unlike some of his contemporaries, Dickens is not interested in minute descriptions of the rooms in which his domestic scenes take place. He does not, like Charlotte Brontë, dwell on colours and furnishings to intensify a particular atmosphere; he will only laugh in passing at Mrs Boffin's sofa and feathers or Mrs Veneering's ostentatious dinner-table appointments – not entirely unlike his own at Tavistock House, if Jane Carlyle is to be trusted. But the fire is insisted upon; it is the focus of every domestic scene; it is a stage property of tremendous symbolical significance.

Nowadays it is too easy to forget the importance, an importance quite impossible to exaggerate, of the open coal fire in the domestic life of the early nineteenth century. Life literally revolved around it; coal, with all its concomitant implications of labour, drudgery, dirt, smoke and soot, was the great life-giver of the home as well as of industry. Without it, life in the urban winter of the British climate would have been not only cheerless but insupportable. In the 1970s the hearth is not of much importance, if it survives at all. Warmth comes through pipes and travels under floors, is controlled by dials and switches. It is taken for granted and is no longer confined to a single life-giving area. Families no longer cluster together through the long evenings, their feet on the fender and their eyes reflectively fixed on the glowing coals.

But to Dickens the fire is not only a source of warmth and life, it is a domestic numen, a magnet drawing the family together, a bond between friends, a promoter of serious reflection, and, as well (since all novelists depend on such devices) an invaluable implement in the manipulation of situation and dialogue. It is powerful in all the novels, and particularly so in *Dombey*, which concerns a home and a parent-child relationship notoriously lacking in love. It is no accident that the rooms, the meals, the atmosphere of Mr Dombey's house are cold.

> It was as blank a house inside as outside . . . Every chandelier or lustre, muffled in holland, looked like a monstrous tear depending from the ceiling's eye. Odours, as from vaults and damp places, came out of the chimneys. . . Every gust of wind that rose, brought eddying round the corner from the neighbouring mews, some fragments of the straw that had been strewn before the house . . . and these, being always drawn by some invisible attraction to the threshold of the dirty house to let immediately opposite, addressed a dismal eloquence to Mr. Dombey's windows.

And at little Paul's christening, on 'an iron-grey autumnal day, with a shrewd east wind blowing', the festive meal is

> a cold collation, set forth in a cold pomp of glass and silver, and looking more like a dead dinner lying in state than a social refreshment . . . There was a toothache in everything. The wine was so bitter cold that it forced a little scream from Miss Tox, which she had great difficulty in turning into a 'Hem!' The veal had come from such an airy pantry, that the first taste of it had struck a sensation as of cold lead to Mr. Chick's extremities. Mr. Dombey alone remained unmoved. He might have been hung up for sale at a Russian fair as a specimen of a frozen gentleman.

When little Paul is removed from his own funereal home to Mrs Pipchin's, and the ghost of a feeling of companionship begins to develop between him and that formidable lady, it is by a toasting-hot fire (kettle steaming, cat purring) that the unexpected improvement in their relationship takes place.

> She would make him move his chair to her side of the fire, instead of sitting opposite; and there he would remain in a nook between Mrs. Pipchin and the fender . . . Mrs. Pipchin had an old black cat, who generally lay coiled upon the centre foot of the fender, purring egotistically, and winking at the fire until the contracted pupils of his eyes were like two notes of admiration. The good old lady might have been – not to record it disrespectfully – a witch, and Paul and the cat her two familiars, as they all sat by the fire together.

The heat of the coals is as palpable as in the uncanny chiaroscuro of Hablôt Browne's illustration.

In the same way, on the only occasion when Mr Dombey establishes something approaching communication with Paul, it is when they are gazing together into one of the few fires mentioned in that frigid household.

> They were the strangest pair at such a time that ever firelight shone upon. Mr. Dombey so erect and solemn, gazing at the blaze; his little image, with an old, old face, peering into the red perspective with the fixed and rapt attention of a sage . . . Mr. Dombey only knew that the child was awake by occasionally glancing at his eye, where the bright fire was sparkling like a jewel . . .

That spark of reflection in the child's eye, that jewel of the fire that shows him awake and alive, is more than a piece of inspired observation; we are to remember it when Paul's life begins to dwindle, and his spark goes out.

So aware is Dickens of the fire, both as focus and symbol, in every indoor scene which is not specifically set in summer, that he constantly resorts to it as a punctuating device. He was extremely sensitive to punctuation, being more than normally conscious, even long before the days of his public readings, of that silent voice which pauses, emphasizes and carries the rhythm in the head of a responsive reader, and at different times carried out his own punctuation experiments. He was, besides, a master of that 'invisible' punctuation of dialogue which is so often the novelist's pitfall, and from which some of the more austere of our present-day writers – the late Miss Ivy Compton-Burnett comes to mind – have saved themselves by avoiding altogether. There are innumerable conversations in the Dickens novels in which the characters gaze into the fire, draw closer to the fire, stir the fire, throw up the ashes, put the poker between the bars of the grate, or otherwise break the monotony of whichever verbal convention is making it clear to the reader which character is speaking. Eugene Wrayburn's conversation with Mortimer Lightwood, late at night in their Lincoln's Inn chambers, is typical of many: '. . . quoth Eugene, stirring the fire.' '. . . said Eugene, smoking, with his eyes on the fire.' 'He stirred the fire again as he spoke, and having made it blaze, resumed.' 'He had walked to the window with his cigar in his mouth, to exalt its flavour by comparing the fireside with the outside . . .' 'There was a silence, broken only by the fall of the ashes in the grate.' These constant references fall so naturally into the general rhythm that we are scarcely aware of them, yet the enveloping warmth of that confidential fireside, the grating of the poker between the bars and the soft fall of the ash are as clearly present in our consciousness as the spoken words.

This is by no means an easy feat. In nine modern novels out of ten the comparable punctuation device is either drinking or smoking, and from innumerable pages in, say, J. D. Salinger's *Franny and Zooey*, one sees to what self-defeating lengths the gimmick can go: 'Franny gave a minimal glance down at her left hand, and dropped the stub of her still burning cigarette into the ashtray . . . She gave a brisk but voluminous drag on her cigarette . . . She tapped her cigarette ash into her cupped left hand . . . Exhaling smoke, he assumed a slightly more relaxed stance . . . Zooey reached for his cigarette again, dragged on it, and then said . . . Zooey gave a great guffaw, then took a drag on his cigarette . . .' and so on, ad nauseam. Dickens's use of the fire has a real value. It not only carries the narrative with easy naturalness, it also brings into presence one of those magical elements without which he almost never seeks to establish the private, protective, comforting atmosphere of home.

Another device, used even oftener and with more emphasis than the fire, is the aura of comfort evoked by food and drink. There is such gusto in Dickens's descriptions of eating and drinking, such a love of the very idea of toasting sausages at the fire or putting lemon-peel into a smoking jug of rum and water, that one might imagine him a gluttonous and hard-drinking man if it were not known from Forster and other sources that, for a notably convivial Victorian, he was abstemious. 'Habits remarkably sober and temperate,' Forster wrote to the Eagle Insurance Company, on Dickens's application for a life policy. Dolby, his reading-tour manager in America, noted that his drinking of innumerable toasts at interminable banquets was done from a cunningly deceptive decanter of toast and water.

> Although he so frequently both wrote and talked about eating and drinking, I have seldom met with a man who partook less freely of the kindly fare placed before him . . . Never once can I call to mind a single instance of his having dulled his brain or made his tongue speak foolishly by such a vice. When sustaining the position of Chairman with its enticing duties he very frequently had by his right hand his own decanter of toast and water; with this he toasted.' And during the first American tour, when Dickens had been twenty-five years younger, his Boston friend James Fields had noticed the same abstemious. 'He liked to dilate in imagination over the brewing of a bowl of punch, but I always noticed that when the punch was ready he drank less of it than any one who might be present. It was the sentiment of the thing and not the thing itself that engaged his attention.[1]

He did – no-one more so – relish good food of the simpler sort, the homely but special dishes that were surely produced in his boyhood home whenever any little windfall or temporary relief from his father's difficulties called for a celebration. It is noticeable in all the novels that whenever the eating of food has a specially emotional connotation the dishes are unpretentious, the sort of food most people nostalgically remember from their childhood. The Wilfers' wedding anniversary dinner consists of a pair of fowls, boiled bacon, potatoes and greens, with a drop of 'something hot' after it. The Boffins, grown rich, have muffins and ham for breakfast. A 'treat'

[1] Quoted by Alfred H. Holt in 'The Drink Question as Viewed by Dickens', *The Dickensian*, vol. xxvii, 1931, p. 170.

meal, for a special occasion, is veal cutlet and ham fried, followed by ale and rum, the latter with boiling water and lemon-peel. Captain Cuttle, to revive and comfort poor runaway Florence Dombey, roasts a fowl at the fire, accompanied by potatoes and sausages, and makes egg sauce and gravy in little saucepans. ('He then dressed for dinner, by taking off his glazed hat and putting on his coat.')

Some of the meals in Dickens's novels are deservedly famous; all of them contribute more than is immediately apparent to the matter in hand. The meal following Paul Dombey's christening is, as we have seen, in more senses than one a cold one, as cold as Mr Dombey's demeanour. Under the Micawbers' kindly influence, on the other hand, whatever the financial crisis, the food is hot and delicious, cooked by Mrs Micawber on (one presumes) the very grate under which she has lain not long since in a swoon, on account of bailiffs; or, as on one occasion, proffered by Mr Micawber at an inn:

> We had a beautiful little dinner. Quite an elegant dish of fish; the kidney end of a loin of veal, roasted; fried sausage-meat; a partridge, and a pudding. There was wine, and there was strong ale; and after dinner Mrs. Micawber made us a bowl of punch with her own hands.

It is that particularly knowledgeable little touch, 'the *kidney end* of a loin of veal', like the 'lamb's fry in private' of another occasion, which gives these Micawber meals their succulent and homely flavour. We feel that Dickens had learned from experience all about the humbler cuts of meat as well as the 'kidney end', and would have made quite a good job of cooking them, the results being as different as possible from the menus in poor Catherine Dickens's only published work, a most indigestible little book to be found today, so far as I know, only on the shelves of the British Museum, and entitled *What Shall We Have for Dinner?*[1] No doubt as a result of the short commons so familiar in the worst periods of his childhood Dickens developed and retained to the end of his life a markedly emotional attitude to the whole subject of food. It was a

[1] See the essay 'Mrs. Beeton and Mrs. Dickens' in *Purely for Pleasure*, Margaret Lane, 1966, pp. 180-6.

symbol of well-being and security, almost – the parallel is inescapable – a substitute for love.[1] It appears not only in his novels –
('Salmon, lamb, peas, innocent young potatoes, a cool salad, sliced
cucumber, a tender duckling, and a tart' as the exquisitely suitable
accompaniment to Ruth Pinch's demure falling in love with John
Westlock) – but also in innumerable letters, described with the zest
and detail of genuine feeling. 'We got a fire directly,' he wrote to
Forster, when he and Catherine and their guide had been 'well nigh
frozen' in the Pass of Glencoe, 'and in twenty minutes they served
us up some famous kippered salmon, broiled; a broiled fowl; hot
mutton ham and poached eggs; pancakes; oatcake; wheaten bread;
butter; bottled porter; hot water, lump sugar and whiskey; of which
we made a very hearty meal.' Not even the bread and butter are
forgotten.

Sometimes, admittedly, and especially in his early days, this
obsession with food and drink as symbols of happiness or good
fellowship runs away with him. In Pickwick, I believe, there are
35 breakfasts, 32 dinners, 10 luncheons, 10 teas and 8 suppers,
while drink is mentioned 249 times. Even in *Our Mutual Friend*,
the last completed novel, the variety of different drinks knowledge-
ably mentioned – shrub, purl, flip, dog's nose, hot port negus,
burned sherry, tea with brandy in it and so on – is quite startling.
A reader who knew nothing of Dickens's own life might well
imagine him, from such a catalogue, to have been a man neurotically
dependent upon alcohol. Such, as we have seen, was not the case.
Once he was past his first youth, when it seemed exquisitely funny
that Mr Pickwick should fall asleep, dead drunk, in an empty
wheelbarrow, he seems rarely if ever to have been the worse for
drink himself, and certainly came to regard drunkenness with
distaste. His dependence on alcohol, such as it was in his later years,
was no more than would have been expected of any man in easy
circumstances, whose work made exhausting demands on his
vitality. But it is painful to read some of his letters home during the

---

[1] Cf. Barbara Hardy's illuminating essay, 'Food and Ceremony in *Great Expectations*'
(*Essays in Criticism*, vol. xiii, No. 4, October 1963) which shows in convincing detail
how the meals described in that novel 'testify to human need and dependence, and
distinguish false ceremony from the ceremony of love'.

last reading-tour in America, when he was not only nervously exhausted but suffering abominably from gout. He was unable, he told his daughter Mamie, 'to eat more than half a pound of solid food in the whole four-and-twenty hours, if so much', and was managing to get along on a liquid diet.

> At seven in the morning, in bed, a tumbler of new cream and two tablespoonsful of rum. At twelve, a sherry cobbler and a biscuit. At three (dinner time) a pint of champagne. At five minutes to eight, an egg beaten up with a glass of sherry. Between the parts [of the reading] ... the strongest beef tea that can be made, drunk hot. At a quarter past ten, soup, and anything to drink that I can fancy.

One cannot imagine his fancying anything more deadly for the gouty condition from which he suffered.

Drink, then, was something Dickens enjoyed as much for the sentiment of the thing as for its actual effect; as one reads the novels, and, still more, the letters, the symbolic aspect even seems to predominate. Food and drink, gaily and lovingly shared in the family circle, are not only a sovereign charm against unhappiness, they are the most potent symbols of security that he knows. And of course, if we are honest, we must admit that the application is universal. All who have any happy memories of childhood, who have still a fleeting nostalgia for that protected state, for the enclosed, secure, more or less *manageable* world which was first made real to us in the age of innocence, must admit that the response to those images which Dickens so often evokes – the life-giving fire, the loving comfort, the things we like best to eat – is basic and profound. Dickens's own response was immediate, and he used these images deliberately over and over again, confident that they would stir his readers' emotions as profoundly as his own. For his own age he hit the target unerringly. His aim is less sure today, since much that seemed good and true a century ago now strikes us as false and mawkish. Dickens was not conscious of any falsity, though a trace of it existed. Even for his own time his emotional nature made him a special case.

It is sometimes said that Dickens made too much, or that too much has been made on his behalf, of the blacking warehouse incident. Concealed from everyone, even from his wife and children, revealed to no-one until he painfully spoke of it to Forster in middle-age, that break in the more or less even story of his child-hood was one of the great traumas of his life. It may even, in its formative pressure on his imagination, have been the most important factor in his experience. At twelve years old, a delicate and peculiarly impressionable child, he had been in a sense abandoned; his home had collapsed under him. It can have seemed, to the child, no less than this: his parents camping out in empty rooms in Gower Street before his father's arrest, then established in the Marshalsea Prison, himself cast adrift in mean lodgings and put to degrading work in a blacking factory. However happy-go-lucky his home had been, with his father's alternate bouts of extravagance and despair, there is no doubt that it was a reasonably happy one. There had been affection, cheerfulness, modest comfort, and at least the illusion of security. Now it had all dissolved as in a bad dream, and the child found himself with 'No advice, no counsel, no encouragement, no consolation, no support, from anyone that I can call to mind, so help me God.'

A great part of the bitterness of his situation came, as we know, from the fact that his parents seemed quite unaware that, *for him*, this was nothing less than a child's tragedy. 'No one,' he wrote in the secret narrative which was eventually shown to Forster, 'made any sign. My father and mother were quite satisfied. They could hardly have been more so, if I had been twenty years of age, dis-tinguished at a grammar school, and going to Cambridge.' How long this hungry and outcast period lasted is not material; in fact it was only nine months, but to a child three-quarters of a year can seem a lifetime. I believe it is scarcely possible to exaggerate the effect of this whole experience on Dickens's subconscious nature. The happy home, the fireside myth of love and security which had been snatched away, became enshrined in memory; as time went by every detail of remembered pleasure was touched with the golden haze of wishful dream. And during those miserable nine months themselves, as though fate were contriving the ultimate in bitter contrast, there were 'the cold wet shelterless midnight streets of London' to be traversed between the Camden Town lodgings and the warehouse basement at Hungerford Stairs; the 'foul and frowsy dens' to be passed in back streets round Drury Lane, 'where vice is closely packed and lacks the room to turn; the haunts of hunger and disease' that must be hurried through on his Saturday route to the Marshalsea; the 'shabby rags that scarcely hold together' on children even younger, even more destitute than himself. These considerable distances were covered, perforce, on foot, and as the child laid the foundations of those daemonic walking habits so characteristic of the man, Dickens was early exposed to a nightly panorama of desolation, poverty and crime which was to flicker ever more luridly before his mind's eye for the rest of his life. Anyone who cares to trace his probable routes from Little College Street, where he was farmed out with two or three other children (illegitimate or otherwise unwanted), to Hungerford Stairs below the Strand, where the blacking warehouse then was, and again across the river into the great squalid slum and commercial wilderness that was the Borough, will – especially with a map of the 1820s – gain some idea of the maze of streets and rookeries through which he trailed in his hours of hungry leisure. What he saw, what he encountered, was never forgotten. The back streets and teeming slums of early Victorian London contained the seeds of all his social indignation, of his pity for the helpless poor and the exploited, of his self-identification with outcast children. They also crystallized, and as it were by contrast fixed for ever in his subconscious that vision of the happy childhood home that was for ever lost.

Such an emotional concept, imprinted in the receptive years of childhood, is not likely to alter much in the light of experience. Real life shows us one thing, the beloved fantasy-memory shows another. Both, when the creative imagination is at work, rise unbidden to the surface and must be dealt with; if they are irreconcilable they must be kept apart; and we certainly get the impression in Dickens's novels that his view of domestic life as he actually observed it was more often than not a wryly sardonic one. He asks us, each time we come to a happy ending, to suppose that David and Agnes Copperfield will live happily ever after, that John Harmon and Bella Wilfer are ideally matched, that Florence Dombey will be happy with Walter Gay, and that even Pip and

Estella will make a tolerable job of it. But of the married couples already encountered he rarely asks us to believe anything so tame and so improbable. There are remarkably few 'nice little dumplings' among the established wives; Mrs Vardon is a highly indigestible one, and most of the wives belong to what Shaw called Dickens's 'gallery of unamiable women.' It is, of course, much easier to be amusing at the expense of someone exasperating or disagreeable, than to make a 'good' character interesting, and the satirical vein in Dickens was always strong. Still, his shrews and scolds and near-idiots, glorious as they are as comic creations, do seem to recur more frequently than one would expect from any law of averages. What home could really be tolerable with Mrs Nickleby's inane inconsequential chatter going on, even though there was 'no evil and little real selfishness' in her nature? How could the Wilfers know any real happiness, even over cold neck of mutton and a lettuce for supper, in the face of Mrs Wilfer's gloves and majestically low spirits? The number of patiently suffering husbands increases as we read on. R. Wilfer is not the only one; he has Joe Gargery, Gabriel Vardon, Mr Chick and Mr Jellyby for company, and many more. We have more faith in the domestic happiness of the Veneerings, perhaps, than in that of the Lammles, or the Podsnaps, but not much; the world of wealth and 'shares', as Dickens saw it, was not one in which the happy hearth could be envisaged. That, always, was inseparable from a comfortable simplicity, not far removed from the middle-middle-class, modest-genteel of the early Dickens home near Chatham Docks. Florence Dombey, watching from the shadowy window of her father's house, catches glimpses of 'rosy children' in the doorway opposite, and knows that it is there. Lady Dedlock, seeing a child run out of a keeper's lodge in the rain, to be caught up in the arms of a man in oilskins, knows that it is there, and is 'put quite out of temper.' The ideal is not peculiar to Dickens, it is universal. What gives it its hallucinatory intensity in his novels is the depth of Dickens's emotional need to reach back to something he had once possessed, and must re-create again and again, for his own comfort.

If we pursue this theme into his own life, we find the pattern repeated with painful emphasis. Delight in the pleasures of home, in food and drink and children's games, even in such practical details as the choice of a wall-paper or the pattern of a shower-curtain, is expressed with an intensity of feeling far beyond the normal. And yet, in spite of all, the marriage, the home, the children, the festivities, all after twenty years are flung violently away, as though the discrepancy between what he had and what he *meant* to have, the lack of that 'one happiness I have missed in life, and one friend and companion I never made', had become finally unbearable.

Reality is no match for the cherished vision. Towards the end of Dickens's life one senses even that the vision itself has begun to fade, that it is called up more mechanically than in the past, and that our response to the idyllic set-pieces (Bella Wilfer as wife and mother, the contentedly trotting Boffins) is less spontaneous. There is no longer the authentic ardour of those earlier years, when he could write to Forster, during a Highland tour, 'The moral of all this is, that there is no place like home; and that I thank God most heartily for having given me a quiet spirit' – strange illusion! – 'and a heart that won't hold many people. I sigh for Devonshire Terrace, and battledore and shuttlecock . . . On Sunday evening the 17th of July I shall revisit my household gods, please heaven. I wish the day were here.' And in the following year, 1842, returned from months of yearning all through the American tour, 'As to the pleasures of home itself, they are *unspeakable*.'

PAMELA HANSFORD JOHNSON

THE SEXUAL LIFE IN DICKENS'S NOVELS

It is due, perhaps in part, to Dickens that so many people believe that the Victorians were totally ignorant about the by-ways of sexual behaviour. The image of the 'family audience' became so strong with him that, as he grew older, he failed more and more to use even those liberties Thackeray and Trollope found available.

In the three early books, *Oliver Twist*, *Nicholas Nickleby* and *The Old Curiosity Shop*, Dickens was not so prim. Nancy, though somewhat distressingly refined, is obviously a prostitute and Sikes her bully. The stag dinner at which Ralph Nickleby forces Kate to preside is not given for the purpose of marrying her to the highest bidder: there is not the slightest reason, seeing she is penniless, why Sir Mulberry Hawk or Lord Frederick Verisopht should ever make her such a proposition. No, she is there because Ralph intends the sale of a virgin for the top price that he can get for her.

Ralph's dinner party has an unmistakeable reek of the Regency stews.

> All she could ascertain was, that there were several gentlemen with no very musical voices, who talked very loud, laughed very heartily, and swore more than she would have thought quite necessary. But this was a question of taste.

Kate is rudely greeted:

> 'Eh!' said the gentleman. 'What-the-deyvle!'
> With which broken ejaculations, he fixed his glass in his eye, and stared at Miss Nickleby in great surprise.
> 'My niece, my lord,' said Ralph.
> 'Then my ears did not deceive me, and it's not wa-a-x work,' said his lordship.

Sir Mulberry Hawk's bet that Kate cannot, within ten minutes, raise her eyes and look him in the face, is a pretty coarse one.

> There was something so odious, so insolent, so repulsive in the look which met her, that, without the power to stammer forth a syllable, she rose and hurried from the room. She restrained her tears by a great effort until she was alone upstairs, and then gave them vent.

(There is by the way, nothing inherently improbable about Sir Mulberry except his silly name.)
When Hawk follows Kate upstairs and tries to make love to her, Ralph does bring himself to intervene: for one overt reason, that he wants her for Lord Frederick, and for another – though this may be said to be in the 'sub-text' – because he now realizes that he has not the slightest chance of making her malleable enough to be sold off. Indeed, she has managed to scare him.

> 'Only listen to me for a moment,' interrupted Ralph, seriously alarmed by the violence of her emotions. 'I didn't know it would be so; it was impossible for me to foresee it. . . . You are faint with the closeness of the room, and the heat of these lamps. You will be better now, if you make the slightest effort.'
> 'I will do anything,' replied Kate, 'if you will only send me home.'

'Well, well, I will,' said Ralph; 'but you must get back your own looks; for those you have will frighten them, and nobody must know of this but you and I.'

As we see, he is even scared for once of what may be thought by the purblind Mrs Nickleby.

(Incidentally, with regard to Trollope's comment that he could not imagine whence Mrs Proudie, her train caught under the sofa castor, found the magnificent phrase, 'Unhand it!' she might well have remembered this from *Nicholas Nickleby*, where Kate, regrettably, cries to Sir Mulberry, 'Unhand me, sir, this instant').

The whole scene at Ralph's dinner is more purely *louche* than anything Dickens had ever written, or was ever to write again. It might well have brought a blush to the cheek of the 'young person' if read aloud in the Victorian family circle, and the young person had the least idea what was going on.

There is also, in *Nicholas Nickleby*, another curiosity: the dress rehearsal for the marriage of Jonas Chuzzlewit and Mercy Pecksniff in the projected marriage of Arthur Gride and Madeline Bray. Gride is a senile Jonas, sadistic, miserly and a punisher. It is not uncommon to find the theme of *punishment through marriage*, or by the enforcement of the body without marriage, in Dickens's novels. The Gride-Madeline story is not so successful as that of the Jonas-Mercy one, because Madeline is a nothing, one of those heroine nullities upon whom Angus Wilson has reflected. But Gride really needs to 'punish' Madeline for her beauty and for his own moral and physical ugliness. (There was a daily beauty in her life that made him ugly.) He will clasp a string of beads around her neck on the wedding-day, but afterwards he will take them away again. Delighted as this repugnant January is with his young May, he means nevertheless to half-starve her and to see that she is miserable. So Jonas, a young man, listens to Mercy's chirping abuse, submits to being called 'dragon' and 'fright', because he knows what he will do with her when he gets her home, and we know it too. It is impossible to imagine sexual intercourse between Harry and Rose Maylie, Clennam and Little Dorrit, John Westlock and Ruth Pinch, but quite easy to imagine it between the young Chuzzlewits, or (more pleasantly) between Dick Swiveller and the Marchioness.

Another example of 'marriage' (in this case adultery) as punishment can be seen in the strange affair between Carker and Edith Dombey, and had Dickens gone ahead with the seduction instead of burking it, we should have seen it clearly.[1] This is proposed punishment by the body, as the Duchess in Barbey d'Aurevilly's story punishes her husband for having her lover strangled by becoming a notorious prostitute and having the fact carved upon her sepulchre.[2] Carker wants Edith because he is hot with desire for her, but also because he needs to wreak vengeance upon her (and Dombey) for the humiliations he had had to endure. Both Carker and Edith are mature characters and there is no doubt that had Dickens been writing in an age when the 'family audience' had ceased to exist, the matter would have been carried to a highly effective conclusion. For we sense that Edith, where her husband is not concerned, may potentially be highly-sexed and that Carker, all glitter and teeth, is certainly so. Furious sexual pleasure, at least, could easily have been achieved in that *cabinet particulier* in Dijon, even when combined with hatred.

Dickens, whose approach to women, child-brides and all, sometimes approaches the sadistic, has more than these three examples of the proposed 'punishment by marriage'. What would have been the fate of, say, Georgina Podsnap had she married Fascination Fledgeby? We know how Nell would have suffered had she indeed become the second Mrs Quilp. Quilp would have bitten her.

He, of course, is in his manic way one of the most sensual of Dickens's creations, and was doubtless a sexual athlete. Did he really keep Mrs Quilp up all night just sitting in a chair while he sat and smoked, or is the burning pipe a sexual symbol? It is remarkable that whenever this monster is away his wife languishes for him, and that she can roundly inform a roomful of her friends that if Quilp were free, there is not one of them who wouldn't accept him. And we do not doubt it. The only person who would certainly not have taken him is Nell, towards whom his behaviour is peculiarly repulsive.

[1] To go ahead was his original intention: he was deflected by Lord Jeffrey.
[2] 'La Vengeance d'une Femme' *Les Diaboliques*, vol. i, 1874.

It is interesting in this connection that the corrected proofs of the novel in the Victoria and Albert Museum clearly show that Dickens originally meant Quilp to be the father of the Marchioness by Sally Brass. Setting the genetic implausibility aside (what would such a child have been like? As 'Sophronia Sphynx,' she turned out to be '*good-looking*, clever and good-humoured' – the italics are mine), one is compelled to feel that any man sufficiently attracted by Sally to beget a child upon her must have been sexually athletic indeed.

However, the original intention is not in doubt, and the relevant passage is quoted in full by the late Professor Gerald G. Grubb in 'Dickens's Marchioness Identified' (*Modern Language Notes*, vol. lxviii, March 1953). Hints of the parentage still remain in the existing text, when it is suggested that both Quilp and Sally Brass could tell the truth if they liked: but this seems to me something residual, overlooked, like small shards of scattered masonry from a long demolished building. Why did Dickens abandon this idea? Professor Grubb thought it a good one, the Marchioness setting 'in motion the jaws of the Haman plot that had been intended to overwhelm Kit, but was destined to overwhelm Quilp and the Brasses.' He believes that Dickens deliberately 'de-emphasized the Marchioness,' failing 'to capitalise on this almost perfect sub-plot' because, on reading his galley-proofs, he realized that the Marchioness was a serious threat to interest in Nell, a distracting force just at the time when the latter was dying in style: and so, 'decided to risk artistic incompleteness rather than raise up a rival of Little Nell.'

This is, of course, arguable. But I rather feel that Dickens, who was by this time becoming increasingly a master of literary tact, decided that the sub-plot was far too mechanistic, far too neatly packaged and sealed. He may even have pondered, as I have, whether it is remotely plausible that the 'good-looking, clever, good-humoured girl' could have been the offspring of these two hideous and unpleasant grotesques. The cleverness she might have inherited: but what else? The fact of her smallness is of no significance, since most of Dickens's favourite women were small to the point of tininess. Furthermore, she displays no corruption through her environment, except a tendency to gaze through keyholes and listen at doors out of sheer boredom and loneliness.

I have said Quilp's behaviour towards Nell is peculiarly repulsive, a judgment that the following passage supports:

> 'How should you like to be my number two, Nelly?'
>
> 'To be what, sir?'
>
> 'My number two, Nelly; my second; my Mrs. Quilp,' said the dwarf.
>
> The child looked frightened, but seemed not to understand him, which Mr. Quilp observing, hastened to explain his meaning more distinctly.
>
> 'To be Mrs. Quilp the second, when Mrs. Quilp the first is dead, sweet Nell,' said Quilp, wrinkling up his eyes and luring her towards him with his bent forefinger, 'to be my wife, my little cherry-cheeked, red-lipped wife. Say that Mrs. Quilp lives five years, or only four, you'll be just the proper age for me. Ha ha! Be a good girl, Nelly, a very good girl, and see if one of these days you don't come to be Mrs. Quilp of Tower Hill.'

Is this simply malevolent teasing, or does it contain the perfectly cold-blooded threat to commit murder to bring about a desirable state of affairs, to provide for himself a new and very young creature to outrage and torment (Mr Jack Lindsay suggests that it does)? It has been pointed out before how symbolic is the picture of Quilp smoking furiously away as he lies in Nell's bed. Nowadays, we all feel Quilp's sexual fascination – at a safe distance: it would be horrible if he really put his head round the door. But there is something of his maker in him, the manic side. Is he really such a hideous dwarf, *or is he some more alluring person in disguise?* Do we adore Quilp because he is a monstrous indiscretion? Had Dickens given away just a little too much of the wilder side of himself? It might seem to us good wild fun to dance a young girl to the end of a pier, as he did the girl Eleanor at Broadstairs, and hold her there till her stockings and dress were soaked, but to the onlookers at the time it must have seemed like madness.[1] (The equation between Quilp and Dickens himself has been made by Mr Lindsay[2].)

' "Such a fresh, blooming, modest little bud, neighbour," said

[1] See Eleanor Christian, 'Recollections of Dickens', *Temple Bar*, April 1888.
[2] *Charles Dickens: A Biographical and Critical Study*, 1950, p. 193.

Quilp, nursing his short leg, and making his eyes twinkle very much; "such a chubby, rosy, cosy, little Nell!" ' The very implausibility of the description makes it all the more repellent.

It is interesting that in this novel Dickens deals also with a most tender, if very oblique, side of the sexual life. Is Dick Swiveller, too, in disguise? Because the fairy-tale (only partially mock) wooing of the Marchioness, after her long spell of sick-nursing, is extremely – and, in Dick's bizarre way, lyrically – tender. She is, in fact, only a child: but an old child, and when he has money enough, he has her educated so that she may grow up to marry him. He is growing her up for himself – as Quilp would have had Nell grow up for the same purpose. But with what a difference!

> Having eaten and drunk to Mr. Swiveller's extreme contentment, given him his drink, and put everything in neat order, she wrapped herself in an old coverlet and lay down on the rug before the fire.
>
> Mr. Swiveller was by that time murmuring in his sleep, 'Strew then, oh strew, a bed of rushes. Here will we stay, till morning blushes. Good night, Marchioness!'

This extraordinary development, or suggested development, of a love-affair between Dick and the child is one of the most delicate things in the whole of Dickens's work, losing nothing by its wildness of spirit and by its sheer oddity.[1]

The sexual by-way most persistently, if tentatively, explored in the novels, is sadism. But when the exuberance of the younger Dickens has tamed itself, and there are no longer dinners with Ralph Nickleby or sessions with Quilp at the Thames-side wharf, something happens which is very surprising, and that is the revelation of lesbianism, the almost bald accusation of Miss Wade, by that otherwise somewhat Pooterish character, Mr Meagles.

> 'I don't know what you are, but you don't hide, can't hide, what a dark spirit you have within you. If it should happen that you are a woman, who, from whatever cause, has a perverted delight in making a sister-woman as wretched as she is (I am old enough to have heard of such), I warn her against you, and I warn you against yourself.'

---

[1] Here we have the often-aphrodisiac master-pupil relationship, even if all that Dick is teaching her is cribbage.

Indeed, Mr Meagles has heard of such: and because he has, then so had most of the Victorians, or this speech would be meaningless to the reader. Very few of them would have read and rejoiced in *My Secret Life*: but that is a far cry from never having heard of the perversions.

In Dickens's work, even a hint of male homosexuality is conspicuous by its absence, or at least, I can trace no hint of it: the adolescent emotional feeling between Steerforth and David (note that the latter is nicknamed 'Daisy') is so much a norm that it would be twisting a word to find any true homosexual impulse there. It has been suggested that something of the sort could lie behind the mutual ragging of Quilp and Tom Scott, but however superficially attractive the thought, I cannot believe this without a most uneasy and implausible stretching of the imagination. Trollope, an incomparably more worldly writer and great psychologist (though not, like Dickens, a towering genius), probably had some idea of repressed homosexuality in Dean Arabin, who has the luck – more than he deserves in the view of some, who do not find his wittiness proved – to fall in love with Eleanor Bold.

But Trollope, like Dickens, also has something to say about suppressed lesbianism, and combines that with the 'marriage for punishment' theme. In *The Eustace Diamonds* the overtly sadistic Sir Griffin Tewett becomes engaged to the Lucinda Roanoke, who has been driven to the match by the greed and impercipience of her aunt. Lucinda loathes Sir Griffin and says so: his very touch is a horror and his kiss a worse one. We know how he would have become avenged for her slights after the marriage – which never takes place, since she sits down in ordinary dress with her Bible on the wedding morning and refuses to budge. She has gone out of her mind. It is not so strongly hinted as Dickens hinted, where Miss Wade was concerned, that Lucinda can love no man: but it is implicit. She is a poor girl constantly under pressure to be forced out of her nature, wholly sympathetic and wholly sad.

The impression is hardly escapable, that Trollope and Dickens were addressing their readers from differing degrees of elevation. Trollope was speaking, at a consonant height, right into their ears and, furthermore, speaking to one person at a time: Dickens came to slant his talk a little downwards, because he was addressing a seated group. Probably his image of his reader was as one who read aloud to other readers of varying ages; therefore, some things were suitable and some were not. There are hardly any characters in Trollope who, when mated, could not have mated physically. Dickens's works abound in couples who seem to be beyond coupling. As Professor Wilson says,

> The contemporary censorship, in fact, went along with, rather than against, Dickens's natural inclinations. His submerged, but fierce, sensuality was to run some strange courses from the days of John Chester until it came to light in the diverging streams of Wrayburn and Headstone. Seduction withheld, deferred, foiled – at any rate never accomplished – produced many interesting and complex characters, who would not have been born in a fiction that reflected the real world where men are more resolute and women are weaker.[1]

But it also resulted in characters who have no active role to play, because they appear to be devoid of any kind of sexual appetite.

Dickens has nowhere such a ruthless creature as Trollope's Lady Arabella Trefoil (*The American Senator*), shopsoiled from many seasons, who hounds silly Lord Rufford remorselessly towards marriage and then, when having behaved indiscreetly he still rejects her, comes like Apollyon over the fields to confront and denounce him. In her case, her strength does not spring from sexual energy but from sheer desperation: if she cannot corral him, then what is her future to be like? Lord Rufford, on the other hand, is an easygoing thoughtless sensualist, and by the mere negative process of not thinking all but delivers himself into her iron hands.

Is there a woman in Dickens's novels strong enough to pursue a man? This was not the role he had for women. Since the death of Mary Hogarth he had lived a fantasy life, all his sexual instincts playing upon the idea of 'the little woman,' 'the child-wife.'[2] It took

---

[1] 'The Heroes and Heroines of Dickens' in *Dickens and the Twentieth Century*, edited by John Gross and Gabriel Pearson, 1962.

[2] This was quite a common Victorian fantasy. See, for example, Maltus Holyoake's article on Captain Mayne Reid in the *Strand Magazine* (vol. ii, 1891, pp. 93-102). Holyoake writes that the Captain's wife was 'so young that she was often taken for the Captain's daughter, and he himself called her his "child wife", which is the title of one of his subsequent novels.'

Ellen Ternan to give him some idea of child-wife reality. Admiring him as we do (and here one must reiterate the claim that he stands next to Shakespeare) one still feels that readers of our day suspect and dislike his avoiding of sexual issues. Even Dora Copperfield seems too infantile to be slept with, whereas mere contemplation of the union between Clennam and Little Dorrit must give rise to the glummest of speculation.

It is possible to consider whether the romantic side of Dickens's temperament did not outweigh the purely sexual: which is why he found it possible to marry dolls together, not considering what might have happened beyond the altar. In the mutually-punishing Lammles he gives some real idea of a totally loveless marriage which need not, I think, in this case have been without physical expression. In Miss Margaret Drabble's phrase, this couple 'had complicity'; and complicity in married life, no matter what the basic subject of it, can be pretty well all-embracing.

They are an interesting pair. We see them trailing each other morosely over the Shanklin sands, each furious because neither has a fortune, and no marriage would have taken place had not both been deceived by the Veneerings in thinking to the contrary. Sophronia Lammle is so sick with rage that she breaks her parasol.

> His colour has turned to a livid white, and ominous marks have come to light about his nose, as if the finger of the very devil himself had, within the last few moments, touched it here and there. But he has repressive power, and she has none.

It is Alfred Lammle who suggests that they shall now speak reasonably. Both, he tells her, have been deceived, and they had better come to terms with the fact as soon as possible.

> 'I cannot get rid of you, you cannot get rid of me. What follows?'
> 'Shame and misery,' the bride bitterly replies.
> 'I don't know. A mutual understanding follows, and I think it may carry us through.'

Here he proposes to her that they shall make a united pretence of felicity to the world, while carrying out their respective careers as adventurers, but this time to their mutual advantage.

'We owe the Veneerings a grudge, and we owe all other people the grudge of wishing them to be taken in, as we ourselves have been taken in ... We agree to keep our own secret, and to work together in furtherance of our own schemes.'

'What schemes?'

'Any scheme that will bring us money. By our own schemes, I mean our joint interest. Agreed?'

She answers, after a little hesitation, 'I suppose so, Agreed.'

They walk back along the sands, but this time together. It should not be so uninteresting a life for the two of them, these birds of prey: and there is no reason to believe that birds of prey do not mate in the same manner as other fowls of the air. At least, no one could claim that the Lammles were not fully mature.

It is impossible that Dickens consciously conceived his long passion for Mary Hogarth, his short ones for Christiana Weller and – one suspects – Madame de la Rue, in any kind of sexual terms. That was buried deep. But Ellen Ternan was not a romantic, child-like symbol: she started a sexual drive in a nature that had at least been romantically deprived, and which was now in desperate need of romantic and sexual love combined. It is impossible to think of her as a very nice young woman, certainly not a loyal one. As Kate Perugini said sadly, animadverting to family cricket, 'She did not play the game.' Her photographs show a pretty, almost Terry-esque, but essentially hard and rather sly young person. It is difficult not to feel that, having been chosen by and having succumbed to, a much older man of great genius, she need not have let him down so horribly in her later remarks to Canon Benham.[1] Ellen was not a sportswoman and it was Dickens's error to think that, in any sense, she ever could have been.[2]

It is to the novels of his later years that Dickens restores an interest in sexual passion.

---

[1] See Thomas Wright, *The Life of Charles Dickens*, 1935, p. 356.

[2] There is still a body of opinion which holds that she did not sleep with Dickens at all, and that the essence of their relationship was that she should remain technically 'pure'. Since there is no evidence either way, we are left with speculation. For myself I do not see why she should not have been Dickens's mistress in the fullest sense: this would better explain her expressed repulsion in her later life than a situation which might have given her the consolation of being technically innocent.

Now, of course, few writers of the highest order are in entire control of their material every moment of the time they are working. Those who appear to have been were Balzac (in his maturity), Tolstoy and Proust. But in his younger years Dickens did not think of character in depth: characters happened to him. It has been observed here that on the evidence of Mrs Quilp, Quilp was probably a sexual athlete; though it is quite unlikely that Dickens thought in such crude terms at all. Mr Mantalini emerges as a far more dubious character than the initial wholly comic conception would seem to justify: and the sensuality of Pecksniff towards Mary Graham comes as something of a surprise since it has not been prepared for.

Mantalini, despite his delectable absurdities, is an inveterate woman-chaser, able only to calm the more than lively suspicions of his wife by his unique brand of flattery – 'The demdest little fascinator in all the world.' It might be possible to imagine that his flirtations are harmless, until Miss Knag, spying on 'some little matters connected with that gentleman's private character,' finds much to impart to Madame Mantalini –

> as to open her eyes more effectually than the closest and most philosophical reasoning could have done in a series of years. To which end, the accidental discovery by Miss Knag of some tender correspondence, in which Madame Mantalini was described as 'old' and 'ordinary,' had most providentially contributed.

Mantalini's pretence that he has poisoned himself, so distraught is he by his little fascinator's lack of faith in him, is no great success: and in the end, which is significant, Dickens sees that he, even he, is punished for his misdemeanours. We last find him turning – or failing to turn – the mangle, beneath a torrent of abuse from a woman much different from his wife.

> 'You nasty, idle, vicious, good-for-nothing brute,' cried the woman, stamping on the ground, 'why don't you turn the mangle?'
> 'So I am, my life and soul!' replied a man's voice. 'I am always turning, I am perpetually turning, like a demd old horse in a demnition mill. My life is one demd horrid grind!'

Comic retribution, but retribution it is. Dickens believes in settling scores, but if Mantalini had been quite the harmless grotesque to whom we are first introduced, then no score – and for him it must have been a heavy one – would have been settled.

With *Great Expectations*, the most important of the post-Ternan novels, Dickens does not yet seem wholly in control. Estella is in fact a very unattractive girl; apart from her beauty we are shown nothing to commend her. (Dickens too often equated physical beauty with sexual attraction, which is why so many of his minor heroines are failures.) Should Pip marry Estella, he is in for another 'marriage of punishment' – his strong masochistic streak will ensure it. But here the emphasis will have shifted, with Estella as punisher, as she has always been taught to be.

'Love means stopping thinking about oneself,' Mr Christopher Ricks percipiently remarks. There can scarcely ever have been a better definition. If Pip continues to think of himself and his dis-qualifications in Estella's eyes, it is only because he relates every-thing to her. It is a true passion, and we feel it as much as any passion of love in the whole of Dickens, including the passion of Bradley Headstone. '. . . I'll never cry for you again,' says the boy,

> . . . which was, I suppose, as false a declaration as ever was made; for I was inwardly crying for her then, and I know what I know of the pain she cost me afterwards.

The childish image is so powerful that when Pip meets her as a grown woman he does not at first recognize her.

> The lady, whom I had never seen before, lifted up her eyes and looked archly at me, and then I saw that the eyes were Estella's eyes. But she was so much changed, was so much more beautiful, so much more womanly, in all things winning admiration, had made such wonderful advance, that I seemed to have made none. I fancied, as I looked at her, that I slipped hopelessly back into the coarse and common boy again. O the sense of distance and disparity that came upon me, and the inaccessibility that came about her!

So Dickens must, though a famous and sophisticated man, have thought of Ellen Ternan at first: of the disparity of age, the inaccessibility caused by his marriage. There was no doubt that he was telling the truth when he made the crazy public statement of her innocence: it was afterwards that (as I believe) she became his mistress. She had been hard to get. Had she, like Estella, no heart?

We feel that whereas John Westlock only wanted to share a roof with Ruth Pinch or Clennam with Dorrit, Pip wanted the physical possession of Estella as much as Carker wanted to possess Edith Dombey.

Edith is a very much more attractive woman than Estella ever was. Like Soames's Irene, she marries, as it were, for a meal ticket: and also, like Irene, cannot bring herself to make any concessions to her husband. Even allowing for Mr Dombey's horrible temperament, one cannot but feel that the household would have been a happier one for him, for Florence, for Edith herself, if the latter had been able to display the least generosity. But where her relations with her husband are not concerned, Edith is often warm-hearted, passionate and outgoing. She could have been more of a genuine love-object than Estella: it is only because Pip is a child that he fails so hopelessly to find the slightest fault with the latter and is trapped by her for life.

It is curious how much at home Dickens is with the wildly passionate nature and how poor at giving it human speech. There is an echo of 'Unhand me, sir!' every time Edith Dombey opens her mouth. She is stilted and histrionic in her utterance, a creature of the stage: a fact which has prevented her from being fully appreciated. Yet in herself she is fascinating, and it is interesting to think how she would have seemed to the reader had she had the faculty of naturalistic expression.

> 'Did I ever tempt you to seek my hand? Did I ever use any art to win you? Was I ever more conciliating to you when you pursued me, than I have been since our marriage? Was I ever other to you than I am?'
>
> 'It is wholly unnecessary, Madam,' said Mr. Dombey, 'to enter upon such discussions.'
>
> 'Did you think I loved you? Did you know I did not? Did you ever care, Man! for my heart, or propose to yourself to win the worthless

thing? Was there any poor pretence of any in our bargain? Upon your side, or on mine?'

One feels that Edith is really rather enjoying the sound of her own voice. What stuff it is, this rhythmic flow of rhetorical questions! Yet Edith in her actions, especially in her treatment of Florence, is wholly real and usually sympathetic. She is not at all an a-sexual creature, such as the Ruth Pinches, the Rose Maylies, seem to be. Free of her wonderful and dreadful old mother, appropriately mated (preferably to one of Trollope's heroes, such as Lord Chiltern) she might have been a normal woman.

But there is no doubt that about younger women Dickens knew little, while Trollope knew all there was to know.[1] Dickens is too great to suffer much even by such a sweeping comparison: yet his young girls of good breeding, with the exception of Bella Wilfer and Rosa Budd, leave him uneasy.

It may be instructive to compare the rejection of Adolphus Longstaff by the delightful American beauty, Isabel Boncassen (*The Duke's Children*, 1880), with the rejection of Carker by Edith Dombey (*Dombey and Son*, 1848). Thirty-two years had, admittedly, passed, but Trollope's hand with dialogue was always much the same.

Here Mr Longstaff, the most languid, most eligible and certainly the most 'hard to get' of the untitled upper class young men in London society, is attempting to propose to Miss Boncassen, who is an expert at fending people off.

> 'How humble-minded you must be when you think me a fool because I have fallen in love with such a one as yourself.'
> 'I like you for that,' she replied laughing, 'and withdraw the epithet as not being applicable. Now we are quits and can forget and forgive; – only let there be the forgetting.'
> 'Never!' said Dolly, with his hand again on his heart.
> 'Then let it be a little dream of your youth, – that you once met a pretty American girl who was foolish enough to refuse all that you would have given her.'
> 'So pretty! So awfully pretty!' Thereupon she curtsied.

[1] A reviewer of *Rachel Ray* called him a 'lady-killer', meaning that he had exceptional insight into the hearts and the domestic lives of women.

'I have seen all the handsome women in England going for the last ten years, and there has not been one who has made me think that it would be worthy my while to get off my perch for her.'

'And now you would desert your perch for me!'

'I have already.'

'But you can get up again. Let it all be a dream. I know men like to have had such dreams. And in order that the dream may be pleasant the last word between us shall be kind. Such admiration from such a one as you is an honour, – and I will reckon it among my honours. But it can be no more than a dream.' Then she gave him her hand. 'It shall be so; – shall it not?' Then she paused. 'It must be so, Mr. Longstaff.'

'Must it?'

'That and no more. Now I wish to go down. Will you come with me? It will be better. Don't you think it is going to rain?'

Here is Carker, in that *cabinet particulier*, brim-full of self-confidence and expecting the prize to fall into his arms.

He was coming gaily towards her, when, in an instant, she caught the knife up from the table, and started one pace back.

'Stand still!' she said, 'or I shall murder you!'

The sudden change in her, the towering fury and intense abhorrence sparkling in her eyes and lighting up her brow, made him stop as if a fire had stopped him.

'Stand still!' she said, 'come no nearer me, upon your life!'

They both stood looking at each other. Rage and astonishment were in his face, but he controlled them, and said lightly,

'Come, come! Tush, we are alone, and out of everybody's sight and hearing. Do you think to frighten me with these tricks of virtue?'

'Do you think to frighten *me*,' she answered fiercely, 'from any purpose that I have, and any course I am resolved upon, by reminding me of the solitude of this place, and there being no help near? Me, who am here alone, designedly? If I feared you, should I not have avoided you? If I feared you, should I be here, in the dead of night, telling you to your face what I am going to tell?'

'And what is that,' he said, 'you handsome shrew? Handsomer so, than any other woman in her best humour?'

'I tell you nothing,' she returned, 'until you go back to that chair – except this, once again – Don't come near me! Not a step nearer. I tell you, if you do, as Heaven sees us, I shall murder you!'

'Do you mistake me for your husband?' he retorted, with a grin.

It was Dickens's tendency towards the stagey that was so often to destroy the very atmosphere of the sexual which he was trying to achieve.

Where he achieved sensuality so brilliantly was with his grotesques, with Mrs Gamp, as reekingly sensual a creature as ever walked upon chimney-pots and parapets, with Quilp, even with Miss Mowcher, whose flirtatiousness with David and Steerforth has just an edge of the unpleasant. With these people he was uninhibited, and through him their direct voices spoke.

Yet he did not achieve the very essence of hopeless sexual passion till he came to Bradley Headstone, in *Our Mutual Friend*. I remarked earlier in this essay that we felt Pip's passion of love for Estella more than any other consonant passion in Dickens, and to this, despite the violence of Headstone's feelings and reactions, I still adhere, since in Headstone's case the element of frustrated *lust* is so powerful: one cannot feel this in Pip, and I have here used the word 'love' to make a distinction.

The famous scene where Bradley, in frustration, dashes his fist on to a stone till it is covered in blood, is not fustian at all. This is the spontaneous consequence of rejection, and we believe in it totally. He is one of Dickens's most menacing and powerful characters, not the less so because the woman he is pursuing is a bizarrely-refined nullity.

What did Eugene Wrayburn eventually make of her? She must have been plastic to the moulding, and I daresay even appeared eventually (forgiven) at Podsnap parties with modest and genteel grace. Eugene himself is an attractive and wholly adult character. His original intentions towards Lizzie, by whose beauty he is bowled over, are far from honourable and it is hard not to believe that it is through a mixture of gratitude and sheer *panache* that he marries her. That this union is basically unconvincing is not his fault: he is a natural creature. The fault lies in the basic improbability of Lizzie. It is fair to admit that, in addition to certain natural and gentle endowments, she attained her ladylike qualities *via* Charlie, who had learned gentility from the schoolmaster; but even so, she is too good to be true. A creation of Dickens's maturity, she is too good to be true even as that curious gentleman of nature,

Oliver Twist, was too good also. We are forced by Oliver's example, I think, to suspect that Dickens instinctively believed more in heredity than in environment. He appears to insist that if we bring the Duke's son up in a slum, he will mysteriously remain, demonstrably, a duke. For myself, I think the hereditary endowment is the more powerful, but not to the extent of creating the outward manner. Lizzie, on the other hand, has no heredity that will explain her. That is why she is so puzzling: nice girl as she is, she has not even Oliver's pitiful shred of excuse for behaving so consistently, in the social sense, as she does.

But apart from the case of Bradley Headstone, sexuality is very much present in *Our Mutual Friend*. Bella Wilfer's flirtatiousness, her 'little me-ishness', stem from the natural sexual impulse. Like so many teases of her kind, she is always glad to stop putting lions through their paces and to put her head in the lion's mouth. When she begs John Harmon's forgiveness, first, for her own imperious treatment of him and second, for the insults of Mr Boffin in his miserly avatar, it is with true masochistic gusto. It is a genuine relief to her to 'come off her perch'; and this is why Bella is among the more interesting of Dickens's heroines. (It is possible that Rosa Budd, judging from the charming scene in which she acknowledges to Eddie that marriage between them would be entirely inappropriate, would have gained a great deal in interest had *Edwin Drood* ever been finished. She does not suffer, as Rose Maylie and Madeline Bray seem to, from a sort of profound unawareness. She is only too aware, hypnotized or not, of the sexual light in which she is regarded by Jasper: she experiences sexual repulsion.)

He, in the murderous quality of his sexual impulse, is not nearly so convincing a figure as Bradley Headstone. Headstone is instinct with the melodrama of life, Jasper with that of the theatre.

We must not, however, should we ever regard Dickens's melodrama as a spoiling factor, forget that life *is* full of melodrama in its happenings, though it is human behaviour in the face of melodrama which makes it what we call 'melodramatic'. Dickens's manic nature predisposed him to it; his histrionic nature dictated its treatment.

It might be said that apart from the dinner party at Ralph Nickleby's, the behaviour of Quilp on the wharf towards Nell, and the confrontation between Meagles and Miss Wade, Dickens showed small awareness of the by-paths of sexual behaviour. Yet he was not an innocent man, as Wilkie Collins must have been fully aware, on those nocturnal perambulations of Paris. It is the family audience which dominates him, starting with the audience of his own family. There were things that he did not judge it good for others to know: despite the genuine restrictions of his age, he took, as I have suggested, far less advantage of such liberty as there was than some other writers of his time. Unlike Thackeray, he would not have been particularly happy with the liberties of France or nineteenth-century Russia, with those of Balzac or (later) of his follower, Dostoievsky. He did not much feel the coercion of his age, or if he did, there is little sign of it. He took small interest in the intimacies of the marital domestic scene (as George Eliot did in the scenes between Rosamond and Lydgate) nor much interest beyond the wedding bells except when, as in the case of Jonas and Mercy Chuzzlewit, the results were sinister. (The books were meant not only to be read but to *be heard*, and it is in a sense not surprising that they read and dramatize magnificently.) Except in scenes of melodrama, Dickens's heightened dialogue sounds surprisingly naturalistic, as anyone will realize who has followed the television adaptations. The truth is that what may seem to be excessive grotesquerie lies far less in the spoken word than in the commentary surrounding it: and when the commentary is removed, say, from *Martin Chuzzlewit*, which was excellently adapted for the small screen, then none of the dialogue seems forced at all. As for Mrs Gamp (and for Flora Finching, in *Little Dorrit*) the stream-of-consciousness technique is very familiar to the modern ear.

Not that Dickens thought himself satisfied – at least, he wrote as if he did not – with the repressiveness of his age: and Professor Edgar Johnson is more inclined than I am to think that it did in fact worry him.

> The same limitations explained the shortcomings of English literature. Mrs. Grundy had her grip on everything, smothering courage and truth. What a dishonest state was represented by some smooth gentleman complaining that the hero of an English novel was always 'uninteresting – too good – not natural, etc.,' in comparison

with the heroes of Balzac and Sand! 'But O my smooth friend, what a shining impostor you must think yourself and what an ass you think me,' when both know 'that this same unnatural young gentleman . . . whom you meet in those other books and in mine *must be* presented to you in that unnatural aspect by reason of your morality, and is not to have, I will not say any of the indecencies you like, but not even any of the experiences, trials, perplexities and confusions inseparable from the making or unmaking of all men!'[1]

Yes, but as Trollope showed, a Johnny Eames, a Lord Silverbridge, a Frank Tregear, even a Frank Greystock, were all possible to create, and none of them lacked naturalness, or were immune from confusions and perplexities.

Professor Johnson continues:

> These feelings, the never-ending toil of his book (*Little Dorrit*), and his deep inward unrest, all generated a desperate craving for excitement. 'Prowling wretchedly about the rooms on the Champs Elysées, tearing my hair, sitting down to write, writing nothing, writing something and tearing it up, going out, coming in,' he said, he was 'a Monster to my family, a dread phenomenon to myself.' Sometimes as he planned another scathing chapter on officialdom, he had a grim pleasure 'that the Circumlocution Office sees the light,' and wondered 'what effect it will have.' Then, his head stinging 'with the visions of the book,' he would feel that need to plunge 'out into some of the strange places I glide into of nights in these latitudes.' One night it was the *fête* of the company of the Folies Nouvelles, 'which I should think,' he told Collins, 'could hardly fail to attract all the Lorettes in Paris.' Another night it would be a cheap public ball, with 'pretty faces, but all of two classes – wicked and coldly calculating, or haggard and wretched in their worn beauty.'

This is that peculiar restlessness which sometimes feels like a disturbance of the digestive organs, and it is possible that Dickens occasionally longed to put his nightprowlings into prose. His books are far from devoid of sexual pursuers. Yet it is noticeable that most of these, such as Uriah Heep, Pecksniff and Gride, are left with nobodies (Agnes Wickfield, Mary Graham, Madeline Bray) to

[1] *Charles Dickens. His Tragedy and Triumph*, London, vol. ii, 1953, p. 859. Johnson is quoting from a letter of Dickens to Forster written in 1856 (*Letters of Charles Dickens*, Nonesuch Edition ed. W. Dexter, vol. ii, 1938, p. 797).

pursue. It was almost as if he feared to risk any real confrontation by opposing a true sexual nature (bad) to another true sexual one, however virtuous the latter might be.

In his work there is no Lord Steyne, and no Becky Sharp, certainly no Rochester and Jane Eyre, no Burgo Fitzgerald and Glencora Palliser, not even a Lord Silverbridge and a Miss Boncassen: for these couples were matched in normal sensuality (actual or potential) as Dickens's couples never were, and never could be.

Does it worry us then, that we find so little suggestion of sexual or sensuous love in the novels of Dickens? Not much, I think; because, unlike Trollope, he was not a true realist. His genius consists in the heightening out of life, to such a pitch that many of his creations stand together in a giant mythology, and we do not expect so much sexual *sensibility* from gods, even from gods disguised, as from ordinary men and women.

To sum up, the sexual life in the novels of Dickens, where it is overt, almost invariably fails to find a reciprocating object. It would be easy to claim that, in the post-Ternan period, lack of reciprocity is dominant, this arising, possibly, out of Dickens's difficulties with his young mistress. But this will not do, since it was always so with him, even from the beginning. Dickens himself seems to have been more sensually-romantic in inclination than purely sexual: which might lead us to speculate whether here we have evidence of a certain timidity. He was afraid of being *turned down*, and so his 'pursuers' always are turned down. Furthermore, Eugene Wrayburn excepted, they are invariably villains: so it may not be totally unreasonable to suggest that there is some powerful guilt in operation here. (It is reasonable to suppose that the sudden rejection, in his youth, by Maria Beadnell, produced something of a trauma which lasted his lifetime. As with the blacking factory, Dickens seems to have got over nothing.)

Dickens came under heavy fire for the Ternan affair: yet few people have credited him with twenty years of restrained behaviour under the pressure of a marriage devoid of all intellectual contact, and with a manic temperament wholly against him. Like Queen Victoria he was determined to be good: but when the breaking stress came upon him he behaved about as badly and certainly as foolishly as it is possible to conceive. One feels really very sorry for all parties concerned.

The most fluent of men in his letters, he still leaves us puzzled. On the one hand the 'periwinkles' and 'lorettes'; on the other the seduced women in the books, who either go drearily round for ever making low moaning noises, or are forced to take their hopes of redemption to the Antipodes. On the one hand Urania Cottage, the home for fallen women that he assisted Miss Coutts to run, and the sensitivity that wanted the girls to have pretty rather than penitential clothes; on the other the charging of the prostitute for swearing[1] and the approval of Captain Chesterton's tread-mill regime at Coldbath Fields prison.[2]

It is very hard to believe that so complex and in a sense so fear-driven a man, where his public was concerned, would have been happy today with the extreme liberties we possess for the publication of almost everything. Had he been born right into it, he might have found some degree of liberating force: but had he grown up into it, as have so many writers now living, he would probably have preferred (as they do) to leave most of the new privileges unused. Yet these must have made a difference, however small, to his treatment of sexual matters, seriously have inhibited the 'child-wife' dreams and the dream of union, as in *Little Dorrit*, for more or less utilitarian purposes. We are all to an extent creatures of our time: perhaps he was abnormally much a creature of his, constantly putting out a hand to touch his shackles and make quite sure, with a sigh of relief, that they were still secure.

[1] See the essay 'The Ruffian' in *The Uncommercial Traveller*.
[2] See Chapter 3 of Philip Collins's *Dickens and Crime* (rev. ed. 1963).

ANGUS WILSON

DICKENS ON CHILDREN AND CHILDHOOD

In 1846, in the eighth chapter of *Dombey and Son*, Dickens wrote of that 'old-fashioned' child, Paul Dombey, that he was

> never so distressed as by the company of children – Florence alone excepted, always.
>
> 'Go away, if you please,' he would say to any child who came to bear him company. 'Thank you, but I don't want you.'
>
> Some small voice, near his ear, would ask him how he was, perhaps.
>
> 'I am very well, I thank you,' he would answer. 'But you had better go and play, if you please.'

In 1861, in the sketch, 'Tom Tiddler's Ground', subsequently published in *Christmas Stories*, we meet an equally 'old-fashioned' child whose attitude is quite the contrary. In this story, primarily written to express Dickens's disgust at the spectacle of a rich man who has turned hermit and lives in filth, we meet Miss Kimmeens, a very young child who, as a result of various circumstances, has been left alone in her boarding-school for a whole day during the vacation. At first, in her panic and loneliness, she begins to blame the rest of the world – the other girls, the staff, the maids, etc. – for her plight; then suddenly she thinks, 'Oh, these envious thoughts are not mine. Oh, this wicked creature isn't me! Help me, somebody! I go wrong, alone by my weak self! Help me, anybody!' Tiny though she is, she sets out upon the high road and, meeting the narrator, is used by him to teach Mr Mopes, the disgusting rich hermit, a lesson in the natural urge and need of man for community with his own kind.

Paul Dombey is one of the most brilliantly drawn children in fiction, playing a relevant and valuable role in a dexterously organized novel that is near to a masterpiece. Miss Kimmeens is a sentimental whimsy in an ephemeral Christmas magazine sketch for *All The Year Round*, originating in an immediate journalistic grievance, for Mr Mopes was founded upon a genuine rich man, Mr Lucas, 'The Hertfordshire Hermit'. It can well be argued that in each instance Dickens is making the same case for the need for human fellowship, since Paul's isolation, his obsession with Florence, are the marks of a dying boy, the victim of an ambitious, uncomprehending paternal love and of a false system of education. Yet there can be little doubt that Paul in his sick will for isolation (no less sick though far less disgusting than that of Mr Mopes wilfully wallowing in filth) commands our interest, our sympathy, our concern, our affection. The children with whom he does not choose to play are as nothing to Dickens or to us. We know that Major Bagstock is slily (or, indeed, rather crudely) insinuating himself into Mr Dombey's affluent company, when he says of Master Briggs, 'He's a fool, Sir . . . a born fool, Sir', and of Paul, 'That boy, Sir, . . . will live in history. That boy, Sir, is not a common production.' The irony that Paul will die soon is obvious. Yet we know, also, that the Major is right: Briggs, for all his neglected state, is an ordinary boy and consequently nothing; Paul is a sick, dreaming inventive boy and, therefore, everything.

Yet when a grown man in Dickens's novels wishes to feed his

jaded, adult self with something of the spiritual health which hangs about children and childhood, it is to ordinary healthy children and their ordinary healthy games that he must have recourse. On Christmas Eve – when, as Dickens says in 'A Christmas Tree' (1850), 'we all ought to come home from the great boarding school where we are forever working at our arithmetic slates', when (*A Christmas Carol*) 'it is good to be children sometimes, and never better than at Christmas, when its mighty Founder was a child himself' – Bob Cratchit, father of a family, downtrodden clerk of Scrooge, 'went down a slide on Cornhill, at the end of a lane of boys, twenty times, in honour of its being Christmas Eve, and then ran home to Camden Town as hard as he could pelt, to play at blindman's buff.'

Evidently to be a child and to be a child again are not in Dickens's fiction quite the same thing – yet both, in their different ways, are the symbols of the spiritual life. We may, perhaps, here distinguish between two sayings of Jesus, the New Testament texts to which much of Dickens's cult of children is related. First we may take St Matthew's 'Except ye be converted, and become as little children, ye shall not enter into the kingdom of Heaven.' Here we think of the saved Scrooge joining in the children's games, of Mr Dick flying his kite or walking with the Doctor as he reads out of his dictionary of Greek roots, of Major Jackman and Mrs Lirriper playing at coaches with little Jemmy. Then we may set beside this, St Mark's 'Suffer the little children to come unto me, and forbid them not; for of such is the Kingdom of Heaven.' Here we may think of Oliver's little friend, Dick, of the schoolmaster's favourite pupil in *The Old Curiosity Shop*, of Little Nell ('It was like passing from death to life; it was drawing nearer Heaven'), or of Paul Dombey ('The old, old fashion – Death! O thank God, all who see it, for that older fashion yet, of Immortality') or of Jo's death ('I'm more cumffler than you can't think, Mr Snagsby'). The life to be gained from childhood association or memory is clearly not the same as the life to come meted out to many of Dickens's lost children.

It may be argued that the dying children – little Dick, Oliver's friend; Smike; the schoolmaster's favourite pupil and Nell; Paul – are early demonstrations of the sacrifice of young lives to faulty systems of upbringing, or of social cruelty and neglect. Jo's career and death are only an extreme version of the same theme. This is true, but there is a further point to note; in the old reprobate view of childhood which Dickens never ceases to attack, death comes to children as a punishment. Mrs Pipchin, the protagonist of all that was wrong in the bringing up of children, having a system 'not to encourage a child's mind to develop and expand itself like a young flower, but to open it by force like an oyster, the moral of these lessons [her readings with her charges] was usually of a violent and stunning character: the hero – a naughty boy – seldom, in the mildest catastrophe, being finished off by anything less than a lion, or a bear.' Dickens's early child heroes and heroines, being good, are, by contrast, rewarded with slow declines into death. They exemplify the Heavenly Reward of the Good and the Innocent, as is graphically shown by the endpiece of *The Old Curiosity Shop* with Nell, the child, being borne heavenward by angels (who are also, of course, children of a kind). The story of Oliver Twist is in the author's own words, 'little Oliver the principle of Good surviving through every adverse circumstance, and triumphing at last.' But Oliver does not need to die, for his Magdalen mother has done that for him earlier in the book – as Smike's grave is the scene of the children's pilgrimages in the happy ending of *Nicholas Nickleby* and the subject of one of Phiz's better attempts at a scene of happy childhood sentiment, so one of Cruickshank's least happy illustrations ends *Oliver Twist*, where Oliver and Rose Maylie, each with a pronounced almost elephantine proboscis, gaze at the tablet to the memory of Agnes, Oliver's erring mother, and

> if the spirits of the Dead ever come back to earth, to visit spots hallowed by the love – the love beyond the grave – of those whom they knew in life, I believe that the shade of Agnes sometimes hovers round that solemn nook. I believe it none the less because that nook is in a Church, and she was weak and erring.

But even apart from his erring mother, Oliver's own goodness is itself often connected with the idea of death – 'he fell into that deep tranquil sleep . . . that calm and peaceful rest which it is pain to wake from. Who, if this were death, would be roused again to all the struggles and turmoils of life,' etc., and, again, the boy was lying, fast asleep . . . so pale with anxiety . . . that he looked like death; not death as it shows in shroud and coffin, but in the guise it wears when life has just departed; when a young and gentle spirit has, but an instant, fled to Heaven, and the gross air of the world has not had time to breathe upon the changing dust it hallowed.

Death in novels before *Barnaby Rudge* (in my opinion the turning point in Dickens's growth from an extraordinary to a great novelist) is hallowing (as well as harrowing) in and for itself. Above all, it is, I think, specifically intended to affect the reader as would an act of mourning. It is true that we are supposed to see Oliver and Rose left better for the contemplation of Agnes's tablet, of Nicholas' children made better by bringing their flowers to Smike's grave, everybody, including pilgrim-tourists made better by the sight of Nell's tomb. But it is all crowded into a last page; it has no vitality in the life of the novels themselves; it is an edifying curtain tableau for us the readers. As such, of course, compared with the joyous progress of Clarissa to her Heavenly Bridegroom it shows a decline in robust Christian faith over a century. Yet even other Victorian deaths of children, for example the near death of Arthur in its effect upon Tom Brown, the effect of the deaths of Russell ('Russell, as he fondly imagined him now, glorified with the glory of heaven, crowned, and with white robes, and with a palm in his hand') and of his own small brother Vernon upon Eric Williams, however little to our taste, however inferior the works of art in which they appear, are integral to their stories. Dostoievsky saw this need clearly. We do not know into what temptations Alyosha Karamazov would have fallen in the never-written sequel to *The Brothers Karamazov*, but when in his final address to the boys at little Ilusha's funeral, he says,

My little doves – let me call you so, for you are very like them, those pretty blue birds, at this minute, as I look at your good dear faces. My dear children . . . you must know that there is nothing higher and stronger and more wholesome and good for life in the future than some good memory, especially a memory of childhood . . . when we recall how we buried Ilusha, how we loved him in his last days . . . that one memory may keep him [the one who remembers] from great evil. . . .

we may be sure that in the unwritten sequel the evil from which Alyosha or any of the boys might have been saved would have been a terrible and real one. Ilusha's funeral (his whole harrowing death) is not there as Nell's end is, like one of Mrs Jarley's waxworks 'classical' and refined, to edify the reader; when the boys at the end of Dostoievsky's novel cry 'Hurrah for Karamazov!', it is not for having made the reader weep, but for offering a meaningful discourse upon an event that will affect volume two which, alas, no reader ever saw. After *The Old Curiosity Shop* Dickens left these theatrical curtains of death behind him, but, as he did so, he really gave up the attempt to weld the ethical system he tried to derive from the New Testament teaching about children into any solid fusion with a metaphysical scheme embracing Eternity. His mind was too rational for the task, his metaphysics as a result too simple. Dostoievsky, with a more crazy, with a much deeper need for God bred of doubt, and an all-consuming love of Christ, more successfully solved the problems of fusion, because he had no revulsion from the irrational distortions of social and ethical thought needed to accommodate the cementing mysticism. But Dickens presents us in his early work with two contradicting edifications – the laughter of healthy children, the deaths of sick ones.

With Paul Dombey, however, a more mature Dickens is now at work: Paul's career is only a portion, though a brilliant portion of a whole story in which Mr Dombey and Florence are the real centre; the boy's death, although its strong accentuation recalls Nell and Smike and Oliver's mother, is a necessary and telling part of the larger theme. As for Jo, he is only the base – though a wonderfully dramatic and successful base – to a large construction of society, and his death is a fitting and, in its context, extraordinarily powerful element in the story of the corruption of that society. And, before Jo's creation, Dickens's venture into self-exploration had already started him upon a new course of the reliving of childhood as a prelude to solving the problems of maturity which was to end in Pip and the rejection at a deep level of most of what he had sought to embody in his earlier child-figures. Yet even here there is a reversion when David writes 'the mother who lay in the grave, was the mother of my infancy; the little creature in her arms was myself, as I had once been, hushed for ever on her bosom.' The journey is a long one between Oliver, 'the principle of Good', and Pip, whose degree of guilt (even from childhood) is complex enough to be the subject of some of the most sophisticated and, more importantly, penetrating of modern Dickensian criticisms (of, for example, the essays of Julian Moynahan and of Dorothy van Ghent).[1] Yet the seeds of Oliver the good and Pip the guilty have common sources in Dickens's scheme of metaphysics, and they are sources which in most ways are in conflict with his general view of childhood as a source of refreshment, of innocent joy and of happy fellowship that pervades description of children and of childhood when in his fiction, his journalism or his public speeches he has to refer to the beneficial effect that they have upon those who remember them, or care for them, or join with them.

Few themes in Dickens's fiction are without their inherent contradictions in this fragmented man who lived an integrated life only by an overwhelming act of will. What matters, of course, is the success with which he uses his many inherent conflicts to force from himself – painfully and gaily at the same time – artistic unities of a very high order. Nowhere does he do this with more variations of success and failure than in his depiction of children, of childhood, and of those adults who are still children at heart. Among his successes are some of the finest portrayals of children in fiction, the more remarkable since he was a pioneer in the field. More importantly, he learned to incorporate these fine child-portraits into full-scale novels of adult concern. Most important of all, in his reverence for childhood, he revered those elements in himself which were the most distinctive marks of his literary genius – deep concern with inanimate objects and their endowment with an autonomous life which is yet sympathetic to the human life lived out among them; fascination with dreaming and half-waking states; belief in meaningful legendary shapes informing everyday real life; a sense of absurdity poised delicately between cruelty and compassion; the forms, and the language of memory and the tricks that it plays upon time, places and persons. In the last, at least, even granted that Sterne

---

[1] Julian Moynahan: 'The Hero's Guilt: The Case of *Great Expectations*', *Essays in Criticism*, vol. x, 1960, 60–97. Dorothy Van Ghent: *The English Novel*, 1953.

had come before him, he was influential, far beyond what he could have guessed, upon the future of the novel as a form of art. In children and childhood, I think, he tried also, as I have written, unsuccessfully to unite his social and ethical views with a metaphysical scheme that could not accommodate them. Finally in the progress of his treatment of children and the childhood vision we can see the (probably largely unconscious) way in which he came to some realization of the conflicts between his private and public ethics and the nature of his intuitive and aesthetic genius. For all these reasons, some examination of the intricacies of his conflicting views and feelings about children and childhood would seem to be one of the most fruitful approaches to an examination of his simple-seeming, highly complex art.

[2]

The sources of his concern for children and childhood are broadly three, and they are, of course, intricately interconnected. They are: the pressure of his obsession with certain incidents in his own childhood; his attempt to resolve the metaphysical debate concerning the meaning and value of childhood that he inherited from the previous century – in this, because he was often so unconscious of the theories behind his beliefs, he was at his most incoherent and contradictory; and his concern with the social and industrial exploitation of children as the most immediately horrible feature of a callous society – in this he was at his most coherent, simple and liberal level, and most at one with other social reformers of his time. In his attitude to education, as Professor Collins has admirably shown, he was more contradictory; this is, I think, because his ideas on education, though apparently part of the third category – his social views – were strongly influenced by his autobiographical obsessions and by his incoherent metaphysical attitude to children.

The most powerful motive of the three is, it must be admitted, the autobiographical. I write 'it must be admitted', for the circumstances of Forster's revelation of Dickens's obsession with the dark months of 1823/4 at Warren's blacking factory were sensational enough and their connection with his (until fairly recently) best-

known and most admired novel, *David Copperfield*, was so immediate that the boyhood trauma has unfortunately attracted the
attentions of his critics and biographers almost to the exclusion of
the other two very vital sources of his concern with childhood.
Nevertheless, if the discussion of the relation of C.D. to D.C., and
of David to Pip, or, indeed, of Charles Dickens to all the lost,
wandering, neglected or repressed children of his novels from Sam
Weller sleeping under the arches onwards, with all their rich
variations of sex (Esther Summerson or Little Dorrit), age (Arthur
Clennam looking back), or circumstance (Paul Dombey in his
castle to Jo at the gate of the rat-ridden burial ground) is by now a
little stale, a little squeezed dry, it is none the less central. To it
attach certain obsessive biographical details, incidental, in fact, to
Dickens's own life, but made by his constant use of them to seem
almost the essence of childhood as a source of intuitive wisdom and
spiritual strength.

The first and most important of these is littleness. In *The Old
Curiosity Shop* we find the elderly narrator saying, when he meets
Little Nell, 'I love these little people; and it is not a slight thing
when they who are so fresh from God, love us.' This sentence
contains a curious mixture of approaches, for the sentiment in
general is Wordsworthian, but the phrase 'little people' carries
connotations of an earlier view of children which Dickens would
certainly have consciously rejected. It is a favourite phrase of
Dickens. Eighteen years after he wrote the sentence I have just
quoted, he spoke at a dinner on behalf of the very indigent Children's
Hospital in Great Ormond Street. In this speech of 1858, he said,
'any heart which could really toughen its affections and sympathies
against those dear little people must be wanting in so many human-
izing experiences of innocence and tenderness, as to be quite an
unsafe monstrosity among men.'[1] The phrase has, perhaps, come
for us to be associated with some rather whimsical view of fairies,
but, used by Dickens, it conjures up the idea of 'old heads on young
shoulders.' As such it became incorporated into the cult of childhood which grew up in Victorian and Edwardian times and was
covered with the sweet charm in which that cult was eventually

[1] *Speeches of Charles Dickens*, ed. K. J. Fielding, 1960, p. 248.

drenched in the days of Barrie and Maeterlinck – an example of a popular usage of this sort of phrase in later post-Dickensian days is in the title of the popular publication *Little Folks*.

But with Dickens's use of 'little' associated with 'people' there is a more complex suggestion of mysterious wisdom. Mrs Wickham, that lugubrious nurse, alarms Mrs Pipchin's niece by classing Paul Dombey with those strange, half-supernatural little creatures who bring death to those whom they fix their gaze upon. Dickens, the rationalist that he always was where popular superstitions, ghosts and so on were concerned (except in one or two instances of personal experience, for example, when Mary Hogarth's spirit appeared to him) is here mocking an old wives' tale, for, of course, it is Paul that dies, not tough Mrs Pipchin on whom he has fixed his glance. Nevertheless, as in so many of Dickens's apparent asides, the suggestion that Paul is somehow gnomic (the pun, though crude, is relevant) sticks, and is a true guide to what we should feel about his intuitive wisdom. So, also, I think, with Little Nell. Dickens writes, 'I had it always in my fancy to surround the lonely figure of the child with grotesque and wild, but not impossible, companions.' But the purpose behind his fancy, I think, was to mark the little girl off as something monstrous (monstrously good) among the giants and the dwarfs and the waxworks; and – very typically – to try to rationalize this suggestion of an intuitive, heaven-sent child's wisdom by making those grotesque companions 'not impossible'. The littleness of the child, then, connects with its 'old-fashioned', intuitive wisdom. And the appeal comes from this juxtaposition of 'little' with 'people'.

There can be no doubt, I think, that this view of gnomic children derives from his reminiscence of himself in those castaway months. A first reading of the autobiographical fragment immediately establishes this emphasis upon his smallness – 'I was such a little fellow', 'Small Cain that I was, except that I had never done any harm to anyone', 'poor little drudge,' 'such a strange little apparition'; and the association of the littleness is always with that 'old-fashionedness', that intuitive wisdom which, for example, knew that the lady sharing the debtors' prison cell with the dirty captain was not his wife, a too early knowledge of the world saved, indeed hallowed, by his accompanying innocence. It is on behalf of this 'little fellow' of Hungerford Stairs and Charing Cross who a few months earlier had known those magical Chatham afternoons of ordinary childhood fun playing with the toy theatre and with his little friends the Stroughills as described by nurse Weller, who a few months later was to know the plain schoolboy fun and companionship described by Doctor Danson and others of his ex-schoolfellows at the inferior Wellington House Academy, but who now for those black months at Warren's was lonely and desolate; it is on behalf of this child frozen in time and place that all Dickens's child portraiture is written. He withheld the episode in his lifetime from everyone (except Forster and, I think, since I am inclined to accept his eldest son's account of the matter, his wife Catherine), but he made sure by his fictions that the boy who had suffered in it should be remembered. He inveighed against the circumstances, social or educational, that could so isolate a child from the happy healing laughter of child companions; but it took him a whole lifetime not to crown that lonely child with a halo of martyrdom (even, in the earlier works, a martyrdom that leads straight to death) and, for all that he cries out (and with utter sincerity) against the abominable distortion that such isolation, neglect, or faulty teaching brings, it is exactly these cut-off children (even those like Lou Gradgrind who have been deprived of the healing springs of childish legend and fancy) who 'wonder', who gaze into the fire and dream dreams, that are worth more than all the Christmas laughter and glee of the ordinary children whom Dickens exhorts his adult readers to care for. Here is the great paradox brought about by his autobiographical fiction.

Glee is withheld from his holy children. Little Nell's only laughter is at the sight of Kit Nubbles's wry, clownish face – not perhaps very kind, but probably a true picture of children laughing together; at any rate, the nearest to childish laughter that any of the fated holy children get, for Oliver's only laughter is a terrible blasphemy, when he bursts out laughing at Fagin's mimicry of the old man whose pockets the boys are learning to pick. Yet it is clear that the laughter of the childish chorus off-stage is 'natural'. When his favourite pupil is dying, the village schoolmaster in *The Old Curiosity Shop* asks the other boys to respect the death-bed by making no noise. But they soon forget their promise and rush across the green huzza-hing and holloaing. ' "It's natural, thank Heaven!" said the school-master, "I'm very glad they didn't mind me." ' It may be natural, but in his novels, we can hardly doubt that what is worthwhile in life is left behind with the dying boy and little Nell (so soon herself to die) sobbing quietly by the bedside. In his journalism, however, his more simple, social belief in the value of childish play and lightheartedness, his memory of the happier parts of his own child-hood assert themselves. In his essays, 'A Christmas Tree', 'The Holly Tree', 'What Christmas is as we grow older', 'Dullborough Town', 'Birthday Celebrations' and others, he recaptures with evident delight the pleasures and the sweet terrors of an ordinary childhood. They are even there, of course, at odd moments in the fiction – particularly with David. But these ordinary delights are mainly celebrated in those feasts he shared as an editor with his family readers in the Christmas Stories. The earlier and more famous Christmas Books have a mixed and very interesting flavour. *The Chimes*, that fictionalized political tract, dwells on the social prob-lem which is the third strand in his approach to the subject of children. *The Haunted Man* has a particular interest in relation to the second, least discussed, metaphysical strand. But the best and most popular of all – *A Christmas Carol* – unusually incorporates, in order, to bring home its lesson, both scenes of exceptional 'Dickensian childhood' merriment, notably the flashback to the Fezziwigs, and the most famous and most striking of all his indict-ments of childhood neglect – 'This boy is Ignorance. This girl is Want. Beware them both.' But the note in *A Christmas Carol* which most underlines the autobiographical paradox I wish to illustrate occurs during the vision that Scrooge is given of Bob Cratchit's penurious but happy family Christmas. 'They had a song, about a lost child travelling in the snow, from Tiny Tim, who had a plaintive little voice, and sang it very well indeed.' Even in Christmas happiness, the lost little boy must not be forgotten; and who more appropriate to remind the happy party of the faith they must not break than Tiny Tim, the ailing, crippled boy with his 'old-fashioned wisdom,' Tiny Tim, of whom we learn, 'somehow he gets thoughtful, sitting by himself so much, and thinks the strangest things you ever heard. He told me, coming home, that he hoped the people saw him in Church, because he was a cripple, and it might be pleasant to them to remember upon Christmas day who made lame beggars walk, and blind men see.' I shall discuss further the contradictions involved in Dickens's adherence to primitivistic idealism about childhood when I examine the other two sources of his treatment of childhood – the metaphysical-historical, and the social; here I simply wish to stress the great emphasis that his obsession with his past self laid upon the magic inherent in those very deprived or unloved children whose state he was deploring. It is, of course, like those socialists of the 'thirties who used to wax lyrical over the moral value of the way of life imposed upon the working class by its deprived economic status, a contradictory sentimentalism; but in Dickens's case, the sentimentalism has a certain underlying sense. He remembered, no doubt, how the seeds of his intuitive genius were already present in the imagination of the boy of twelve, and how, although that genius might have been utterly lost through the neglect and incomprehension of his parents, it was in fact fed and developed by the half-knowledge of an ugly world that he gained by this very neglect.

Parental failure is an old theme in the English novel, dating from the callous incomprehension of the Harlow family for their finer bred daughter Clarissa. But the eighteenth-century novelists, at any rate, felt no interest in this conflict where it affected those non-beings, children. The first novelist's description of a lonely child's neglect, the first almost sentimental description of the child's little world built up to defend its loneliness against unloving, uncomprehending adults is in that proto-Victorian novel *Mansfield Park;* yet the almost Wordsworthian description of Fanny's little room and prized little objects when she was a child is for Jane Austen only an early prelude to the history of Fanny Price's fight for the true values of Mansfield Park in an adult world against adult wordly wisdom. Nevertheless the childhood pages of Fanny's history are a prelude to the stories of Florence Dombey and Jane Eyre and Maggie Tulliver. But, of these heroines, it is notable that, although she grows up to marry Walter Gay, Florence alone never really leaves her childhood, she does not solve her problems by growing up (or like Maggie evade them by death), she simply waits until her father is so reduced to a childish state that he needs her – child though she still is – to lavish upon him the parental love that he had always denied her. This curious story brings us to the heart of another paradox that comes from Dickens's concern with the harshest years of his childhood. Just before his father entered the Marshalsea, the young, intelligent, promising Charles had been made, as he says, 'a little drudge'; and he looked back with amazed horror to the way that his otherwise loving father could have so exploited him. But worse was to come, for when John Dickens went into the Marshalsea, not even the little Charles's drudgery was wanted – alone, forgotten, underfed (save for the happy family Sunday reunions in the prison) he was cast into an outer darkness far worse than the intimate relationship which drudgery implies. Now Dickens's novels are more full than any others of parents who fail their children. Indeed the only *children* who fail, fail not their real parents but their little mother-sisters (Tom Gradgrind, Fanny and Tip Dorrit, Charles Hexam). Indeed the only substitute-parent whose influence ultimately succeeds in saving his child is that divinely child-like adult Joe; and, I shall suggest, Joe's teaching to Pip implies a denial of those very ideas of the divine wisdom of children, their intuitive and imaginative election. Joe's conception of duty, however gentle, belongs to a much older scheme of things than the magic which surrounds Paul and Sissy Jupe and Little Nell. For the rest all the parents (and even surrogate) parents in Dickens's novels fail. In the main, they fail through selfishness – they are the exploiters – Mrs Nickleby, John Chester, John Willett, Nell's grandfather, Mrs Skewton, Good Mrs Brown, Mrs Jellyby, Mr Turveydrop, Mr Dorrit, Mr Dolls; or they are the neglecters, those who cannot love – Ralph Nickleby, Mr Dombey, Mr Gradgrind, Mrs Clennam, the Podsnaps. On the whole it seems clear that Dickens, looking back at the bad years of childhood, thought that he preferred the relationship of drudgery to the non-relationship of neglect. We may imagine that Florence or Lou would have suffered much drudgery in order to be needed like Little Dorrit or Little Nell; and we know that Little Dorrit and Little Nell would evade many benefits rather than give up their drudge's roles. The despair of those bad years must have bitten very deeply into Dickens to have reduced his range of choice of a child's relationship to that of a drudge rather than that of an outcast. But, of course, there is much talk of the loved children – yet they are mainly off-stage, as with all the many, happy loved children who surround poor lonely Florence when she visits Sir Barnet Skettles. There are, it is true, the rather dimly conceived Dr Manette and his Lucie; and more convincingly, if a little cloyingly to our taste, Bella Wilfer's relationship to her father which is used efficiently to play its part in the softening of her character. Yet these are but a handful of successful loving parent-child relationships. For the rest, where love holds sway, it tends to be as ruinous as exploitation or neglect, as with the subtle picture of David and his Mamma, or with Mrs Steerforth's icy indulgence of her beloved James, or even with Dan'l Peggotty's devotion to his niece Emily; or, in a later novel, the Meagles's partiality that destroys both Pet and Tattycoram. But these examples of spoiling children perhaps belong to that element of an older, sterner view of children, one in which they can so easily prove reprobate – a view indeed that is reflected in the early *Sketches by Boz* and *The Portraits of Young Couples* where well-to-do children are spoiled, noisy nuisances, and poor children as in the Newgate sketch or in 'Criminal Courts' are the ungrateful jailbait off-spring of loving, too indulgent mothers. To this I shall refer in my discussion of Dickens's place in the history of theories of children.

The most autobiographical sketch of a child-parent relationship in all Dickens's fiction is, of course, the relation of David to his surrogate parents, the Micawbers. Here John and Elizabeth Dickens receive far kinder treatment than in *Little Dorrit* or in *Nicholas Nickleby*. Yet the character of Mr Micawber is not without its darker overtones, even though the generally sweet tone of that novel (surely, for all its extraordinary, almost revolutionary analysis of childhood thoughts, the most false of all his major books) demands a final sugaring over of the cracks in that otherwise impressive 'Dickensian' edifice. And, perhaps logically, Dickens's sweetening of his father through Micawber leads to his only betrayal of himself as he had been in the neglected, lost boy of 1823–4. Not in the character of David who gets all the compassion the author felt for his past small self, but in the strange comic treatment of Wilkins Micawber junior. This boy is placed in exactly the cruel position that Dickens had suffered as a small boy of twelve, yet, for the purposes of the novel, he is entirely facetiously treated – 'Master Micawber, whom I found a promising boy about 12 or 13, very subject to that restlessness of limb which is not an infrequent phenomenon in youths of his age.' Such might have been the comic description of that 'little drudge' the promising young Charles Dickens in his Bayham Street days by the most imperceptive, unfeeling of visitors. It is a measure of the degree to which his need ultimately to establish Mr Micawber as 'good' leads Dickens into a falsification of humanity with a betrayal of that very obligation to avenge his small, past, lost self that is the obsessive urge from which the whole book springs.

But in part the refusal to face the effect of Mr Micawber upon his own children, rather than upon the surrogate child, David, into whom Dickens had thrown all of his past self that he cared to think about, springs from the fact that *David Copperfield* belongs to the end of that period in which Dickens had so little analyzed his obsessive sense of grievance about Warren's that he could not or would not separate the professionally insulted and injured from those who had been truly cruelly treated by the injustice of society. This realization is surely at the centre of the increasing stature and growth of maturity in his greatest novels from *Bleak House* to *Great Expectations*. To treat it in total would be to describe Dickens's moral, spiritual and artistic growth; yet children and divine idiots (or those who are as little children) are so essential a part of his work, that the place they play in that separation of the sheep (the genuinely exploited) from the goats (the injustice-seekers) is a vital one.

Mr Micawber may be our starting point. In Dostoievsky he could become a mixture of sheep and goat, part exploited, part exploiting his own exploitation, a shabby, boastful truthless clown who yet utters the divine truths, saved perhaps by some innate childlike quality, some divine idiocy. This is too much for Dickens's simple system, and, let it be said to his credit as a man and ultimately perhaps as a writer, too big a distortion of what he felt to be the truth, above all, what he felt to be justice. Scoundrels and blackguards cannot be saved by some inner childlike grace, so Mr Micawber can only suffer the occasional slur (David's warning to Traddles, for example), for the rest he must remain a good, if absurd, childlike man who will eventually be saved for society only by responsibility and hard work in Australia. The real injustice to his children may be forgotten. But Dickens had been plagued enough by John Dickens's irresponsibility and childish selfishness, even though he loved him, to see another blacker side. And as he grew richer, more famous and more open to exploitation, he learned that the number of John Dickenses inside and outside his family was considerable, and many of them spoke with the unworldly voices of little children. So in his next novel *Bleak House* we have a whole mountain of irresponsible children-adults of whom Mr Skimpole is the wonderful apex. And they are all condemned. Even so Dickens has hardly diagnosed their malady – hypocrisy, selfishness, self-indulgence, posturing we see; but the real motive force of injustice-seeking, of battening upon the sense of guilt and the compassion of the hardworking, responsible members of society only becomes clear in that wonderful novel about the corroding force of self-pity and hugged grievance *Little Dorrit*, and, before this, by the brilliant revelation that Mr Bounderby's story of his childhood spent upon the pavement of the Opera House is all a fraud. But it has been there in a suppressed form from early on, in the nature of the little child exploited as a drudge parent by the irresponsible real parents, in the too early forcing of worldly cares upon the child's innocent mind. The meaning is evaded from the start, when we learn of the neglected, cruel boyhood of Sam Weller's street pavement nursery, without attaching any guilt to that wise old childparent Tony Weller. It almost comes to the surface when, with Nell's grandfather, we are told that second childhood is not the same as being a child – 'Lay death and sleep down, side by side, and say who shall find the two akin? Send for the child and the childish man together, and blush for the pride that libels our own old happy state, and gives its title to an ugly and distorted image.' Yet, throughout his early books, he does exactly this, as we have seen in the quotations from *Oliver Twist* – sleep becomes death, and death a long sleeping – the child has the wisdom of an old hand, the old and childish a child's heart.

Such a confusion, of course, could never survive the need to show how young Charles Dickens had nearly been lost through the irresponsible selfishness of John and Elizabeth, parents who were both so young at heart. The contradiction was bound to make a hash of any general theory that 'except ye shall be as little children' could be a model for the whole of adult life. There are, of course, genuine divine fools, adult children whose saintliness convinces us – Mr Pickwick, Mr Toots, above all, and (though the picture is more complex) Joe Gargery; they may stand beside Prince Myshkin or Lizaveta Prokofyevna Epanchin in their perfection; but at the last Dickens is forced to see the text not as a general rule for life for ordinary men, but rather as a licence to indulge the spirit of child-hood refreshment at the winter solstice – at Christmas and Twelfth Night; or, indeed, at festive times throughout the year. But inevit-ably the examination of this text meant an examination of the other, the logic of examining the irresponsibility of the childlike adult with his grasshopper demands on a world of ants meant an examination of living upon the memory of past grievance, of the absolute inno-cence of the exploited child. Out of this deeper self-inquiry into the autobiographical obsession comes the more complex picture of childhood presented in Pip and, with that, some attempt to subordi-nate in allegory Dickens the intuitive genius to Dickens the hard-working craftsman. Not only adults, but even the exploited child may hug injury too closely as we see with Pip – 'Within myself, I had sustained from my boyhood a perpetual conflict with injustice. I had known from the time when I could speak that my sister . . . was unjust to me. To this assurance . . . I in great part refer the fact that I am morally timid and very sensitive.' In the strange, ambigu-ous story of 'George Silverman's Explanation' (1868) we find a final more sinister account of the destructive effects of a neglected and exploited childhood. The child gives place to the man. We may disbelieve the new hierarchy of *Great Expectations* as much as the old, we may find it a sad conclusion, but it produced his most perfectly shaped novel. Most people have agreed that this victory for logic is at the cost of much of his magic (naturally so, since the child has been dethroned), but we may marvel at how great is the power of intuition that so much of the magic remains in the last novels when the illusions of his central autobiographical thesis have been largely demolished. The collapse of this child worship was perhaps inevitable for, apart from the sheer drive towards artistic truth, even for a man as little given to abstract thought as Dickens, the sheer incompatibility of the many views of life to which he consciously or unconsciously gave credence must have made it so. To conclude this essay on his treatment of children and childhood, I must recapitulate much of what I have said, but in terms of his relation to the general thinking of his age about these subjects. In this discussion, my debt to Mr Coveney's *Poor Monkey* will be clear to all who know that enlightening book;[1] yet his chapter on Dickens set as it must be in a subordinate context leaves room for further discussion. With this discussion of this second stream feeding Dickens's views of childhood I shall also combine such aspects of the third stream – his concern for contemporary society's exploitation of children – only as it affects his treatment of children and his childhood in novels. His practical work to save children from the effects of want and ignorance – the two spectres he saw as the centre of the nightmare jungle of Victorian poverty – lies outside the scope of this essay, and is anyway treated very fully in Humphry House's *Dickens World* (1941) and in Professor Collins's two books,[2] of which the one on education seems to me especially enlightening.

[3]

In the main, whatever his doubts about the efficacy of Parliament, the decency of English legal institutions, and the dangerous pampering of evil men inherent in much penal reform, Dickens was, for all his flashes of authoritarianism, a whole-hearted radical progressive. As such he rejected most decidedly (with his usual boisterous vehemence) the two main primitivisms in which from the early eighteenth century onwards, with the growth of philosophical

---

[1] First published in 1957. Revised edition (1967) entitled *The Image of Childhood*.
[2] *Dickens and Crime* (rev. ed. 1963) and *Dickens and Education* (rev. ed. 1964).

reverence for intuition as a mode of cognition, artists and historians and others had sought (and indeed still do seek) to find refuge from a rational, scientific universe whose increasing complexity they can only dimly comprehend and whose materialist values they find distasteful. No golden age of simple moral decency, of integrated intellectual standards and so on ever caught Dickens's credence. His view of history – the result, no doubt, of poor education – was crude in the extreme – all the past was 'the bad old days'; in all English history only Oliver Cromwell and King Alfred were allowed moral worth. Such ignorance, however, saved him from those primitivistic historical myths by which many far more educated men have distorted the history of culture in a desperate effort to preserve themselves from acceptance of their own ignorance in our modern scientific world. Nor was he more favourable to that other eighteenth-century version of the Golden Age – the Noble Savage. His dislike of African missionary work was in large part due to his belief that Exeter Hall Evangelicalism used the needs of some of the heathen Africans to protect itself from recognition of the needs of the heathen poor at their own doorstep (of Jo who, but for Allan Woodcourt, would have died in total ignorance of God and of Our Saviour). But his rejection of the Noble Savage was also a direct result of his dislike of all glorification of separation from our fellow men, of hermits (as we have seen in 'Tom Tiddler's Ground'), but also, in vehement essays, of tramps and of vagabonds, and, of course, of those bêtes noires who spoiled his beloved Italy and Switzerland for him, Roman Catholic friars and monks.

Having, however, renounced the more conventional primitivisms of the Golden Age and the Noble Savage, he fell victim to a large extent to the primitivism of childhood as a pre-Adamite Eden, the more strongly because circumstances – of his own concern for his own past, of the current campaigns to remove at least the greatest enormities of childhood exploitation – disguised, to a great extent from him the logic of the theory he was espousing.

That he was, however, plunged into the heart of the controversy about the place of the child in God's scheme and in man's society is apparent, I think, when we see that two features attach so often to his child victims which, having, as far as we can tell, no autobiographical connection, cannot be seen as a purely personal obsession. The first of these is the presence of Calvinist gloom that often hangs around his little heroes and heroines – David Copperfield, Clennam, Pip. 'The gloomy theology of the Murdstones made all children out to be a swarm of little vipers (though there *was* a child set once in the midst of the Disciples) and held that they would contaminate one another.' This, of course, is the reprobate view of children inevitably common in the Christian world from the triumph of Augustine over Pelagius, receiving fresh impetus in the sixteenth and seventeenth centuries from the teachings of Calvin (or of Jansen). There were strivings against it in the seventeenth century, among the cultured from the influence of Neo-Platonic ideas, among the ignorant where eccentric sectarianism found foot. But for a widespread revolt against the notion of the child born in sin we have to wait until the second half of the eighteenth century, when the primitivisms of the revived Golden Age and the Noble Savage were well under way. Of course, in practice, it is not to be supposed, that in any but the many severely religious households, the child of the eighteenth century was held down by Murdstonian chains. As I was preparing this essay, I was reminded of how easily the image of childhood's healthy pleasure (even licence to children) was accepted, by seeing at Houghton Hall a conversation piece by Hogarth of the Chol-mondley family in which a small boy is vaulting a little table covered in books, while pursued in play by a slightly older brother, the adults sitting in solemn pose beside the sportive scene. Of course there is licence, possibly even ridicule, in this portrait by Hogarth as there is in his portrait of the Herveys, yet the scene is still there of the children absorbed happily in their own healthy play – not even requiring that check of high spirits required by that beloved aunt of the late eighteenth century, Jane Austen, in her reprimand of the spoiled Middleton and Musgrave children. Probably, in practice, in all but pious homes, the reprobate view of children meant no more than ordinary, with occasional severe, discipline; but it did certainly mean a lack of interest in children or childhood, a concern, as with Lord Chesterfield, about how they could acquire manhood's grace as soon as possible. In this the enemies of Dickens's children all unite – as Mr Dombey thinks,

'Six years old! Dear me, six will be changed to sixteen before we have time to look about us', and kindly Doctor Blimber has no answer to any child's problems, but 'Bring him on, Cornelia, bring him on.' Such a reprobate view of children persisted throughout the nineteenth century, only at last giving place to Peter Pan's power when Freud's polymorphous pervert was already in the wings. Nor was it always on the side of brutality or even of overloading of the childish mind with learning. From our viewpoint Doctor Arnold may seem at times both a moral bully and a monstrous torturer of the child mind with overburdening classical learning. But this is not how thousands of his pupils saw him; from the studious Dean Stanley to the hearty radical Tom Hughes, champion of boys' natural and healthy inclination to a bout of fisticuffs, 'The Doctor' was remembered as a civilizing humane influence, caring for individual boys and their future as had never been known before. And, if we can believe the glimpses we get into early nineteenth-century Eton after the doors of the schoolhouse were locked at night, it would seem to have been a hell akin to Fagin's kitchen, save that the inmates – tortured and torturers alike were from upper-class homes. From all this Doctor Arnold rescued his boys, yet he did so with a total disbelief in the divine nature of childhood, free from any of that beautiful view of 'boy nature' which was to reach its heights in Forest Reid or Hugh Walpole's *Jeremy*; his view was far nearer to the reprobate –

> My object will be . . . to form Christian men, for Christian boys I can scarcely hope to make; I mean that from the natural imperfect state of boyhood, they are not susceptible of Christian principles in their full development upon their practice, and I suspect that a low standard of morality in many respects must be tolerated amongst them, as it was on a larger scale in what I consider the boyhood of the human race.[1]

The primitivism of children is here accepted but is made to accord with Dickens's view of the ignoble savage. Dickens was less logical. He associated such views on the whole with less benevolence than Doctor Arnold's – with the near sadism of the Murdstones, the cold

[1] Letter to the Rev. John Tucker quoted at the end of Chapter ii of Dean Stanley's *Life of Arnold*.

cruelty of Mrs Clennam, the self-righteous bullying of Uncle Pumblechook. There is no evidence that Dickens himself suffered from such a Calvinist, reprobate view of children. Neither Elizabeth or John Dickens were at all likely to be frequenters of the sort of Evangelical or Nonconformist places of worship where such doctrines were taught. In an essay, 'City of London Churches', in *All the Year Round* he speaks of his childish sufferings listening to hte long sermons of the Reverend Boanerges Boiler. If this picture is genuinely autobiographical, it must presumably belong to his (in general) happy Chatham days, but it is difficult to reconcile the account with what we know of his family life. Much later, it is true, indeed after the attacks on the Reverend Stiggins, his favourite sister Fanny was converted to so strict a Congregationalism that her husband, Burdett, gave up his promising career as a singer. We know that Dickens found their new Puritanism a trial. But this is in the early 'forties and has nothing to do with his childhood. Paul Dombey is reputed to have been modelled upon the invalid child of the Burdetts; but then, again, Paul is not a victim of Calvinist gloom and reprobate teaching about children, but of another side of the eighteenth-century view. All in all, I think we have to conclude that the Calvinist ethos surrounding the Murdstones and Salem House, and Mrs Clennam, and Mrs Gargery is not autobiographical like the other obsessive details of childhood I have described. It suggests that Dickens was consciously incorporating a principal theory of childhood which he knew that he was opposing.

The same I believe to be true of his repeated attacks upon what might be called a secular version of the Calvinist dogma, namely, the idea that children must be transformed as quickly as possible into useful men and women by cramming them with factual orderly grammatical education. Sometimes this is attacked in its old public school classical form as with Dr Blimber's constant driving home of the dreaded Romans, so that the boys talked dead languages in their sleep, or as in the disastrous Winchester education of Richard Carstone – presumably Dr Strong's classical reign was, by contrast, such a heavenly one, because, instead of cramming the boys with Greek learning, he kept it all for his dear old dictionary of Greek roots. Sometimes this factual reign was more modern, more, in the

Dickensian account, Benthamite, as with the schools under Mr Gradgrind's supervision, or with the withered dead education that Bradley Headstone ladled out, as the fires burned within him. Whatever its form, Dickens is here making the general case that we know so well from John Stuart Mill's particular account of his own upbringing. But it is not at all a part of Dickens's own childhood. Neither of the schools he attended was probably very good – William Giles's, however, was agreeable and he was grateful for it; Mr Jones's was very bad and Dickens took all occasions he could to say so. But neither can have been a forcing house of any kind whatsoever. Once again, I think, we must see what may look like a personal obsession in his fictional accounts, as a conscious recognition of the theoretical battle he was fighting.

In only one particular is his hostility to the factual, cramming type of education associated with the reprobate view of childhood or the secular deviation from, it connected with Charles Dickens's own childhood. If he knew that to his childhood fancies he owed his intuitive and imaginative powers, he also knew that those powers had been fed upon fairy story and legend. Upon every sort of education that killed the fairy story whether in the name of reprehending lies or of inculcating fact he came down with all the force of his disapproval, that is, until Pip is admonished for his lies. Among the bogeys of his childhood that he attacks directly is *Sandford and Merton* by Thomas Day, the most popular child's book, perhaps, of his own early years.[1] Wherever legend or fancy reigned, he tells us, Mr Barlow's voice could be heard drawing morals from it, or enlarging upon its factual information, in short, killing the power of imagination. The indictment is reasonably fair. Yet it is not quite so simple as it looks. Thomas Day, though he perverted it, was a disciple of Rousseau's *Emile*, the very gospel of the eighteenth century from which, at first sight, Dickens's views of blessed childhood would seem to spring. Certainly Rousseau, and even more Pestalozzi, would have deplored the continuous pedagogic (and moralizing) purpose to which Mr Barlow, the tutor of Harry Sandford and Tommy Merton, puts every event of the day. Mrs Pipchin's stories in which bad boys are devoured by lions, to which I have

[1] See *The Uncommercial Traveller*, Chapter xxxiv ('Mr. Barlow').

already referred, are only exaggerations of the misfortunes – being rolled on by angry sows or stung by bees – to which spoiled, rich Tommy Merton falls prey (I suspect Dickens had his old enemy, Mr Barlow, in mind when he described Mrs Pipchin's moral tales). But when Dickens, looking back, attacks Harry Sandford as a little hypocrite, his childhood distaste for Mr Barlow's moralizing leads him somewhat astray. The important point about Harry Sandford, the hero of the tale, is that he is the healthy, vigorous son of a farmer whose natural boyish goodness is contrasted with the weak, pampered, over-civilized effeminacy of Tommy Merton, the sugar-plantation owner's son, reared on the evils of slave labour. This is the true gospel of Rousseauism which was to be spread far and wide by *Paul and Virginie*, a book to which, once again, Dickens seems to make rather slighting reference by making it the book which Flora had borrowed from Arthur in 'those foolish far off days'. Yet the rescuing of children from their reprobate state, or from the nullity to which a secular form of this view had damned them depended greatly upon that healthy, vigorous (ultimately revolutionary, anti-aristocratic, Godwinian) view of nature which Rousseau provided. The Wordsworthian view of children of *The Lyrical Ballads*, even that later remembered boy who imitated owls and knew so well Winander, is far nearer to this concern for a vigorous, healthy, natural childhood than the sickly, pale little people who are the heirs of Wordsworth in Dickens's pages.

[4]

We know all too little of Dickens's relation to the Romantic poets – a little of his admiration for Wordsworth, a good deal of his hatred for Byron. We know that Coleridge was his forerunner in hating the contemporary moralizing or pedagogic meddling with legend and nursery story. We may, I think, legitimately connect his declared admiration for 'We are seven' in conversation at a dinner to celebrate the conclusion of the publication of *Nicholas Nickleby* with the Smike's grave tableau ending of that novel and with the child who shows Nell his brother's 'garden' in the graveyard (*The Old Curiosity Shop*, Chapter LIII). I have no doubt that Mr Coveney is right in seeing Dickens's novels as the heirs of Wordsworth's

poetry in their celebration of children and childhood. From the
sketch 'The Poetic Young Gentleman' of his early years to 'Mugby
Junction' of 1866, Dickens, despite his high admiration for Tennyson
and many other poets, is constant in his dislike for a commonplace
regard for poetry as more 'inspired' than novels. I think this is
surely a half-conscious sense of the degree to which his own novels
were poetry (sometimes bad conscious poetic prose, in the main
infused poetry of a very subtle kind). He, if any novelist, surely
was the heir of the Wordsworthian romantic tradition, and especially
in what concerned memory, dreams, childhood influence, fancy as
a superior force to reason, and so on. Unfortunately this influence
is not chronicled (unless future letters reveal much more than
seems likely), whereas his reminiscence of the hold that the
eighteenth century picaresque novels had upon him has, like other
contents of *David Copperfield*, or the autobiographical memoir, been
endlessly repeated. So far as childhood goes, it is only in the whimsical side of *Tristram Shandy* that we can find ancestors among the
eighteenth century novelist, notably as regards the opening chapter
of *David Copperfield*. It should also, I think be remembered how
much the underlying theme of *Tristram Shandy* carries a note of
protest against the exploitation of his childhood self by the selfish
concerns not only of his father, but even of simple, good Uncle
Toby. Dickens's debt to Wordsworth is, I suspect, at its highest in
the years from *Oliver Twist* (which may indeed have been his
earliest conceived novel) to *Barnaby Rudge* where the eponymous
hero (notably, in his exchange with Mr Chester about the truth of
the antics of clothes hanging on a clothes line) seems to be heir to
Wordsworth's idiot boy tradition. But there is one basic difference
which surely explains the more morbid direction in which Dickens's
child-cult took him. Despite much Cockneyish expressed devotion
to the superior emotional and moral effect of the rustic scene,
strongest in his early novels (*Oliver*, *Nicholas*, *The Old Curiosity
Shop*, and *Barnaby Rudge*) but liable to erupt at intervals in his
later works, Dickens remained primarily an urban novelist,
Barnaby Rudge's divine idiocy is seen in relation to an urban
riot and found insufficient. Above all, however his children
may seek their natural setting of rural beauty (and indeed do find

death-rest there) urban evil does not leave them undisturbed –
Fagin and Monks (in apparition form?) gaze down upon the drowsy
Oliver, his evil father's agent passes Smike in his last peaceful
countryside retreat, Nell shrinks behind the pillar of a country town
as Quilp hurries by, Barnaby (the grown up child) is pursued to his
rural bower by the evil blind man, Stagg. To this pervasive theme I
shall return, but it does separate children from Wordsworthian
innocence, freshness and rural health, and tie them to the sinister
morbid city.

This shadow of urban evil, of course which springs from a deep
sense of a dualistic world, is much strengthened by the impulses of
social reform, which are the third source, as I have suggested, of his
portrayal of childhood. Without all that we now associate with Lord
Shaftesbury, we should not have the story of childhood exploited
from Oliver to Jo. Inevitably (even with the bowdlerization that
still surrounds Oliver and Nell) sickness, disease and death must
play their part. In this Dickens is more truly the heir of Blake than
Wordsworth, although, alas, we have, so far as I know, no record
of his reading the poet of childhood innocence condemned to hell.

It is here, however, that the conflicts between Dickens's metaphysical views become most apparent. He seems in *Oliver Twist*
to believe in some form of absolute good and of absolute evil. Yet
his words in his preface about Sikes do not suggest that he accepst
the idea of innate evil, only, as he says, of 'some insensible and callous
natures, that do become utterly and incurably bad'. Yet in the
famous conversation between the landlady of the French inn and
her Swiss customer concerning Rigaud-Blandois, Dickens seems to
subscribe to some idea of human beings evil from the start. The
point is important when he eventually seeks to resolve it in *Great
Expectations* with an allegory of a child, Pip, whose good impulses
are personified in Joe and whose bad impulses are acted out by
Orlick. From his earliest work, however, he seeks to evade the
dilemma by placing corruption at society's door, and leaving the
moment of corruption conveniently vague. In 'A Visit to Newgate'
(*Sketches by Boz*) he describes the boy prisoners – 'There was not
one redeeming feature among them – not a glance of honesty . . . we
never saw fourteen such hopeless creatures of neglect, before.' But

he was to see many more, from the Dodger who is, after all, only 'about his own [Oliver's] age' (i.e. twelve) and four feet six of corruption (highly likeable corruption, be it said), through Squeers's school ('what an incipient hell was breeding here'), to the outcry of his 1863 essay in *The Uncommercial Traveller*, 'The Short Timers', in which he speaks of 'myriads' of neglected 'children who awfully reverse Our Saviour's words and are not of the Kingdom of Heaven, but of the Kingdom of Hell.' One child, in particular, plays a peculiar part in this borderline of his view of innate evil. This is the street arab of *The Haunted Man* in 1848:

> No softening memory of sorrow, wrong or trouble enters here, because this wretched mortal from his birth has been abandoned to a worse condition than the beasts . . . All within this desolate creature is barren wilderness . . . Woe, tenfold, to the nation that shall count its monsters such as this, lying here, by hundreds and by thousands . . . a harvest that mankind MUST REAP. . . . Open and unpunished murder in a city's streets would be less guilty in its daily toleration, than one such spectacle as this.

Here the idea of hugging insult and injury is treated as a directly moral good that Redlaw, the haunted man, seeks to evade to his own peril and to that of all those he meets. The street arab, however, is eventually on the way to being converted and softened by the play of other children.

> It was sad to see the child who had no name or lineage, watching the other children as they played, not knowing how to talk with them, or sport with them, and more strange to the ways of childhood than a rough dog. It was sad, though in a different way, to see what an instinctive knowledge the youngest children there, had of his being different from all of the rest, and how they made timid approaches to him with soft words, and touches, and with little presents, that he might not be unhappy. But he kept by Milly, and began to love her . . .

Here we are near to some scheme which suggests that the child untouched by civilization like the savage is born a beast; and yet at the last, Dickens draws back from so absolute a conclusion and suggests that the bestiality is the fault of society. Yet this violent hating little child certainly seems to trail no clouds of glory as he comes. He has not even the sportiveness of Quilp's familiar, Tom Scott. At the last, I think, Dickens was to resolve this problem most successfully when he brought Ignorance and Want together in Jo. Some modern readers may find his response to the Lord's Prayer both too histrionic and too unprepared a conversion; I should not agree. It seems to me that from the first appearance of Jo with his 'not knowing nothink' coupled with his 'he wos werry good to me' we are beautifully prepared for a nature broken and bewildered by his bestial life – 'Where can I possibly move to, sir, more nor I do move?' – to his bewildered unhappiness at being the source of Esther's smallpox. Only in Jo does Dickens successfully combine convincing condemnation of society with credible pathos of childhood; only here do we feel that he has given way neither to his hatred of crime as a manifestation of man's evil side by handing over too easily young criminals like Dodger to perdition, nor to his wish to personify man's good side at the expense of all reality as in Oliver Twist.

Yet the struggle between some idea of an innate evil in the world from which children cannot be wholly immune and the belief in a pre-Adamite childhood innocence is not resolved until *Great Expectations*. I suspect that such a resolution was in some degree impossible because of a deep suppression of any concept of sexuality in children. It is hardly possible for a modern reader to credit that his treatment of Quilp's feelings towards Little Nell can be free from conscious sexual overtones – 'You look very pretty today Nelly, charmingly pretty', 'what a nice kiss that was, just upon the rosy part', 'so small, so compact', 'such little feet' – yet I am not sure that in Dickens's conscious mind, and more surely in the mind of his readers the sexual overtones of this are not nullified by 'say Mrs Quilp lives five years, or only four, you'll just be the proper age for me'. Given the facts of child prostitution in Victorian England, it is hard to be sure. What is quite clear is the evasion of adult sex by which Dickens pleased his readers in presenting pictures of childhood romances – the whimsical charm that is woven around the boy-girl romance of Emily and David, or the more intolerably 'cutely' served up story of the elopement of eight-year-old Harry Walmer with his seven-year-old sweetheart in 'The

Boots' Story' in 'The Holly Tree Inn' (1855). These seem to me examples of the most unattractive aspects of Victorian sexual evasion, akin to the many oleograph pictures of little sweethearts that adorned their walls, making 'romance' charming because, being between two children, it could have no nasty physical overtones. Such connections between the sexual overtones of Dickens's fiction and his attitude to evil in childhood must inevitably be conjectural, and are better left, if they be attempted at all, to psychoanalytical experts.

What is clear, however, is that his social concern with the exploitation of poor children is directly connected with the mental exploitation of children of all classes – in the end, the most fruitful of all his approaches, for from it comes (from Paul and David and Louisa and Pip) his most important contributions to the psychology of children and to the fictional techniques of memory. It is in the context of industrial exploitation that we first meet the evils of the suppression of fancy, when Miss Monflathers admonishes Nell who is distributing the leaflets for Mrs Jarley's waxworks – 'Don't you feel how naughty it is of you to be a waxwork child, when you might have the proud consciousness of assisting to the extent of your infant powers, the manufactures of your country?'. This crude economic motivation is an introduction to the admonition of Sissy Jupe eleven years later, but Mr Gradgrind's rejection of the circus is considered more in the light of its mental than its physical exploitation; it is connected directly to Louisa and all that she had missed –

> The dreams of childhood – its airy fables; its graceful, beautiful, humane, impossible adornments of the world beyond: so good to be believed in once, so good to be remembered when outgrown, for then the least among them rises to the stature of a great Charity in the heart, suffering little children to come into the midst of it, and to keep with their pure hands a garden in the stony ways of this world, wherein it were better for all the children of Adam that they should oftener sun themselves, simple and trustful, and not worldly-wise.

Indeed the central gathering of all three influences may be found in

David Copperfield, where the historical and metaphysical is represented by Murdstone's Calvinism and his factual Gradgrindish
mental arithmetic, with the economic exploitation at Murdstone
and Grinby's and with the most conscious power of autobiographical obsession. What is found less in David, however, is the
ill health, the morbidity of the other child heroes. Dreamy he is,
and alone, but there is not that constant exploration of the sickly
fancy, of the half-dreaming state of the dying child (of Oliver
[though he ultimately gets well], of Nell, of Paul) which crude,
at first, and peculiarly and improbably adult in Oliver – 'there is a
drowsy state between sleeping and waking . . . at such times a
mortal knows just enough of what his mind is doing to form some
glimmering conception of its mighty powers, its bounding from
earth and spurning time and space, when freed from the restraint
of its corporeal associate. Oliver was precisely in this condition . . .'
– reaches in Paul an extraordinary power of analysis. And even in
David the best passages of child psychology lie close (though often
half-humorously seen) to death – his vanity at being marked off in
school by his mother's death, his analysis of his emotions at the
association of his mother's coffin with the amatory exchanges of
Minnie and Joram, even his strange fear of his real father buried in
the churchyard next door to the Rookery. It is this aspect of
Dickens's treatment of childhood, in which legend, the telling of
nursery stories, the macabre, the pleasures of convalescence, the
surrender to death, dreaming, half-dreaming, and solitariness are all
associated that tie his work irrevocably to Proust's Marcel. It is a
great artistic achievement, and it is almost entirely morbid. In it are
inextricably confused a concern for childhood as a human condition
worthy of respect (logical, rational, progressive), a belief in childhood as a healing force (New Testament Christian, irrational, anti-
Augustinian) and some primitive belief in an absolute evil that,
ultimately, leads to an authoritarianism, a strict morality more
usually associated with the Calvinism he so fiercely rejects.

When at last in *Great Expectations* he tracks down his own self-
pity and the cherished gentilities that go with it, a more strict
(though always loving) code gains sway. Pip, the imaginative,
dreaming boy must be torn from that sick room of Miss Havisham's

(the very realm of fairy story, of morbidity, of solitary rejection of the world's busy cares and responsibilities). Exactly those stories, grotesque, poetic and childish that have marked Paul Dombey's refutation of the calculating materialist world, that presumably have made David a novelist of fame, must now be relinquished. When Pip tells his stories of the black velvet coach and the dogs and the veal cutlets, drawing upon the same fancy that had made him at the opening of the book visualize his parents and his brothers and sisters from the shape of their tombstones; when only doubt about being believed prevents him from adding a balloon in the yard of Satis House or a bear in the disused brewery, he is told once and for all, however lovingly, by Joe, his good half, that 'lies is lies' and 'that ain't the way of getting out of being common, old chap'. It was, of course, exactly by his wonderful poetic talent for such absurd flight that Dickens himself stepped out not only from the company 'of common boys and men' but of all but a handful of his compatriots of every century.

Is the moral resolution on the side of health in *Great Expectations* centred in the author's changed attitude to childhood, a rejection of his own creative powers, of the poetry within him? To some extent, I think, we must say so. The conflict in Dickens between faith and work, between intuition and sensible thinking, between inspiration and hard work at craft marks his whole career. From the days of his advice to the young poetic tyro, Harford, in the early 1840s, Dickens was always suspicious of a lazy reliance on inspiration. He was always jealous of the honour of the profession of writer, he could be scathing about those who supposed that it could be undertaken without imaginative talent, but what he preached to his contributors in and out of season was hard work at their craft. It is hard work and a modest success to which all Pip's ambitions at last must come. There is surely some doubt, in this great novel of self-revaluation, of his own great genius; above all, in the fierce attack upon those who make puppets of others or mould them into idols (Jaggers, Magwitch, Miss Havisham, Pip's own treatment of Estella) there is surely some doubt about that exercise of will which Dickens must have come with all his family trouble to question in himself; with that egoistic will that wore down his wife and children he may surely have come to associate the whole power of shaping real life into fictions.

The cruel realization makes a perfect novel; and, since his intuitive childish genius was so far developed, his later novels do not suffer from any rejection of his poetic, comic powers. Yet there is less stress upon childhood's claims in his last two works, a more mature concern for young people and adolescents which make the heroes and heroines of *Our Mutual Friend* and *Edwin Drood* more subtle and serious than their predecessors. He can allow a cripple just the disturbing sadism of Jenny Wren without losing compassion for her patient courage. Here he is greatly superior surely to the exaggerated pathology of Dostoievsky's invalid girl, Lise Hohlakov, enjoying in imagination her pineapple compôte while a four-year-old child is crucified. The only attempt in these last novels to use children as a source of ennoblement is in little Johnnie's softening of Bella with his 'Boofer lady'. It is, in the whole, an embarrassment that fails but its failure does not seriously damage the book. In periodical writings, it is true, where he needed to woo his public's love, he flatters the more whimsical side of the childhood cult in his 'Holiday Romance' (1868) with its 'quaint', rather strained, attempts to reproduce the imagination of the nursery and the schoolroom in story form but even at this journalistic level, he had left behind the terrible sickly sentimentalism of 'A Child's Dream of a Star' of the early 'fifties – 'supposing all the children upon earth were to die, would the flowers and the water, and the sky be sorry?' His last fictional child is surely one of his strangest, for Deputy recalls Tom Scott, indeed he is described as Durdles's Imp; yet he can hardly, for all his fierceness, be seen as the savage infant of *The Haunted Man*; he is, so far as the story tells us a primeval force, neither good nor bad with his song, so necessary to the drunken Durdles, yet so triumphant in its malicious glee – 'Widdy Widdy Wen I ket ches Im out ar ter ten'.

NOTES
ON
CONTRIBUTORS

WALTER ALLEN is Professor of English at the New University of Ulster and the author of several novels, the most recently published being *All in a Lifetime* (1959). His critical works include *The English Novel* (1954), *Six Great Novelists* (1955), *George Eliot* (1964) and *Tradition and Dream* (1964).

PAMELA HANSFORD JOHNSON's first novel appeared in 1935. Among its successors were *An Error of Judgment* (1962), *TheHumbler Creation* (1959), *The Unspeakable Skipton* (1959) and *The Survival of the Fittest* (1968). She published 'Three Novelists and the Drawing of Character' in *Essays and Studies*, 1950, and a study of Ivy Compton Burnett in 1953. Her *Six Proust Reconstructions* (1958) was fallowed by an essay on Proust in *Essays by DiversHands*, 1963.

BARBARA HARDY is Professor of English at Royal Holloway College (University of London). She published *The Novels of George Eliot. A Study in Form* in 1959 and *The Appropriate Form. An Essay on theNovel* in 1964. She has collected several of her essays on Dickens in *The Moral Art of Dickens* (1970).

JOHN HOLLOWAY, Fellow of Queens' College, Cambridge, and University Reader in Modern English, published *The Victorian Sage* in 1953 and a book of literary essays, *The Charted Mirror*, in 1960. He contributed an essay on *Hard Times* to the symposium *Dickens and the Twentieth Century* (1962) and wrote an introduction to *Little Dorrit* in 1968.

MARGARET LANE, President of the Dickens Fellowship from 1959 to 1961 and again in 1970, is the author of *The Tale of Beatrix Potter* (1946), *The Bronte Story* (1953) and a book of essays, *Purely for Pleasure* (1966), which includes studies of *Oliver Twist*, *Great Expectations*, and 'Mrs. Beeton and Mrs. Dickens.' Among her most recently published novels are *ANight at Sea* (1964), *A Smell of Burning* (1965) and *The Day of the Feast* (1968).

MICHAEL SLATER, Lecturer in English at Birkbeck College (University of London), has been Hon. Editor of *The Dickensian* since 1968.

C. P. SNOW is the author of a sequence of eleven novels collectively entitled *Strangers and Brothers*. The final volume in this series, *Last Things*, will appear later this year (1970). From 1964 to 1966 Lord Snow was Parliamentary Secretary at the Ministry of Technology after a long period (1945z50) as Civil Service Commissioner. A major speech of his devoted to Dickens was published in *The Dickensian* in 1968.

RAYMOND WILLIAMS, Fellow of Jesus College, Cambridge, and University Reader in Drama, discusses Dickens in his *Culture and Society* (1958), *The Long Revolution* (1961) and in his new book, *The English Novel from Dickens to Lawrence* (1970). He contributed an essay, 'Social Criticism in Dickens: Some Problems of Method and Approach,' to *Critical Quarterly* in 1964 and wrote an introduction to *Dombey and Son* in 1970. He has published two novels, *Border Country* (1960) and *Second Generation* (1964).

ANGUS WILSON is Professor of English Literature at the University of East Anglia and a Vice-President of the Dickens Fellowship. He discussed Dickens in his Northcliffe Lectures on 'Evil in the English Novel' in 1961 and his essay on 'The Heroes and Heroines of Dickens' was reprinted in *Dickens and the Twentieth Century* (1962). He has written of the power exercised over him by Dickens in his own career as a novelist in 'Charles Dickens: A Haunting' (the *Critical Quarterly*, 1960) and *The Wild Garden* (1963). His most recently published novel is *No Laughing Matter* (1968) and he is also the author of *The World of Charles Dickens* (1970).

INDEX

MR. PICKWICK'S RECEPTION by Sol Eytinge, Jr.
(for *Every Saturday*, No. 15, April 9, 1870.)